**St. Louis Community
College**

Library

5801 Wilson Avenue
St. Louis, Missouri 63110

SISTERS
AND WIVES

Contributions in Women's Studies

SISTERS
AND WIVES

The Past and Future of Sexual Equality

KAREN SACKS

Contributions in Women's Studies, Number 10

Greenwood Press
Westport, Connecticut   ●   London, England

3-25-80

Library of Congress Cataloging in Publication Data

Sacks, Karen.
    Sisters and wives.

    (Contributions in women's studies; no. 10 ISSN 0147–
104X)
    Bibliography: p.
    Includes index.
    1. Women.   2. Women—Africa.   3. Sex role.
4. Women—Social conditions.   I. Title.   II. Series.
GN479.7.S2   301.41'2   78–75241
ISBN 0–313–20983–9

Library of Congress Catalog Card Number: 78–75241
ISBN: 0–313–20983–9
ISSN: 0147–104X

First published in 1979

Greenwood Press, Inc.
51 Riverside Avenue, Westport, Connecticut 06880

Printed in the United States of America

10 9 8 7 6 5 4 3 2 1

COPYRIGHT
ACKNOWLEDGMENTS

CONTENTS

ACKNOWLEDGMENTS

In the process of writing this book, my focus shifted away from counting and evaluating women's places relative to men's and toward finding another way of seeing, toward trying to reconceptualize human organizations with women at center stage. Many people contributed to this effort along the way. William O'Barr, Z. I. Giraldo, Naomi Quinn, Tom Reefe, Carol Smith, Catharine Stimpson, and Denise Soffel all found good material for me to read. Iris Berger, Judith K. Brown, Cynthia Enloe, Elizabeth Hansen, Judy Hilkey, Lila Leibowitz, Sue Levine, Nate Raymond, Dorothy Remy, Bill Sacks, Muriel Dimen-Schein, Gerald Sider, Catharine Stimpson, and Nina Swidler all read, wrestled with, and strengthened parts of the manuscript at various stages. I am grateful for their comments, arguments, and support. Louise Lamphere read several versions of the manuscript and consistently encouraged me to rethink the entire study; her help was invaluable. At Clark University, Lynn Olson, assisted by Denise Soffel, typed and photocopied a long line of drafts. Pat Reefe typed and Lanier Rand Holt proofread the manuscript and both saved me from many grammatical disasters. Dianna Grinstead, Sylvia Terrell, Naomi Quinn, and Richard Fox of Duke's anthropology department made it possible to xerox the book. My family, Sylvia and Jack Brodkin, Bernice Sacks, Ruth and Irving Rapfogel, and Bill Sacks all provided much needed time and encouragement at critical stages. Carol Stack and my co-members of the Center for the Study of the Family and the State at Duke University nurtured and gave me the space to put the last bits together. Finally Benjamin and Daniel Sacks introduced me to a new world of neighborhood and kin networks over the years and provided invaluable insights into both women's and children's places.

SISTERS
AND WIVES

INTRODUCTION:
SOURCES AND USES
OF THEORY

The search for women's overall or fundamental position long ago or far away is an outcome of the confrontation between social darwinist anthropology and the feminist and socialist movements over sexism here and now. I use social darwinism to stand for a world view, the key elements of which include an interpretation of the natural world from an industrial capitalist perspective, as inherently competitive and hierarchical, a belief that such an order is necessary for survival, an interpretation of human social relations as necessarily natural in this sense, and either an advocacy of inequality as natural and progressive or a despair in being unable to overcome our distasteful but inevitable natures. In this world view, nature is an unconscious metaphor for industrial capitalist social relations.[1] Women have been fighting for equal rights for well over one hundred years. The center of struggle lies in changing institutionalized patterns of behaviors and allocations of social roles. All behavior is informed and shaped by ideas, by ways of seeing the world, as well as by standards for what is right and wrong, moral and immoral. A marxist and feminist anthropology can affirm the reality of equality in other times and places and increase our understanding of how to obtain such a social order for ourselves. This book is an attempt to develop such a way of seeing and of informing our actions. But there is something hollow and unreal about simply laying out a marxist and feminist perspective as if it were a self-contained package. Ideas cannot be detached from the social and intellectual experiences that birthed them. Marxism and feminism are really ways of seeing oneself in relation to an industrial capitalist social order. They are world views born of cumulative and analyzed struggles of the working class and of women to end their oppression.

Marxist and feminist perspectives have had to confront social darwinist perspectives, for this is how industrial capitalists have interpreted the world. They are diametrically opposed ways of seeing the same social order(s), and they represent opposed class views and needs. But it has never been an evenly balanced opposition. Communists and plutocrats alike have been early and heavily socialized to view the world through social darwinist lenses, to ask social darwinist questions. That marxist and feminist perspectives have been sustained, developed, and put into practice at all attests to their roots in working-class and women's realities and attests to human abilities to create ways of seeing that speak to one's own needs and experiences.

To develop marxist feminist perspectives on women requires confronting and working through the social darwinist and sexist perspectives with which we have been socialized. Those perspectives are summed up in everyday contexts as stereotypes about how people act or think and why they act and think as they (supposedly) do. Stereotypes are powerful. Even marxist analyses, particularly with respect to women, have not always analyzed the complex reality of class and sex struggle, but often the distorted and simplified social darwinist stereotype of that reality. Thus the starting point of any marxist feminist analysis needs be to confront the dominant stereotypes. These stereotypes come out most sharply in discussions of women's essential being or universal condition. Much of the support for social darwinist stereotypes about "essential woman" comes from anthropology, a field that studies the social orders and cultures of the long ago and far away. As an academic discipline, anthropology has played a significant role in shaping and reinforcing ideas about women's place, nature, and roles (Fee 1974; Martin and Voorhies 1975: 144–77). Until recently, however, anthropology's message has been almost unrelievedly antifeminist and social darwinist in that it has insisted that women have always been and therefore must always be the second sex. Recently a new kind of anthropology has begun to develop, challenging antifeminist perspectives and creating marxist and feminist perspectives for seeing and acting on the world.

This book contributes to these efforts. It is a counterpoint—between what capitalist Euroamerica has said about the precapitalist world it sought to expropriate and refashion in its own image and what part of that world was really like. The resolution of that counterpoint is how the history of humanity looks with the female half at center stage.

The book is in two parts, indicating two aspects of a unified whole. The first part analyzes anthropology's contribution to generating social darwinist stereotypes, particularly those about essential woman, and shows how precapitalist reality contradicts its official academic stereotypes. Chapter 1 is long because it counts and analyzes the ways in which anthropology has interpreted women's place through social darwinist lenses. It is not about the totality of the discipline, for there have been dissidents and resisters in the past, and certainly feminism has become a significant perspective in recent years. Instead I concentrate on those aspects of our intellectual socialization that we need to overcome, for they do not sit well with feminist perspectives. To illustrate, I include some feminist analyses that were undertaken from social darwinist perspectives. I think they come to social darwinist conclusions in spite of themselves. Social darwinism speaks about biology and roots its explanations in tangible or intangible but nevertheless innate attributes. But these explanations are simple assertions and have not progressed beyond this stage for a century. Thus social darwinism is not really about biological roots of male and female places. Rather biology is its unconscious metaphor for social relations. What it has said with respect to social relations is that wifehood-motherhood is at once women's essential and defining social relation and that it is necessarily a relation of dependency.

The validity of an idea is not determined by who holds it or by whether it serves feminist ends. It is determined by how well it explains reality—past, present, future. Feminists and marxists seem haunted by an unrealistic fear: What if the social darwinists are right when they assert that women have never been the social equals of men? I think this fear has retarded inquiry into the question of women's position. Instead of tackling the problem head on, many have often found it easier to make end runs or apologies, conceding that women are subordinate but reasoning that culture, not biology, has put us in that position or that the conditions for equality have not yet been created. These may be consoling or inspirational thoughts, but they are not scientifically convincing or helpful, for they do not speak to what it is in culture that supposedly demands women's subordination. Is it changeable? How do we know? What is it in past and present forms of organization that has made women subordinate? Why should anyone expect it to change in the future? Chapter 2 refutes social darwinism at the level of social relations rather than engaging the debate at the level of biological metaphor. Empirically women's social relations are neither universally dependent nor universally subordinate; women have been making culture, political decisions, and babies simultaneously and without structural conflicts in all parts of the world. I discuss women's relationships as sisters, mothers and wives to show that there is not a universal, single, essential relationship that everywhere defines woman and to show that women's social relations include economic autonomy and political and economic decision making. Together the first two chapters are about undoing the hegemony of bourgeois lenses for viewing women's places in precapitalist societies and industrial capitalism alike. Because social darwinism has no room for equality or for change in women's places, it is logically deficient even as an explanation for inequality and its persistence. Even more significant for my own thinking was my realization that the mental category "essence of woman," which I carried in my head, was a social darwinist stereotype and not reality. Until that time, I had been necessarily asking the wrong questions, about some mythical, albeit social, essence of women's and men's relationships. And like others, that essence centered around motherhood in both its biological and social dimensions.

In the second part of the book, I ask different questions, marxist ones, about how women's and men's relations to the means of production create different social relations among them and create complex and multifaceted social beings who do not have universal gender-based essences. These questions are explored in the context of analyzing women's places in precapitalist social orders of Africa.

My goal is to find the kinds of productive relations that give women the economic, political, personal, and sexual equality we seek for ourselves today. My thesis is that the central relations are sisterhood and wifehood, relationships that I think were critical for women's lives in the precapitalist world. *Sister* is a kind of kinship shorthand for a woman member of a community of owners of the means of production: an equal, an adult among adults, a decision maker. *Wife* is shorthand for a woman's relationship to her spouse—she may live with him on her family's productive estate (garden lands or pasture, for example), and he may work for her family—or the reverse—she lives at the estate of her husband's family and works for them. (There are, of course, many more kinds of wifehood.) In the first case wife is generally a relationship of dominance; in the second it is generally one of subordination. In a search for equality, the relationship of sisters—to their brothers and to each other—is the critical one to understand. But the necessary condition for sister relations to exist was a corporation of owners, a social order based on groups of kinspeople who owned the means to their livelihood. Differences in the roles of men and women were compatible with sexual equality (Sacks 1976a). This kind of social order, which anthropologists have variously called tribes, bands, chiefdoms, acephalous societies, or lineage societies, among others, has characterized much of human history and was broken up only a few thousand years ago by the rise of states or class societies. States destroyed the possibility of sister relations and hence of equality of women and men, particularly in the underclasses. In Africa, and I suspect elsewhere, the rise of class societies involved the breakup of these kin corporations by ruling classes, who substituted themselves as private owners or as a class of hereditary state officials for kin ownership. Ironically, as ruling classes eroded men's base of power—their land ownership— they simultaneously undercut the basis of sister relations and hence women's power and autonomy. Women were transformed from sisters and wives, to wives (and sometimes daughters), to perennial subordinates. Motherhood, as a social relationship to the means of production, underwent profound changes as a result of changes in women's other relations to the means of production. It went from a relationship of adulthood to one of dependency.

But every historical or evolutionary current has eddies and countercurrents. The rise of states was not an event but a process, and an uneven one in time and space at that. It is still a process. The other side of that process is that kin corporations were not totally destroyed overnight. Rather they have been and continue to be slowly subverted, transformed, and overcome—only to struggle toward rebirth repeatedly as a defense against ruling-class attacks, as a means of spreading the risks of existence, or as a way of holding one's own against poverty. Women, as sisters, mothers, and wives, have been the central actors in these struggles. This history has yet to be written. Urban anthropologists and sociologists have begun to look at its very recent history under industrial capitalism, in studies of kinship networks within the working class (Stack 1974; Young and Wilmott 1962; Joseph n.d.; Brown 1975; Bott 1957; Sacks 1978). But proletarian kin networks lack their own means of production and hence are very different from kin corporations of the prestate and precapitalist world.

Many class societies, including preindustrial capitalism, did not fully sever the underclasses from control over the means of production. In the history of capitalism, that process was greatly accelerated with the rise of industry (Braverman 1974). In the histories of other class societies, it began under other conditions; and in the histories of still others, ruling classes never gained more than a weak and precarious control over the means of production.

I would like the book to show something of this complex history. It is what I think human history would look like if we put women at its center. It is very different from the prevailing views of human social history, of women, of family and kinship. Different chapters speak to different parts of this history, but they do so unevenly because the data are uneven: historians and ethnographers alike ask about some things and take others for granted. In a sense, the thesis reaches beyond the data to guess at a dynamic way of conceptualizing women's relations to the means of production, and the consequences of these under different modes of production for women as actors, shaping their own lives and their society's transformations. This is an evocative book; it is meant to open a discourse, not to provide the last word on it.

Chapter 3 elaborates a marxist perspective on women in precapitalist modes of production, suggesting that sister relations and the autonomy of adulthood it connotes were critical relations for women in preclass societies and that sisterhood sprang from women's membership—by birth—in a community of owner-producers. Married women's relations as producers enhanced or detracted from the exercise of sisterhood depending on sociohistorical particulars. In this respect, the production of food and tools is central, as are the relationships centering on their production and ownership. Relations of reproduction—of a new generation of people—of motherhood (and fatherhood) I see as derived from and determined by women's and men's relations to the means of production. This is just the opposite of social darwinist priorities, which insist that all women's social relations are explained by the biological relationship of motherhood.

I set out two modes of production for nonclass societies: communal and kin corporate. These were derived from looking at women's social relationships in precolonial African modes of production. Chapters 4–6 analyze three nonclass African societies. The Mbuti, gatherer-hunters of Zaïre with a communal mode of production and a more or less single community of owner-producers, made no political and economic distinction between sisters and wives. Instead they combined them in a set of age relationships, the most central of which was that of parent-producer-adult. The Lovedu and Mpondo of South Africa both had kin corporate modes of production with patrilineal corporations; wives lived on and labored for the husband's estate. Sister and wife were contrasting productive relationships in both societies. But in Lovedu, the former predominated and shaped wifehood, whereas the reverse was the case in Mpondo. The reason for the contrast rests with differing productive forces and male productive relationships. In Mpondo men of many patrilineal corporations constituted a productive team for the acquisition of livestock. Their relation to these means of production was one of clientship to a chief. Among Mpondo, but not among Lovedu, clientship coexisted with kin corporations as a productive relationship for men but not for women. And clientship was the framework for much of Mpondo political economy.

In Chapter 7, I turn to class societies and the rise of states. I see states as political organizations of class rule, but I do not see clear types of modes of production in African class societies. Instead the critical dimension underlying the persistence or destruction of sisterly places seems to be the extent to which ruling classes expropriated kin corporations. Women's resources for retaining or creating these places in the face of such attacks seem to reside in their work organization. Chapters 8 and 9 discuss women in African states and proto-states. Chapter 8 describes the development of the kingdom of Buganda, sketching the historical process by which a ruling class undercut corporate kin groups and transformed clanship into the framework by which a hereditary class of owners came to rule the kingdom. In the latter nineteenth century, Buganda was the most powerful and cohesive of the states in East Africa. Its ruling class had perhaps proceeded furthest in its destruction of corporate kin control of the means of production. Commensurate with this was the almost total obliteration of sister relations and the elevation of wifehood. As with women in industrial capitalism, Baganda women were defined by the state as wives and wards. Chapter 9 contrasts the city of Onitsha, where women were more sisters than wives, with the kingdom of

Dahomey, where sisterhood was much weaker though not obliterated as in Buganda. In Onitsha corporate lineages controlled the land securely. Sisters' place was reinforced by the collective organization of West African women's principal work, internal marketing. Dahomean women shared in this pattern, but in that kingdom, lineages were much reduced as landholding corporations. It appears that women's marketing organization was important for sustaining something of sisterly relations among the peasantry.

Finally, in a brief conclusion I summarize the shifts in perceptions and conceptions generated by studying women's places in precapitalist African social organizations: to center on productive relations instead of gender as a key analytic concept; to see family, kinship and affinal relations as productive relations; to presume women may have several and contradictory productive relations rather than a single essential relation to the means of production; to see the history of class societies as a struggle between ruling classes and corporate family organizations for control over productive means; and to look for the ways in which kin groups, as well as task groups, have been organizations for class struggle.

Most of the book shows women in other places and times exercising many of the rights, roles and relationships that contemporary feminists have been demanding. They are important to understand not because they inspire but because they teach us about the kinds of changes that are necessary in our struggle for equality. The book tries to contribute to a marxist way of seeing those paths.

CLASS ROOTS OF THEORY

Feminism, socialism, working-class consciousness, imperialism, and anthropology grew up together over the course of the nineteenth century. Their roots are all intertwined, so that to understand anthropological ideas about women requires references to the complex social changes entailed by the development of industrial capitalism in the United States and Western Europe. Older domestic forms of production were being replaced by new wage labor relations for a large part of the population, including women. Thus proletarianization was one side of the process. The rise of a bourgeoisie, owners of the new, industrial means of production, was the other side. Accompanying the economic transformation was a transformation in political theory: the rise of liberal democratic ideals, laissez-faire, the rights of man, and Jacksonian democracy. The new order meant different things to different people. To the young bourgeoisie, it brought wealth, promise, power, and real democracy. To the growing proletariat of both sexes, it brought relative and in some places absolute impoverishment (Hobsbawm 1969), a more inhuman form of exploitation, no legitimate power, and no real democracy. The rise of industry marked the beginning of a shift in the control over means of production in capitalist society. Over the course of the nineteenth century in the United States, family farms, home production, and family industry gave way to shops and factories, enterprises, and agrobusinesses. In colonial and preindustrial times, family-based property had underwritten a certain amount of sisterly places for women. Albeit as junior partners (to a husband or father) women inherited property, brought it to a marriage, forming a joint estate, and managed it as "femmes soles" in both America and Europe (Goody 1976; Lerner 1969, 1971; Clark 1919). Families were kin corporations to the extent that they held their own means of production. While the shapes of Euroamerican and African kin corporations differed greatly, both underwrote social relationships where women were political and economic decision makers, autonomous beings, at least in some respects.

As production came to rest in nonfamily, noncorporate loci, family ideals and family relationships changed radically, often painfully. Family ideals of industrial capitalism probably had less in common with those of preindustrial capitalism than the latter did with precolonial African corporate patrilineages. New legal practices made married women dependents of bourgeois or proletarian husbands. Proletarian daughters became wage earners for their families (Scott and Tilly 1975). Wives and daughters lost legal control over property and became socially more circumscribed and economically more dependent on male kin and affines.

Beginning with women of their own class, and extended to all women, the bourgeoisie adapted older notions to create a political theory specifically about women; the "cult of the lady" became the uniform ideal for all women (Lerner 1969). Ladies came into being as bourgeois and middle-class women were deprived of socially productive roles with the demise of the domestic mode of production. The new home and the family in it were no longer a productive unit, and domestic relations were being transformed to mesh with the rising industrial mode of production. In the family, women's economic dependence on men was heightened, though in different ways for women of each class. In society, Jacksonian democracy meant an absolute decline in women's legal rights as adult persons either through the creation of new restrictions or through the resurrections of old ones (Ibid.). The cult of the lady was a cultural representation of women's place in the new order. The world was now made up of two spheres: the competitive, public marketplace and the private, loving home, a refuge from the first. Nature made men actors in the first and women guardians of the second. This cult's coherence and rationale came from a panoply of ladies' books and magazines, medical literature, and their male complement, success manuals, whose role was to accommodate both women and men to their places in the new order by providing them with models to emulate (Ehrenreich and English 1973; Hilkey 1975; Smith-Rosenberg 1971, 1974; Welter 1966).

Many bourgeois and middle-stationed women resisted their assigned place in the new order and struggled at least for equal rights with their male counterparts. In so doing, they were forced to develop and articulate a world view, a morality that justified equal rights for them. Similarly their opponents were impelled to do the same to support their denial of equality. This confrontation was one source of feminist and antifeminist theories. But the feminist theories produced in this confrontation shared with their opponents an agreement on a general capitalist world view—with the significant exception of equal rights for women. The bourgeois social order and most of its values, particularly the home-marketplace dichotomy of society, was not challenged.

There was another source of opposition to the industrial capitalist order that ultimately developed a more radical and coherent feminist theory and promised a praxis far more threatening to the bourgeoisie. To the working class of both sexes, the capitalist order was hardly a blessing. Prosperity, power, and freedom were clearly not for them. Working class women were doubly oppressed by both class and sex. From its beginnings as a struggle for greater political and economic democracy, the working class movement developed its own feminist practice and theory, linking sex oppression to class oppression. This feminism has roots in the French Revolution, in antislavery, in working women's economic struggles, in the French uprising of 1848 and in utopian socialism (Rowbotham 1972, 1973; Sacks 1976b; Flexner 1968). "By the 1840s connection between social revolution and the liberation of women had been made. It had fixed in people's minds. But the actual basis for connection was still only vaguely worked out" (Rowbotham 1972: 58).

By the time of the first women's rights convention at Seneca Falls, New York, in the United States, women's rights were associated with radicalism, socialism, and a general anticapitalist spirit. The women who met at Seneca Falls and the early women's rights conventions were in communication with their sisters, Jeanne Deroine and Pauline Roland, French revolutionary feminists jailed in the 1848 revolution (Davis 1970: 17–19). At midcentury there was no clear line between socialist and conservative feminism either in theory or in practice. Out of the developing confrontations of radical, working-class, and feminist praxis with the bourgeois order came the sharpest and most coherent intellectual confrontations of feminist and antifeminist theory. Thus from the activities of the two opposed classes came two opposing views of the world and of women's place, nature, and future in it.

THEORETICAL CONFRONTATION

I cannot summarize the full range of this intellectual confrontation, but at the same time it is not possible to deal only with the parts that affect views of women. They do not separate well because so much of the theory and practice for and against sexual equality is an integral part of acceptance or rejection of the capitalist social order. As feminist and class struggles heightened in the latter nineteenth century, so too did the understanding of their interrelatedness.

Anthropology as an academic discipline has come down squarely on the bourgeois side. Its dominant theories about the long ago and the far away with respect to women stem clearly and consistently from passionately held class- and culture-bound notions that family and society are and have always been different spheres and that women are and have always been what industrial capitalist society says they are. Anthropology has thus helped translate a popular ideology, the cult of the lady, into a pseudoscientific theory about the benefits and necessity of sexism. It has consistently attacked both feminism and socialism in one breath in the name of the bourgeois family. Indeed some of the major figures in nineteenth- and twentieth-century academic anthropology have exhibited reactionary hysteria in their opposition to equal rights for women. Quotations from three of these founding fathers—Herbert Spencer, Bronislaw Malinowski, and E. E. Evans-Pritchard—illustrate the political convictions underwriting major perspectives in anthropology. Herbert Spencer characterized prebolshevik socialism in this way:

Are we on our way to a condition like that reached by sundry Socialist bodies in America and elsewhere? In these, along with community of property, and along with something approaching to community of wives, there goes community in the care of offspring: the family is entirely disintegrated. We have made sundry steps toward such an organization. Is the taking of those which remain only a matter time? . . .

Have these parental and filial bonds which have been growing closer and stronger during the latter stages of organic development become untrustworthy? and is the social bond to be trusted in place of them? Are the intense feelings which have made the fulfilment of parental duties a source of high pleasure, to be now regarded as valueless; and is the sense of public duty to children at large, to be cultivated by each man and woman as a sentiment better and more efficient than the parental instincts and sympathies? Possibly Father Noyes and his disciples at Oneida Creek will say Yes to each of these questions; but probably few others will join in the Yes. [1910: 718–19]

Spencer, who opposed the feminist movement of his time, had earlier addressed specifically those "who wish to change fundamentally the political *status* of women" (1884: 381):

There cannot be more good done than that of letting social progress go on unhindered; yet an immensity of mischief may be done in the way of disturbing and distorting and repressing by policies carried out in the pursuance of erroneous conceptions. [Ibid.: 401]

Bronislaw Malinowski in 1931 had this to say on the Soviet Union and feminism:

Adultery is not a legal offense. Bigamy is not punishable by law. In juridical theory it is, therefore, possible in Soviet Russia to establish what the sociologist calls "group marriages" or communal unions. That is to say, several men and several women may run a communal household, and indiscriminately share as much of their lives as they like. . . .

Some revolutionary reformers, notably the enthusiastic German socialists of the nineteenth century, preached free love and sexual communism by reference to the ape man and his matrimonial entanglements. These writers have, in fact, influenced modern Russian theory and practice, and here you see how anthropology has affected, not to say misguided, practical affairs.

. . . .

I have shown that the fight in defense of marriage is nowadays on two fronts; parental communism versus the family, and sexual communism versus marriage. The communistic legislator objects to marriage, because marriage is, for him, a capitalistic institution, a sort of economic enslavement of woman. He is also out to undermine the individual influence of the home, that is, of the child's own parents, because to him the State, the Community, the Workers' Union ought to educate the future citizen from his early childhood. The modern Hedonist and Misbehaviourist is bent on destroying the home since this is to him the synonym of boredom and repression. . . . The anthropologist is, then, faced with a question: Is communal parenthood compatible with human nature and social order? I flatly deny that it is.

. . . .

Women now claim freedom. They want to share more fully in our national life. . . . But women still have to become mothers and they still desire motherhood as deeply as any savages or any mid-Victorians. . . . Now the question of the future is whether women will cease to be interested in maternity. If women still intend to keep up the vocation of maternity, will they still insist on carrying it on under the system of individual maternity, or will they prefer to give over the children to creches and communal institutions? Will a woman, however intelligent, feminist, or progressive, consent to undergo the hardships and dangers of childbirth in order to give over her child to a glorified foundlings' hospital or State incubator? Here again you know my answer: maternity is individual, has been individual, and will be the most individual of social forces. Finally, if woman is still to be a mother and an individual mother at that, will she choose to have her sweetheart as a mate and as a father to her children? Will she still desire him to stick to her and to share the responsibilities of parenthood? These three questions contain the essence of all marriage problems, past, present, and future. It is incorrect, I think, to regard the marriage contract as established mainly in the interests of the husband. It is quite as much at least a charter and a protection to the woman. Most men would consent to be drones easily enough; but no sound social order can allow them to do this. And there, I think, is the most fundamental point of the debate, namely, that marriage and family are based on the need of the male to face his responsibility and to take his share in the process of reproduction and of the continuity of culture.

. . . .

I believe that the most disruptive element in the modern revolutionary tendencies is the idea that parenthood can be made collective. If once we came to the point of doing away with the individual family as the pivotal element of our society, we should be faced with a social catastrophe compared with which the political upheaval of the French revolution and the economic changes of Bolshevism are insignificant. [Montagu 1956: 21–22, 42–43, 50–51, 76]

Evans-Pritchard told an audience of British feminists in 1956: "I must confess at the outset that I may incur your censure either for never having properly understood the feminist movement or for lack of enthusiasm towards it" (1965: 38). He noted that the political milieu of the 1950s differed from that of Herbert Spencer's time and even the interwar era within which Malinowski wrote.

Gone are the days, at least for the time being, of such speculative and uncritical evolutionary theorizing. Gone also are the days of vigorous feminism and an anti-feminism which formed part of that battle in which the protagonists of all so-called progressive movements and their opponents were mixed up in a general melee. [Ibid.: 40]

Thus Evans-Pritchard's target is feminists themselves. Where Spencer and Malinowski blamed socialists for agitating against motherhood, family, and civilization, Evans-Pritchard blamed feminism for male homosexuality and general problems in the family.

Consequently, the mother too possessive of her son and the daughter too emotionally tied to her father do not seem to figure in the primitive family, and the various maladjustments to which they give rise appear to be absent, or at least relatively so.

The maladjustments to which I refer, and which are only too obvious in our own society, and even more so in the United States, are well known to you in the literature of psychology and psychiatry; and they are perhaps more suitable subjects for professional than public discussion. I feel, however, that I ought to mention one of them, male inversion, because it concerns the subject of discussion, and also because it has, according to all reports and surveys, reached proportions which have caused grave concern, even alarm. It was only the other day described by a leading American psychiatrist, Dr. Kardiner, as a "wholesale flight from the female"; and most psychiatrists seem to agree that one of the main factors in the production of the phenomenon is the domineering mother, and the consequently meek father. This symptom of deep-set social dysnomia is altogether absent in primitive societies or, where it is present, is a very rare occurrence, or a temporary expedient, or plays a cultural role, and consequently is not a social problem. [Ibid.: 48]

Like Malinowski, Evans-Pritchard set up a stereotypic primitive woman, whom he meant to be natural woman.

... the adult primitive woman is above all a wife, whose life is centered in her home and family. . . . A visitor to a primitive society will also observe that parents have as many children as possible. . . . Primitive wives do not know of means by which conception can be prevented. . . .
  In primitive society the spheres of activities of the sexes are clearly demarcated. . . . If this demarcation is for primitive women a restriction it is also a protection. . . . In primitive societies men invariably hold the authority. . . .
  Primitive women do not see themselves as an under-privileged class as against a class of men with whom they seek to gain social equality. They have never heard of social equality; and also they do not want to be like men. [Ibid.: 46, 50–52]

All would have been well, he believed, had it not been for outside philosophies, some espoused even by anthropologists:

In our own society the matter is not so simple, because woman's position became a subject of philosophical speculation in the eighteenth and nineteenth centuries and involved in all sorts of liberal and egalitarian movements; and there arose the ideas of the "subjection" of women and their "emancipation," ideas which received great impetus from J. S. Mill's famous essay of 1869 and were later forcibly expressed in the feminist movement. . . .
  . . . to claim, as some writers do, for example, Dr. Margaret Mead and Simone DeBeauvoir . . . that the temperamental and social differences between the sexes are simply a product of cultural conditioning is a reification that explains nothing. [Ibid.: 52, 55]

Evans-Pritchard concluded:

I find it difficult to believe that the relative positions of the sexes are likely to undergo any considerable or lasting alteration in the forseeable future. Primitive societies and barbarous societies and the historical societies of Europe

and the East exhibit almost every conceivable variety of institutions, but in all
of them, regardless of the form of social structure, men are always in the
ascendancy, and this is perhaps the more evident the higher the civilisation....
Feminists have indeed said that this is because women have always been
denied the opportunity of taking the lead; but we would still have to ask how it
is that they have allowed the opportunity to be denied them, since it can hardly
have been just a matter of brute force. The facts seem rather to suggest that
there are deep biological and psychological factors, as well as sociological
factors, involved, and that the relations between the sexes can only be modi-
fied by social changes, and not radically altered by them. [Ibid.: 54–55]

Evans-Pritchard's counsel in the face of this alleged inevitability is
something akin to "relax and enjoy it":

In so far as the problems of the relation of the sexes are not those just of sex as
such, but of authority, leadership, control, co-operation and competition, they
are problems which occur in every department of social life and in every sort
of society; and they cannot be solved by an insistence on absolute equality but
rather by recognition of differences, exercise of charity, and acknowledge-
ment of authority. Otherwise antagonism is unavoidable and peaceful, harmonious, social life impossible; and far from the acceptance of authority en-
tailing inferiority, it expresses the only true form of equality obtainable in
human relationships, an equality of service. . . .
    I have only to add in conclusion that however insufficient this lecture may
be—and I would be the first to acknowledge its deficiencies—it is less
inadequate than most discussions about women. I have read much in
preparation for it, but I must admit that it is only too evident with little profit.
[Ibid.: 56–57]

SOCIAL DARWINISM AND MARXISM

Not all anthropologists were so antifeminist and antisocialist as
these three, but even those who were not were trained in a theoretical
tradition whose political sources were the reactionary convictions of
these and other men. It has been these traditions that anthropologists
have in turn presented to the public as theories of human evolution and
culture and women's place in it.

No one was as successful as Herbert Spencer in weaving an integrated theory of the benefits and the inevitability of industrial capitalism. Indeed his perspective has dominated twentieth-century anthropology. Just as Spencer's thought represented the perspective of an

industrial bourgeoisie, the works of Karl Marx and Frederick Engels represented that of the industrial proletariat. Where spencerian paradigms have dominated institutionalized higher education, marxist ones have shaped the course of working-class resistance and revolutionary movements. The nineteenth-century clash between Spencer and marxism best exemplifies the range and depth of the continuing confrontation about both capitalism and women's place, past, present, and future.

Nineteenth-century social thought was oriented toward the natural sciences—as opposed to religion or abstract logic—in its search for explanatory principles or laws. It was also concerned with questions about the origins and evolution of human social organization. Its unifying question was to understand the roots of Victorian capitalist social organization. It inquired into the evolution of forms of social organization just as Darwin inquired into the evolution of species. Information on the many shapes of social life around the world was being provided by travelers, missionaries, and the advance guard of colonialism. Non-Western societies were taken to represent something like living fossils of life in earlier epochs of humanity. And from the information available, Spencer and Engels, like others of their time, reconstructed the evolution of human social organization and sought the laws underlying their own society. But they did so through the class perspective of their own social milieu. The bourgeois and academically dominant views affirmed the soundness and naturalness of the social order in their analyses of the long ago and far away, while marxists sought the genesis and agents of contemporary oppression in the past and sought the means for future liberation in the present.

Herbert Spencer, perhaps the most articulate and influential ideologue of laissez-faire capitalism, saw the world through the eyes of the dynamic and expanding bourgeoisie. To this class as to Pangloss, theirs was the best of all possible worlds. Their right to rule and to prosper appeared divinely ordained, but Spencer showed that these privileges were actually an inevitable working out of natural law. It was the spencerian paradigm, later known as social darwinism, that came to dominate academic social science. Its premise was that industrial capitalism was the most advanced and benign social order humanity had ever developed and that this development was the product of a struggle for survival in which the less fit were eliminated by their betters. Although many nineteenth-century academic social

scientists were critical of their own society, they agreed that meddling
with class, race, and sex relationships was a far greater evil than mud-
dling along. The natural law of survival of the fittest was not to be
tampered with.

Spencer saw much to criticize in the status quo, but he believed that
if left to the working out of natural law, it held the prospect of developing the greatest freedom and happiness for the socially fit. The poor—
workers and colonized people—were not so fit, else they would not be
poor. Their ultimate demise was necessary for the progress and improvement of the species. From this vantage point, Spencer surveyed
humanity's climb from a savagery that was the antithesis of the good
life. Women also partook in this general improvement. The development of families based on private property and monogamous marriage
freed women from men's brutality and from hard productive labor,
thus allowing them to become better mothers and thereby contribute
to improving the species. For Spencer a goal of evolution was to separate reproduction from production and to separate the family and
women from the latter as advocated by the cult of the lady. The psychological traits that women developed to survive in a savage early
milieu—guile, flattery, obsequiousness, and an attraction to men of
power—became fixed in women's character and made them still very
much unqualified for the equal rights demanded by radicals and feminists of his time. Women's biological evolution was stunted to reserve
"vital power to meet the cost of reproduction" (1884: 374). This affected modern women's mental capacities and resulted in

a perceptible falling-short in those two faculties, intellectual and emotional,
which are the latest products of human evolution—the power of abstract reasoning and that most abstract of the emotions, the sentiment of justice. . . .
    The remaining qualitative distinctions between the minds of men and wom-
en are those which have grown out of their mutual relations as stronger and
weaker. [Ibid.: 374–75]

Marxist analysis was opposed to Spencer's at virtually every point.
It saw capitalism through the eyes of a growing and oppressed industrial working class. It articulated and unified the concerns and cri-
tiques of earlier socialists and of working-class resistance, becoming
for this class what academic social science became for the bourgeoisie. But it was not until Engels's *Origin of the Family, Private*

Property and the State (1891) that women's specific oppression and its genesis and relationship to capitalism were articulated. In looking at human prehistory, Engels, like Spencer, noted that private property and families based on it came into being relatively late. But Engels saw private property as responsible for destroying not savage disorder but a communist social order in which men and women were equals and in which "pairing marriage" was an egalitarian relationship between a man and a woman: "In the old communistic household, which embraced numerous couples and their children, the administration of the household, entrusted to the women, was just as much a public, a socially necessary industry as the providing of food by the men" (Ibid.: 120). The development of private property first caused the subjugation of women to men through unequal or monogamous marriage and then of the unpropertied to the propertied. For women as for the proletariat, freedom lay in the destruction of the monogamous family based on male private property upon which capitalism rests and a return to an egalitarian communism on an industrial base.

We are now approaching a social revolution in which the hitherto existing economic foundations of monogamy will disappear. Monogamy arose out of the concentration of considerable wealth in the hands of one person—and that a man—and out of the desire to bequeath the wealth to this man's children. . . . The impending social revolution, however, by transforming at least the far greater part of permanent inheritable wealth—the means of production—into social property will reduce all this anxiety about inheritance. . . . This revolution will create the conditions for the development of egalitarian and "individual sex love" between men and women. [Ibid.: 123]

Neither Marx nor Engels was part of the academy, and Engels's work has been anathema to standard anthropology curricula since it was written. It is interesting to note that Lewis Henry Morgan, the American evolutionist whose work formed the basis for Engels's analysis, has faced a kind of red-baiting by association. Although he has been officially designated the founder of the anthropological study of kinship (Haddon 1910; Lowie 1937), his evolutionary scheme (based heavily on the study of kinship systems) has been criticized more severely than similar ones by lesser figures. Robert Lowie, for many years the quasi-official American historian of anthropological theory, claims rather sulkily, that Morgan "has achieved the widest intellectual celebrity of all anthropologists" due not "to his solid achievement, but to a historical accident." Because Engels relied on him, Morgan's work was

promptly translated into various European tongues, and German workingmen would sometimes reveal an uncanny familiarity with the Hawaiian and Iroquois mode of designating kin, matters not obviously connected with a proletarian revolution. Even in America Morgan's book has long been most accessible in the inexpensive reprint issued by a Socialist firm in Chicago. [Lowie 1937: 54]

In all discussion of Morgan and evolutionary thought Engels's name was never mentioned. Indeed the marxist tradition has developed outside the academy in working-class groups and in communist parties, as Lowie noted. Explicitly marxist approaches have been tabood in anthropology until quite recently. Their current influence inside the academy is largely a result of those working-class and anticapitalist struggles outside the academy.

But it has been Spencer and social darwinism and not Engels that has been the mold for anthropology's treatment of women. Social darwinism has insisted that the subordination of women is natural and inevitable because it is based on innate biopsychological characteristics. It blames the victim. In present and past anthropology, this view has been as constant as anthropology's mention of the female half of humanity and more constant than its sustained inquiry into the position of women. Although Spencer was the most comprehensive and consistent theoretician of social darwinism in his time, a host of other academic contemporaries worked in this mode (Lubbock 1870; McLennan 1865; Durkheim 1893; Thomas 1907; Sumner and Keller 1932). More recently, though no more convincingly, others (Tiger and Fox 1971; Tiger 1969; Wilson 1975; Harris 1975; Divale and Harris 1976) have resurrected social darwinist evolutionary sequences and laws to argue anew for male dominance. But social darwinist assumptions about women have persisted even when questions about origins, processes, and causes were in disfavor (Malinowski 1927; Montagu 1954; Evans-Pritchard 1965).

The separation of family and production, or home and work, is a historically recent and culturally specific development. Yet bourgeois theories of women and the family are predicated on insisting that this dichotomy is an original and necessary condition for human existence. It is most commonly expressed as a natural and inevitable incompatibility between motherhood and culture creation or political decision making. Because this theme has dominated anthropology's theorizing about women in such a variety of mainly social darwinist ways, it is important to ferret out the class-ethnocentric assumptions behind the appearance of cultural relativism and eclecticism. For example, men and women are often said to possess sexual temperaments, which are then used to explain the social roles assigned to them. Thus Victorians claimed that sexual self-control and an ability to transcend the earthly and sensual plane of existence were innate male traits. This temperament explained why men were the political and economic decision makers in society and why women could not be. With somewhat changed sexual norms in the twentieth century, sociobiologists claim that men are innately promiscuous and genetically programmed to impregnate as many women as they can. The most successful men in this endeavor (those least able to transcend the sensual plane of existence) are also those most influential in political and economic decision making.

These contradictions would be perplexing if we confined ourselves to examining the history and nature of these ideas without reference to the class perspectives that give them birth again and again. Embedded in the diametrically opposed notions or stereotypes of male and female temperament lies the same ideology of women's necessary political and economic subordination.

NOTE

1. In an important paper, Haraway (1978) has explored the ways in which capitalist perspectives have shaped the modern field of primatology, and how, in turn, these social constructs of nature have been influential in legitimating and reinforcing the social order that birthed them.

Chapter 1

ANTHROPOLOGY AGAINST WOMEN

Social darwinism in one or another form has been the dominant and often the only anthropolgical approach to the question of women's place. It ascribes different innate characteristics to men and to women and explains cultural forms, social evolution, and the relations between the sexes as caused by these alleged differences. A more recent variant has been to see certain relationships as inherent in culture itself. Its major thrust emphasizes an overwhelming uniformity in the pattern of woman-man relationships: men are dominant as a gender and women are subordinate as a gender. The particular innate causes have varied. Sometimes they are physical; at others they are emotional, cognitive, or functional. All rest ultimately on the biological fact that women bear and nurse babies. Despite a bewildering variety and complexity of theory, all seem to be variations on the following syllogism:

1. Making babies and shaping culture are incompatible.
2. Women make babies.
3. Therefore only men can make culture.

The variation takes place mainly in the first point in the reasons motherhood is alleged to be incompatible with equal social rights for women. As production moved out of the home with the beginnings of capitalist industrialization, women came to be equated with motherhood, and motherhood came to mean the opposite of production. The cult of the lady summarized how family and society were natural and complementary opposites, as were men and women, and how the natural temperaments of each sex suited them for the division of labor being engendered by industrial capitalism. In the nineteenth and twentieth centuries, physical and emotional characteristics associated with motherhood were stressed in both social science and in popular explanations: Women were said to be too weak, stupid, and emotional (Spencer 1884; Thomas 1907) to exercise equal rights because their developmental energies were all channeled into their wombs. With the refutation or abandonment of innatist approaches elsewhere in anthropology, the complementary separateness of the spheres came to be stressed: motherhood itself, rather than women's temperament, was alleged to be functionally incompatible with equal rights. Women could not be in two places at once, and family and society were universally and necessarily separate places. Thus women had to stay home. Since the late 1960s, there has been a return to stressing sexual characteristics. Cognitive traits have joined a resurrection of physical and emotional traits and continued beliefs in a natural division between home and work. Culture is said to associate women with inferior things; women are alleged to be biologically unable to work in groups, or, closest to Spencer, are supposedly too weak and pregnant to compete directly for a place in the pecking order which is society.

It is important to stress that social darwinism or an innatist approach is not monopolized by antifeminists. Innatism has been a central part of the capitalist world view for the last century (Chase 1977; Higham 1963). Unfortunately but not surprisingly, much feminist thought has been shaped by it. The reason is not surprising since innatism has been central to arguments in favor of a general capitalist status quo. It explains the status quo by blaming its victims. When sexism is challenged, the most expeditious argument against it often involves accepting the innatist world view but altering it to accommodate equal rights for women by exempting women from blameworthy traits. And indeed, as Kraditor has shown (1971), this was the major outlook and dominant tactic of the American feminist movement between 1880 and 1920. Although this was a minor theme in past anthropology (Mason 1894; Montagu 1954), it has become a significant one in the contemporary anthropology of women (Rosaldo 1974; Ortner 1974) and indeed underlies some contemporary radical feminism (Firestone 1970). It is an unfortunate position for feminists to take because it is virtually impossible to make a logical case for equal rights from innatist premises.

The works of Herbert Spencer and J. J. Bachofen in the nineteenth century were the most complete elaborations of social darwinism and best exemplify its range with respect to the women question. Subsequent anthropology has merely played variations on their basic themes, replacing discredited innatist assumptions with other equally baseless ones. Bachofen and Spencer, although very different from each other, shared the basic assumptions of the social darwinist world view: that men and women are psychologically different from each other; that their own capitalist social order, the progressive outcome of the struggle for survival, is better than all others; that family and society are different spheres; and that women's psychology incapacitates them from playing extrafamilial roles. Thus men must rule for the good of the society and women and for the future of the species. Within this general framework though, they differ profoundly. Spencer's ideas have been the underpinning of most prescriptively sexist arguments, while Bachofen's have underwritten and inspired much ostensibly profeminist but nevertheless innatist arguments. Spencer's ideas and attitudes have been by far the more popular of the two in academic anthropology.

SPENCER

Herbert Spencer's version of social evolution differed from that of most of his contemporaries in that he was explicit about what made societies evolve or progress. For him the prime mover was the struggle for survival. Starting with the assumption that "primitive groups of men are habitually hostile" (1910: 631) and that warfare was the norm for most of human history, he argued that the fittest organizations persisted at the expense of the less fit. Fitness was judged partly by tautology—the organizations that survived must have been the fittest—and partly by how well a society's institutions were geared to rearing its children and caring for its adults. These latter are Spencer's criteria for examining the evolution of the family and, derived from it, the status of women.

According to Spencer, in earliest times "savages" lived miserably; they had high mortality rates, practiced infanticide, matured early, and died early. There were no families and no social order. A woman's postreproductive life was short, ending in violence and/or deliberate desertion. Wife lending was common, chastity devalued, and incest prohibitions absent (Ibid.: 611–18). Spencer recognized that "advance" in sexual relations did not always correspond to "advance" in social evolution, but he insisted that "progress" from "lower" to "higher" forms of domestic organization could be clearly shown by comparing the extremes of this brute savagery with the Victorian middle-class family.

Spencer believed that women had always been the personal property of individual men. He argued that just as carnivores own their prey, so too did men own women. Women were part of the booty of war and hence the property of successful warriors. Exogamy developed from the desire of all men to have what the best warriors had— "foreign" wives. Thus from warfare came capture of wives. Peaceful or weak tribes, by contrast, took their women from within their own group (endogamy) for fear of bringing down the wrath of the strong should they steal women. As the strong exogamous tribes expanded, they created conditions favorable to "internal exogomy" where the daughters of captured wives were acceptable as prestigious spouses. This system led to matrilineal kinship, where relationships were traced through women.

Spencer believed that actual promiscuity reigned but that it was checked by individual men's claims on individual women. Under these circumstances, the only real parent was the mother, since men had no incentive to develop parental ties. This situation also contributed to matrilineal kinship. But Spencer saw matriliny as an inferior institution because children without an institutionalized male protector suffer, and this works against group survival. Natural selection favored those groups that best regulated sex relations and thus best reproduced their members. In the struggle for survival, they won out over groups that did not.

For Spencer, polygyny, polyandry, and monogamy were all equally early ways of regulating sex and child care, and each arose as a response to particular ecological conditions, but they were not equally good for ensuring species survival. Various forms of polyandry were favored under conditions of poor resources, where several men were required to support a limited number of children: "just as there are habitats in which only inferior forms of animals can exist, so in societies physically conditioned in particular ways, the inferior forms of domestic life survive because they alone are practicable" (1910: 659). The deficiencies of polyandry were that it diffused male parental responsibility and produced a limited number of children (Spencer does not say why). But as an inferior form and one producing fewer children, it has been mainly supplanted by more advanced domestic forms.

Polygyny was better than polyandry in that it developed parental feelings in fathers as well as in mothers. Monogamy was the general condition of marriage even in polygynous societies because only men of high prestige could obtain and keep more than one wife. Particularly in areas where the necessary labor was suitable for women to perform, wives further increased a man's prestige by increasing his wealth. Polygyny had still another survival advantage: the normal conditions of endemic warfare gave rise to a shortage of men. Polygyny enabled a warlike society to marry all its women, increase its population, rear a large number of warriors, and hence prevail against societies without polygyny. We shall see that this notion has been resurrected in contemporary social darwinism by DiVale and Harris (1976; Harris 1975).

The development of domesticated animals was a critical boost to the development of a proper family "defined, compact and organized" in that it became centered around property and acted as a unit of labor under patriarchs. It was from this line that modern, progressive society developed: "This organization which the pastoral group gets by being at once family and society, and which is gradually perfected by conflict and survival of the fittest, it carries into settled life" (Spencer 1910: 715). At this point society developed by cooperation among well-defined families, and, in time, "paternal despotism" was undermined:

Individuals of the family, no longer working together only in their unlike relations to one another, and coming to work together under like relations to state-authority and to enemies, the public co-operation and subordination grew at the expense of the private co-operation and subordination. And in the large aggregates eventually formed, industrial activities as well as militant activities conduced to this result. [Ibid.: 716]

The contrast between militant and industrial societies is central to Spencer's sociology. The former are warlike, the latter peaceful. Evolution has moved humanity from a state where the former was the norm to one where the latter is the norm. Industrial society does not mean that war is absent, however; it means only that the bulk of the male population is engaged in productive activities rather than in fighting. Thus both Victorian England and Rome at the height of its empire were industrial because their wars were fought with specialized soldiers, far away, and because the bulk of the population was left at home to pursue industry. Expansive, or imperialist, warfare thus was compatible with social progress. Conditions of peace, the importance of industry, and the renewal of a balanced sex ratio favored the expansion of monogamy, a necessary condition for improvement in what Spencer believed women's status ought to be.

But as we have seen, Spencer was strongly opposed to equal rights for women, and his scenario of evolutionary progress and species survival rationalized his political beliefs. Spencer insisted that society and family operate on different principles. Families operate on the

law that the least worthy shall receive most aid, [this] is essential as a law for the immature: the species would disappear in a generation did not parents conform to it. Now mark what is, contrariwise, the law for the mature. Here individuals gain benefits proportionate to their merits. The strong . . . profit by their respective superiorities. . . . The less capable thrive less, and on the average of cases rear fewer offspring. The least capable disappear. . . . And by this process is maintained the quality of the species. [Ibid.: 720]

The "society stands to its citizens in the same relation as a species to its members" (Ibid.). Thus ethics of family and society are opposite: the former is based on generosity and the latter on justice and merit.

However fitly in the battle of life among adults, the proportioning of rewards to merits may be tempered by private sympathy in favor of the inferior; nothing but evil can result if this proportioning is so interfered with by public arrangements, that demerit profits at the expense of merit. [Ibid.: 721]

Spencer's insistence on the differences between family and society are important for understanding his views on women's place.

Perhaps in no way is the moral progress of mankind more clearly shown, than by contrasting the position of women among savages with their position among the most advanced of the civilized. At the one extreme a treatment of them cruel to the utmost degree bearable; and at the other extreme a treatment which, in some directions, gives them precedence over men. [Ibid.: 725]

Savage women, however, were just as brutal as the men; women were beaten bloody only because they were weaker. Spencer points out, only in passing, that women had political authority in some of these "savage" societies. But the norm was for women to be private possessions of a man. Their condition improved somewhat when men had to work for a wife's parents or pay for their wives, a system that gave women greater value and decreased the likelihood of abuse (Ibid.: 732–33). But the major conditions for women's elevation were the rise of monogamy and industrial society. When these conditions obtained, even among "savages" as they occasionally did, women's position was better than where they were absent.

That approximate equalization of the sexes in numbers which results from diminishing militancy and increasing industrialism, conduces to the elevation of women, since in proportion as the supply of males available for carrying on social sustentation increases, the labour of social sustentation falls less heavily on females. And it may be added that the societies in which these available males undertake the harder labours, and so, relieving the females from undue physical tax, enable them to produce more and better offspring, will, other things being equal, gain in the struggle for existence. [Ibid.: 743]

For Spencer, women's destiny seems to be freedom from productive labor so they may become mothers of the fittest. Women's rights as people and their access to authority and personal freedom seem secondary.

Spencer regards male and female nature as very different. These differences evolved from "adaptation to the paternal and maternal duties" (1884: 313) and from adaptation of women to men and men to the social conditions of existence. Women's biological evolution was stunted to reserve "vital power to meet the cost of reproduction" (Ibid.: 374). This has affected women's mental capacities, resulting in

. . . a perceptible falling-short in those two faculties, intellectual and emotional, which are the latest products of human evolution—the power of abstract reasoning and the most abstract of the emotions, the sentiment of justice. . . .

The remaining qualitative distinctions between the minds of men and women are those which have grown out of their mutual relations as stronger and weaker. [Ibid.: 374–75]

Men who were strong, brave, unscrupulous, and "intensely egoistic" survived in the struggle for existence with other men. Given such men, the women most likely to survive and rear children were those who developed the ability to please, to hide their feelings, to persuade and cajole, and to discern quickly the mood of those around. Women's intellect depended "almost wholly" on such feminine intuition. But women also developed another trait crucial to survival of the species: an attraction to men of power. This trait is still manifest in women's "admiration of power in general" and respect for the "symbols of authority, governmental and social" (Ibid.: 378). These masculine and feminine traits were fixed in humanity by inheritance of acquired characteristics by the same sex.

Spencer expected that the progress of civilization would make these traits ultimately cease to be adaptive and that the mental differences between men and women would decrease. But he took great pains to show that this analysis did not imply granting political or social equality to women because women are not mentally ready for equality with men. First, women respond to appeals based on pity rather than on equity and thus would exacerbate the awful tendency for the pitiful to be given aid; "often as much aid if their sufferings are caused by themselves as if they are caused by others—often greater aid indeed" (Ibid.: 379). Second, women focus on the immediate over the abstract. Thus mothers can see only a child's immediate problems, while fathers see beyond these to the shaping of their child's future character. Women's judgment in social affairs is weakened by this same defect. Third, since women love power, they act to strengthen government and church. Doubt or criticism of power and authority is lacking in women—and hence so too is respect for freedom or "the ability to carry on his own life without hindrance from others" (Ibid.: 380). Thus granting equal rights to women would have disastrous consequences for the future of the society, of women, and of the species itself. Spencer was unalterably opposed to tampering with what he insisted was natural law and hence to the demands of feminists in his society.

Spencer saw evolutionary struggle as selecting for those attributes and organizations that maximized species survival. Because women bear children and because they are always smaller and weaker than men, the struggle destined each sex to different spheres of life and to develop the psychological attributes and desires consonant with their social function and place. Thus evolution produced the following, in Spencer's view:

1. Separate family and social spheres run according to different laws.
2. An intellectually inferior female sex who relies on intuition and obsequiousness for mental functioning and thus is incapable of participating in the social sphere.
3. A female sex whose function is to bear children in the family sphere under the protection and possession of a stronger, wiser man.
4. A male sex whose strength and intellect has adapted it to produce the world's wealth, make its decisions, and protect its own bearer of the next generation.

From this analysis, two political conclusions followed:

1. Real, or practically meaningful, sexual equality lies in each sex's doing what it is innately suited for. Thus equality was redefined to mean complementarity instead of equal rights. The latter was a social contradiction and hence unreal.
2. Demands for equal rights come from socialists who are bent on destroying both the family and private property and hence destroying civilization. Socialism flies in the face of natural law.

Herbert Spencer is little cited in twentieth-century anthropology. Indeed both his celebration of laissez-faire capitalism and his notion that military conquest is a demonstration of social superiority have been in disfavor for quite some time, though they have become fashionable again recently. But his major themes with respect to women have been recreated anew by subsequent schools of anthropology: the functionalist approaches, which dominated anthropological inquiry from the 1920s to the 1960s; the neoevolutionists, who became quite influential in the 1960s; and finally the sociobiology of the 1970s.

FUNCTIONALISM

The functionalists saw themselves as advocating a scientific orientation and as throwing off the shackles of their predecessors' unbridled speculation into origins. The exciting questions of humanity's past and future were abandoned—sometimes as unknowable, sometimes as unworthy of scientific study. Instead inquiry focused on how societies functioned, on how cultures maintained themselves. Biological analogy remained, but instead of its being to the origins of species, it was to the homeostasis of an organism and to the integration of its systems. For most nineteenth-century evolutionists, such analyses were part of their larger focus on social change. However, functionalism took the part for the whole and tended to portray the homeostasis it described as natural and inevitable.

In both the United States and in Europe, functionalism was based on an almost consistently antireductionist position: that social facts—in particular, cultural patterns and variations—could not be explained by alleged biological or biophysical differences. In the United States, the work of Franz Boas was extremely important in demonstrating that biology and culture varied independently and that biology could not explain the organization of particular cultures. Boas was quite influential in discrediting racist arguments that some populations and their cultures were inherently fitter than others. Since Boas, anthropology has consistently discredited notions of biopsychological inferiority and superiority, as well as biopsychological explanations of cultural variation. In other words, innatism and social darwinism are not accepted as scientific explanations.

But this antireductionist principle has not been applied consistently to analyses of social roles of women and men. On the one hand assertions about alleged mental inferiority of women were rejected. And following the boasian tradition, Mead (1935) explicitly debunked assertions about sexual temperament, showing that culture rather than biology shaped personality, often to the disregard of sex lines. Thus innate sexual psychology was rejected as a causal explanation. Instead innate function was retained as the explanatory principle. Certain basic and universal male and female roles, statuses, and relations were asserted to follow necessarily from the biological fact that women bear children and men do not, and these universal social consequences were further asserted to be necessary for the preservation of orderly social life. The functionalists' necessary consequences are identical to Spencer's evolutionary consequences: male dominance in the family and society. Like Spencer too, leading functionalists rejected an equal-rights definition of equality as meaningless. Which sex

made decisions was insignificant compared to the fact that each sex
needed the services that the other provided.

On the woman question, then, the functionalists worked well within
the spencerian innatist and antifeminist tradition but with some theoretical and methodological differences. Spencer saw "the primitive"
as the antithesis of "civilization" and, in accord with his time, traced a
path of progress for women. The functionalists refused to equate contemporary noncapitalist cultures with original humanity. Instead they
emphasized what they believed to be universal patterns of sex roles
and family organization. Spencer "proved" the rightness of the
Victorian sexual status quo by pointing to its success in conquering
and expanding against cultures with "inferior" family and sex role
organization; the functionalists "proved" it by showing that because
all cultures shared the same basic patterns of organization with reference to women and men, this pattern must be a natural one inherent in
the human condition. Although Spencer called it superior and the
functionalists called it universal, they agreed on its content and on its
necessity: (1) Women were basically wives and mothers. This stemmed from women's maternal nature, or function. (2) Families were
properly or basically monogamous and nuclear. (3) Men were the
rulers and decision makers of society and the family. In sum, women
made babies; men made culture and society.

There is a striking difference, however, between the anthropology of
the functionalist era and that of Spencer's time. The latter recognized
both sexes and devoted considerable descriptive and explanatory
effort to explore sexual differences (Bachofen 1861; Lubbock 1870;
Maine 1861; Mason 1894; McLennan 1865; Morgan 1877). But the
functionalists almost completely ignored women in both description
and theory. (Ronhaar 1931 is a rare exception.) To the extent that
women appeared at all, it was as wives and mothers of men. The most
likely explanation for this difference is that there was no active feminist movement to bring the matter to anthropology's attention. In its
absence, anthropological assumptions about women's fundamental
functions, roles, and statuses were derived from the prevailing norms
and world view of their own society and were largely implicit.

There are two kinds of sources for reconstructing anthropological
theories of women. The first is from the bits and pieces of the assumptions that litter functionalist studies of kinship. The second lies in confrontations between functionalists and those outside their academic

milieu. Because there was virtually no debate within academic social science during this period, it was principally in this latter context that anthropologists were called upon to explain the reasoning and theory behind the assumptions they made in their professional analyses.

In the functionalist school, standard kinship analyses emphasized systems of tracing group membership by descent, generally uni-lineal—through the male line (patrilineal) or the female line (matri-lineal). In both types men were assumed to be the holders of authority. In the functional examination of matrilineal descent groups, Malinow-ski's Trobriand Island studies set the pattern.

Even today his are some of the clearest statements on the general position of the male in matrilineal societies, his equivocal relationship to his wife and children, the special importance of his relationship with his sister and sister's husband, and the conflict between a man's loyalties to his natal and his conjugal kin. [Schneider and Gough 1961: xii]

One aspect of this pattern has been a focus on social relations among men, almost to the exclusion of women. Indeed the treatment of women's social relations is limited to their reproductive capacity and to the social relations of motherhood to which it gives rise. The second aspect, from which the first stems, is that women are assumed to have no power or legitimate authority.

This pattern is made explicit in Schneider's introduction to *Matrilineal Kinship*, which is perhaps the most sustained discussion of the social structure of societies based on matrilineal descent groups.

There are, finally, three conditions which are, by definition here, constant features of unilineal descent groups regardless of the principle in terms of which the descent group is formed. They are the "constants," of course, strictly in the sense that the theory requires them as characteristics of descent groups. These three constants in combination with matrilineal descent, give matrilineal descent groups their distinctive characteristics. These are: first, women are responsible for the care of children, with every child being the primary responsibility of one woman; second, adult men have authority over women and children; and third, descent group exogamy is required. [Ibid.: 5]

Matriliny is not seen as a mirror image of patriliny. In patrilineal groups, male kin can live together, bringing their wives to live with them. Because men are property managers and family and lineage decision makers, patriliny is a fairly simple and efficient way of organizing social groups. But a matrilineal kin group cannot be organized simply by having the women of the lineage bring their husbands to live with them. The reason is that women are never the decision makers. Hence in matrilineal (but not patrilineal) organization, the lineage must retain control of both its male members (to make decisions) and female members (to bear the lineage's next generation). Patrilineal descent groups can give up control over their female members. In patrilineal systems, a man can have undisputed authority over wife and children and have his household as part of his lineage. Much attention has been paid since Malinowski's work to the "fact" that marriage in matrilineal societies pulls men in two directions: to wife and children on the one hand and to their own kin group on the other. This structural ambivalence was said to give rise to a characteristic brittleness of marriage in matrilineal societies.

The functionalist treatment explains the alleged nature of marriage relations in matrilineal society by the assumption of universal male authority. Unfortunately these polarized lenses filtered out situations of brittle marriage in patrilineal societies just as it filtered out situations of shared authority among men and women in both patrilineal and matrilineal societies. Both were described in the ethnographic literature of the time. (See Chapters 5 and 6).

E. E. Evans-Pritchard's essay, "The Position of Women in Primitive Society" (1965), while it is unusually crude in its argument, is one of the few works by a major functionalist anthropologist to address directly the question of female-male social relations. Evans-Pritchard tried to show why his study of other cultures argues against feminism in his own society. "Primitive" women are said to be happy to be excluded from the running of their societies: "She does not desire, in this respect, things to be other than they are" (Ibid.: 45). Because women are happy in what they perceive is an inferior position (Ibid: 52), so too are their men. Evans-Pritchard contrasts this harmonious state of affairs with the much less harmonious relations between men and women in his own society, where many women are not happy with their place. He asserts that women's rejection of subordinate female roles is the cause of male homosexuality and contrasts this situation with the alleged rarity of male homosexuality in non-Western cultures (Ibid.: 48).

Evans-Pritchard turned next to the division of labor and basic sex roles. All societies have a division of labor based on sex; this gives rise to a division of socializing on the same basis; thus "the sexes do not intrude on one another all the time" as they do in the West (Ibid: 49). Moreover husband and wife do not compete with each other. Evans-Pritchard recognizes that separation does not mean equality, for women are confined to the household: "If this demarcation is for primitive women a restriction, it is also a protection" (Ibid: 50). If the house is women's place, the authority within it is always male. Evans-Pritchard is at ease with this situation because when a man is clearly in charge, the inevitable household conflicts are more restricted; "they do not constitute a fundamental challenge to man's position in the home." There is less to fight about in "primitive" households than in our own, where "the area of possible disagreement [covers] the whole social life of the family both within and without it, and [causes] suffering to the woman as well as to her husband and children" (Ibid.: 51). Women's place is in the home, and men are the authority both in society and in the home. These places, or sex roles, are universal and must be adhered to in order to preserve social harmony. Finally Evans-Pritchard asserts that this universal order rests on biology, and hence is natural as well as proper (Ibid.: 54–55).

Despite its anachronistic-sounding conservative tone, Evans-Pritchard's essay summarizes some of anthropology's key assumptions about enduring and universal sex roles. The most important of these are that women's place is always a domestic one, that men's sphere is social, and that only men hold social and domestic authority. These have been repeated in contexts innocent of prescriptive intent: "It is sufficient then, to define the male sex role as having authority over the statuses occupied by women within the context of each of these spheres" (Schneider and Gough 1961: 7).

The second set of assumptions that forms part of the core of functional thinking about women concerns the family. The work of Bronislaw Malinowski, one of the fathers of the functionalist perspective, speaks most clearly to the question of family structure and male-female relations within the family. Malinowski's functionalism was more securely rooted in biology than was that of most of his contemporaries. In his view, impulses are biological drives that have been given cultural form. Cultural institutions are responses to impulses rather than directly caused by biological drives (1927: 210–11). Much of Malinowski's work focused on the institution of the family,

which he believed to be essentially monogamous. Thus plural marriages for him simply established compound nuclear families; that is,
one man was the father-husband in two nuclear families, each made up
of husband, wife, and children.

Like other institutions, the family was based on impulses: "No human impulse is so deeply rooted as the maternal impulse in woman . . .
and I believe that it is bound up with the institution of marriage"
(Montagu 1956: 78–79). Similarly men have a matrimonial impulse
to protect the pregnant female. The human family needs a male, and
"this biological need is expressed in the principle of legitimacy which
demands a male as the guardian, protector and regent of the family"
(Malinowski 1927: 253–54). Since parents and children are a social
unit, with responsibility for the education of the child, Malinowski,
like Evans-Pritchard, believed that there must be an authority figure:
"the father or some other male must become invested with authority at
later stages" (Ibid.: 254). "The male aspect becomes gradually the
principle of force, or distance, or pursuit of ambition and of authority"
(Ibid.: 257).

In 1931 Malinowski and Robert Briffault held a series of radio
debates on marriage over the BBC (Montagu 1956). Malinowski
presented a view of the family and marriage that was becoming the
prime one held by social anthropology. Briffault was a widely read and
liberal critic of society yet could not secure a regular academic position (Montagu 1956: 5). He is important here for his attempt to force
anthropology to speak to the issue of marital oppression of women in
capitalist society. Malinowski's major theme was that the family—
composed of one mother, one father, and children—is the foundation
of all culture and that all communist (or any other) attempts to tamper
with it are futile and, moreover, dangerous to humanity. Communist
ideas, according to Malinowski, stem from old (he meant socialist-
communist) and mistaken notions of group marriage. Hence bad anthropology, which Malinowski believed Briffault represented, has had
unfortunate practical social consequences.

Malinowski's first talk focused on the Soviet Union's transformation of marriage and family law. Malinowski, who criticized the
Soviets for attempting legally to make marriage voluntary, claimed
that the Bolsheviks' ideas about sexual freedom and group marriage
were adopted from anthropological interpretation by unnamed "nineteenth century German socialists." Certainly the most influential of

these were Engels and Marx. It is hard to imagine either as a proponent of the sexually exploitative promiscuity Malinowski conjured up. Indeed Engels (1891:57) explicitly denounced such bourgeois interpretations of the past. Malinowski was engaging in a common red bait: obfuscating Soviet attempts to end patriarchal inequality by raising that old bogey of the bourgeoisie, "sexual [actually sexist] communism."

Briffault attempted to pull Malinowski away from such stereotyping by pointing out that criticism of marriage and family came mainly from women in England who objected to their subordinate position. This, he said, is the essence of the issue he and Malinowski were discussing. Nobody, said Briffault, was arguing for the abolition of marriage and family; rather they simply wanted to do away with its oppressive characteristics. Briffault's concern with other cultures was to show that male family rule was a late invention. He claimed that Malinowski's anthropology, or functionalist anthropology, was doing a disservice to marriage and the family because it taught that "as things are now, so they have been from the beginning, and ever shall be" (Ibid.: 32). By such teachings, academic anthropology was buttressing an oppressive state of affairs rather than helping to modify it. His basic challenge was that Malinowski's anthropology, by dealing only in eternal verities of marriage and family and ignoring historical change, would simply reinforce the problems being criticized.

In the ensuing debate, Malinowski proved him right. First, he homed in on group marriage, insisting that marriage has always been individual, "a legal contract between one man and one woman. . . . Polygamy . . . is a series of individual contracts" (Ibid.: 42). In Malinowski's view, marriage protects women by forcing men to take responsibility for family affairs that they otherwise would not do. Women need no coercion to marry because of their "maternal impulse." Men, however, need to be coerced into their domestic roles, a position that leaves women to be the coercers. By implication, then, it is impossible for marriage to be oppressive to women. Malinowski gave little direct comment on what he believed was the content of male-female marital relations, though he seemed to be denying that women have any reason to protest. Where Briffault insisted that marriage and family had been less oppressive to women in the past and suggested that it could and should become so in the future, Malinowski simply insisted on the impossibility of collective parenthood or marriage and became quite emotional at the thought of the "red menace" to civilization: "But an idea like that, once it is taken seriously and applied to modern conditions, becomes positively dangerous" (Ibid.: 76).

At the end of his final talk, Malinowski dealt directly with the question of sexual oppression.

It is a distortion of the truth to attack marriage on the plea that it is an enslavement of woman by man. The analysis of primitive marriage I gave you shows that marriage is a contract safeguarding the interests of the woman as well as granting privileges to man. A detailed study of the economic aspects of marriage reveals in fact, that the man has to prove his capacity to maintain the woman. . . .

The laws of marriage and family express, among other things, the demand that the male should face his responsibility and should take his share of the duties and burdens as well as of the privileges connected with the process of reproduction. [Ibid.: 79]

Malinowski's argument is that women want children and require male protection to rear them; they thus accord men domestic and social privileges in exchange for this protection. Malinowski was reiterating Spencer's theme that unequal social status stems from women's need for protection. In Spencer, but not in Malinowski, women needed protection from men, an interpretation that appears to be a "protection racket," where the victim pays the oppressor for relief. In this situation women are hardly the equals of men. But Malinowski drew the implausible conclusion that marriage is an egalitarian relationship. In this too he echoes Spencer's and Evans-Pritchard's insistence that complementary functions, and not equal rights, are the proper way to view equality. In that way, both sexes will be happier and the future of society assured.

There is thus unbroken tradition asserting that bourgeois family relations, particularly the need for male authority, were rooted in natural law. When Evans-Prichard dredged up the specter of male homosexuality and unspecified general misery as the consequences of feminist meddling with nature, Malinowski warned that women would be seduced and abandoned if they forsook the protection of the bourgeois family to pursue the Bolshevik goal of egalitarianism.

In some ways the functionalist argument for the necessity of male dominance seems an advance over Spencer. The latter needed to

assert that women were intellectually inferior to men for his argumen.
to hold together. The functionalists arrived as their conclusions without reference to intellect. But their advance is illusory because they replaced an innatist argument with an unsupported assertion that baby
makers cannot be decision makers.

NEOEVOLUTIONISM AND SOCIOBIOLOGY

In two ways recent work on women in anthropology has more in
common with writings of the late nineteenth century than it does with
the work of the immediate past. First, there is a return to nineteenth-
century questions of evolution and social change. This includes a will-
ingness to apply what has been learned about nonstate social organizations, about nonhuman primates and about human and prehuman
history to speculate on human origins and patterns of social evolution.
Second, anthropological attention has again been directed toward the
woman question. As feminist activity and inquiry have challenged anthropology's earlier social darwinism, these themes have been given
new form and with an equally prescriptive antifeminist message.

Recent anthropology has presented a view of human social evolution very different from Spencer's and much closer to Engels's in several respects. There is no evidence for any primordial state of endemic
warfare; rather, among collecting societies, organized warfare seems
to have been rare or absent. In addition, social ranking based on
strength or wealth also seems to have been absent (Service 1966; Lee
and DeVore 1968; Bicchieri 1972). Although all known societies
practice marriage, this institution among collecting societies, and
among many nonstratified cultivating societies, appears more like
Engels's description of "pairing marriage" than like Spencer's description of possession of women by men. Even nineteenth-century
speculations about primitive promiscuity are being reconsidered for
presapiens history, based on study of Old World monkeys and great
ape social organization (Lancaster 1975; Lee and DeVore 1968; Slocum 1975). Finally, most twentieth-century neoevolutionists stress
the at least relative egalitarianism of gathering-hunting societies and
trace the bifurcation of society into classes—rich and powerful, poor
and powerless—based on differential access to the means of subsistence (Sahlins and Service 1960; Fried 1967; Adams 1966).

This agreement in neoevolutionary thought, however, does not

⌄ow how women fit into the picture; by and large it was drawn with reference to men. Only in the last few years have there been sustained attempts, which vary greatly, to see how women might have fared in human evolution. Here the focus is on the return to spencerian notions in two forms: cultural ecology and sociobiology. Both argue, though in different ways, that the subordination of women is a necessary outcome of the struggle for survival.

Marvin Harris, in a widely used textbook, *Culture, People, Nature* (1975), argues that sexism was the fittest form of society under the ecological conditions prevailing for most of human history. Harris claims that a state of primeval warfare and aggression is the explanation for contemporary patterns of sexism and even the physical dimorphism of men and women. Like Spencer, Harris roots warfare in the struggle for existence. He believes that warfare has always been with humanity, even before sedentary life, though its purpose in nomadic collecting societies was not territorial acquisition. With sedentization and horticulture, warfare became endemic, more violent, and aimed at annihilation of other groups and acquisition of territory. Indeed Harris believed that endemic warfare and persistent attempts at intergroup annihilation were the norm in the preindustrial, preclass world: "War-linked, male centered institutions, prerogatives and ideologies seem to be present in the great majority of ethnographically known cultures" (1975: 269).

The relationship between warfare and male supremacy rests on natural selection, which favors greater population density, particularly of warrior aged males, "among societies that persistently try to annihilate each other" (Ibid.: 259). Because a society's land base has a finite carrying capacity, a state of warfare favors female infanticide to maximize the number of males reared and to balance out the sexes in later life resulting from the fact that many men will be killed in warfare. In order to persuade a society to kill female babies, cultural forces must glory males and devalue females, who perform valuable labor. This is the source of sexism and patriarchy.

In order to rear fierce and aggressive warriors, males are rewarded with sexual privileges that depend on women being passive and submissive. . . . Males repeatedly denigrate women's work and confer prestige on their own, the relative prestige of hunting versus collecting being the prime example. . . .

The masculine male-war complex leads further to the control over gardens and property by male members of domestic groupings, to the prevalence of ideologies in which descent through males is more important than descent through females. [Ibid.: 269–71, 271–72]

Finally, between graphs of male and female Olympic records labeled "Can the Gap Be Closed?" and a photo essay captioned, "There is evidence of a close correlation between warfare and aggressive male sports," Harris suggests, "It seems plausible to infer that the present degree of sexual dimorphism is a result of selection against tall, heavily muscled women in the past" (Ibid.: 269). Nowhere is there any indication of what in the culture or life circumstances of women might provide the selective pressure against tall, muscular women.

Harris's argument rests on two somewhat contradictory assumptions. Either people make war because they are innately aggressive, as in the explanation of warfare among collecting societies, or they make war because they generally live in a state of chronic shortage of resources and consequently need to destroy competitors for them. Harris applies the latter explanation, which seems to be his principal assumption, to warfare among sedentary societies. However, it is contrary to current evidence and prevailing opinion (Adams and Nissen 1972; Sahlins 1972; Lee and DeVore 1968). In fact, it is probably more likely that major known upsurges in warfare in the nonstate world have been products of capitalist expansion, directly or indirectly, and systematic alienation of resources. This has been demonstrated for the North American plains (Secoy 1953) and the upper Nile pastoralists (Sacks 1979) and has been suggested for the Amazon basin (Davis and Mathews 1976; Murphy and Steward 1956). To project instances of warfare waged under these conditions back to a primeval human condition is ahistorical and grossly inaccurate. In addition, the pattern of male dominance that Harris alleges to be an ancient one seems more a product of male bias in theory building than the reality of nonclass societies.

Where Harris asserts and illustrates the warfare-male dominance argument in his textbook, Divale and Harris (1976) purport to demonstrate it. They claim that their cross-cultural comparison of prestate societies shows that warlike societies practice female infanticide and devalue and subordinate women in other ways. They argue that warfare for scarce resources was probably endemic in the prestate world and that this condition probably explains the universal subordination of women.

In this article as well as in Harris's textbook, the Yanomamo of Venezuela are presented as a classical case of male supremacist society, practicing female infanticide as an adaptation of endemic warlike competition for scarce resources. Though the Yanomamo have been presented by their principal ethnographer as almost a caricature of fierce machismo (Chagnon 1968a), Chagnon asserts that territorial conquest was neither a cause nor a consequence of Yanomamo warfare (1968b: 110). Apparently warfare was not long endemic among all Yanomamo, only among some. Chagnon (1976: 213 quoted in Fjellman: 1977) suggests that warfare is a recent introduction, brought with shotguns, to some Yanomamo villages. Moreover, Davis and Mathews (1976) in a critique of the Yanomamo literature, have argued that warfare as well as a variety of health and nutritionally adverse conditions have been created or exacerbated by twentieth-century capitalist penetration into the Amazon basin. On women's subordination and female infanticide, only the latter is open to dispute. Subordination and poor treatment of women does seem to be the case, but Fjellman has shown that the critical data, on infanticide, are open to question:

The actual countable data on the frequency of Yanomamo infanticide come from two demographic papers by Neel and Chagnon (1968) and Neel and Weiss (1975). This information consisted of oral reports from missionaries of the Unevangelized Field Mission. I can find what looks like information from four villages (Divale and Harris use 26 Yanomamo localities). . . . Out of 220 live births, there are reported to have been 14 infanticides (6.4 per cent) among a people who claim to remove defectives. Furthermore, *none* of these reports mention anything about the sex of the infants killed (1977: 11).

The remaining evidence is anecdotal,

but is mainly an inference from sex ratio data. Neel and Weiss (1975) find a sex ratio of 140 male children to 100 female children. They use this to infer that female infanticide must be taking place. . . .

1) Their sex ratio data is amalgamated data, gathered with great difficulty over a ten year period. This data neutralizes local differences. Furthermore, the Yanomamo have approximately the same sex ratio as is reported for the Xavante, who are not said to commit female infanticide. . . .

3) If the basic sources infer the incidence of female infanticide from sex ratios, then these scales are not independent. Thus, any statistical test performed to show that high sex ratios and female infanticide are associated is illegitimate. Female infanticide is already coded from sex ratios. [Ibid.: 12]

Fjellman's critique goes beyond the Yanomamo case and shows that Divale and Harris have drawn an inappropriate sample, used misleading statistics, and have not made full reference to their sources of data. For example, their data come from 574 localities (by Fjellman's count; Divale and Harris give 561) in 112 societies. But a small number of Cuna in Panama are represented by 92 localities, and a large ethnic group of Edo in Nigeria are represented by one locality. Harris and Divale give 26 Yanomamo localities with data on infanticide, but Fjellman's search of the literature turned up only four.

Hirschfeld, Howe, and Levin (1978) have also criticized Divale and Harris's methods and use of statistics on many of the same grounds. In addition, they reexamine Divale and Harris's use of the Cuna (who make up one-sixth of their sample) and Aymara data and find them guilty of double counting, using data recognized in the literature as unreliable, including states in what was said to be a nonstate sample (the five Aymara localities), and misclassifying the Cuna with respect to warfare. Divale, Harris, and Williams's (1978) reply does not satisfactorily answer these points. Hirschfeld, Howe, and Levin also found that the remainder of Divale and Harris's South American data, when analyzed by other methods, showed no correlation between warfare and skewed sex ratios.

The Divale and Harris study has been widely criticized on other grounds. First, the presence or absence of infanticide is guessed at from sex ratio statistics. These statistics, particularly on small populations, are not accurate. Fjellman (1977) points out that females between ten and fourteen (the critical years for the Divale and Harris argument) are recognized as being generally underreported throughout the world. He also points out that other reasons than female infanticide, such as labor migration, could account for lowered sex ratios, particularly among adults. Second, they have been criticized for asserting that male dominance is a universal, or near universal, condition (Lancaster and Lancaster 1978; Brown: forthcoming).

Whyte, in a cross-cultural study of women in preindustrial societies, found more evidence for women having "higher status in cultures

with constant warfare" (1978: 129) than for the hypothesis that they
had lower statuses:

... in cultures with frequent warfare there is less joint social life between men
and women. ... The strongest associations tell us that in cultures with frequent
warfare women have more domestic authority, somewhat more ritualized solidarity, and perhaps more value placed on their lives. [Ibid.]

Whyte seems to speak to Divale and Harris as well as to other neospencerians:

This last relationship, although modest in size, is important to note because
many ethological speculations current these days assume that when men
spend much of their time in warfare they will also tend to brutalize their
women. ... but in fact we find that women are treated somewhat *better*, with
wife beating not encouraged, in cultures with frequent warfare than in other
cultures. [Ibid.]

Indeed the brunt of Whyte's study is to stress the cross-cultural variety
in women's positions from culture to culture and to undercut any
theory that starts from the premise of universal subordination or inferiority of women.

Spencer has been most fully resurrected by the recent field called
sociobiology, laid out in greatest detail in E. O. Wilson's (1975) textbook of the same name. Sociobiology shares the same world view as
the nineteenth-century social darwinists: society is the product of a
warlike struggle for existence in which the less fit—societies and people—lose out to the fittest. Some societies, like some people, are inherently fitter than others. The new twist is that sociobiology locates
the cause of this variance in the genes and postulates a large number of
behavioral genes, among them, altruistic genes, upward-mobile genes,
homosexuality genes, and aggressive genes. No sociobiologist has attempted, however, to find a chromosomal locus for any of these.
Nevertheless Wilson claims that some cultures are inherently fitter
than others because the gene pool of their members is fitter: "Although
the genes have given away most of their sovereignty, they maintain a
certain amount of influence in at least the behavioral qualities that
underlie variations between cultures. ... In short, there is a need for a
discipline of anthropological genetics" (Ibid.: 550).

Human social and biological evolution are virtually the same in
sociobiology's scheme: better people rise to the top of their society just
as better societies eliminate the less fit, biologically as well as culturally. Not only are the inferior eliminated, but the process by which this is
done is alleged to have become genetically fixed. Because he assumes
that individuals and societies alike consciously act to maximize their
"genetic representation," Wilson assumes that a society of intelligent
beings would see the advantages of eliminating its neighbors and
taking their territory. Early hominids, he believes, were capable of intelligent action. Having defined what constituted intelligent action,
and that humanity's ancestors were intelligent, it follows that they
must have acted on that knowledge. Moreover they are said to have retained a "tribal memory" of their successful course of action to have
kept repeating it, thereby spreading their own "genetic representation
in the metapopulation" (Ibid.: 573): "Such primitive cultural capacity would be permitted by the possession of certain genes. Recipro-
cally, the cultural capacity might propel the spread of the genes
through the genetic constitution of the metapopulation. Once begun,
such a mutual reinforcement could be irreversible" (Ibid). From this
logic it follows that imperialism and warfare are part of the human
(male) genetic program or "biogram." Social systems are not at fault;
they are simply the working out of genetic necessity.

The same process of genetic selection is said to operate within societies to raise better people to both worldly and reproductive success.
Thus in contemporary capitalist societies, the rich and powerful are
not rich and powerful because they inherited wealth and power but because they inherited superior genes, which lead to superior behavior
and success. Sociobiology hopes to "identify the behaviors and rules
by which individual human beings increase their Darwinian fitness
through the manipulation of society" (Ibid.: 548).

Darwinian fitness is not used simply to mean reproductive success
(begetting more progeny). Indeed reproductive success and worldly
success are used almost interchangeably, with the latter often imply-
ing the former. Thus the !Kung Bushmen are described as having "best
people" who are outstanding entrepreneurs, who are male, and, like
men in industrial nations, either achieve success before the age of forty
or accept a lower status for the rest of their lives. !Kung also have
the equivalent of social darwinism's undeserving poor, "who never try
to make it, live in run-down huts and show little pride in themselves or

their work" (Ibid.: 549). Aside from being an outrageous distortion of
!Kung organization and values (E. M. Thomas 1959; Lee 1968,
1969, 1974), this theory envisions social organization as essentially
hierarchical in wealth and influence and in sex roles and relations as
well. The best people make it because they are inherently better than
others. Wilson carries his argument to its logical conclusion: "A key
question of human biology is whether there exists a genetic predisposition to enter certain classes and to play certain roles" (Wilson 1975:
554). He again assumes there must be such a predisposition. Here he
follows Herrnstein's story about how the rich are rich because they are
genetically smarter than others. The logic is that *if* there were such
things as genes responsible for success, they *could* be "rapidly concentrated in the uppermost socioeconomic classes" (Ibid.).

Like its predecessors, sociobiology sees the nuclear family as the
building block of society. However, the basis of family organization,
or perhaps its first cause, seems not to be quite what Spencer or Malinowski envisaged. Wilson adopts Desmond Morris's (1967) discredited notion that men made families because they were attracted to
women's breasts, buttocks, and year-round sexuality (Wilson 1975:
548). Family organization is based on male possession of a sex object,
and kinship derives from exchange of such possessions: "As males acquired status through the control of females, they used them as objects
of exchange to cement alliances and bolster kinship networks" (Ibid.:
553). Thus sociobiology agrees with Spencer that women are the
spoils of struggle, the possession of individual men, and that the best
men control the most women.

For Wilson, women's basic role seems to be universally or eternally
the role Spencer credited to women in bourgeois society.

The populace of an American industrial city, no less than a band of hunter-
gatherers in the Australian desert, is organized around this unit [the nuclear
family]. In both cases the family moves between regional communities, maintaining complex ties with primary kin by means of visits . . . and the exchange
of gifts. During the day the women and children remain in the residential area
while the men forage for game or its symbolic equivalent in the form of barter
and money. The males cooperate in bands to hunt or deal with neighboring
groups. If not actually blood relations, they tend at least to act as "bands of
brothers." Sexual bonds are carefully contracted in observance with tribal
customs and are intended to be permanent. Polygamy, either overt or explicit-

ly sanctioned by custom, is practiced predominantly by the males. [Ibid.: 553–54]

This describes the pattern of subsistence provision neither in contemporary America nor in Australian collecting societies. Women in the latter societies ranged about as far afield as the men and provided at least half of the food supply (Kaberry 1939; Gale 1970). In the United States women now constitute almost half of the labor force (U.S. Department of Labor 1974), though they are not paid half the wages. In sociobiology and the rest of the spencerian tradition, but not in reality, women's primary role is to rear children and stay at home while men go off in groups to deal with social issues. This seems to be the basis of the human sexual division of labor. Human social relations seem to be characterized by an evolutionarily long history of aggressive dominance behavior, with males dominating females (Wilson 1975: 552).

Wilson sees sexual selection as fixing in at least the male sex those innate characteristics that fit men for running society and ruling its female half. Moreover, women are alleged to have selected these traits fairly passively:

Polygyny is a general trait in hunter-gatherer bands and may also have been the rule in the early hominid societies. If so, a premium would have been placed on sexual selection involving both epigamic display toward the females and intrasexual competition among the males. The selection would be enhanced by the constant mating provocation that arises from the female's nearly continuous sexual receptivity [*sic*]. Because of the existence of a high level of cooperation within the band, a legacy of the original *Australopithecus* adaptation, sexual selection would tend to be linked with hunting prowess, leadership, skill at tool making, and other visible attributes that contribute to the success of the family and the male band. Aggressiveness was constrained and the old forms of overt primate dominance replaced by complex social skills. Young males found it profitable to fit into the group, controlling their sexuality and aggression and awaiting their turn at leadership. As a result the dominant male in hominid societies was most likely to possess a mosaic of qualities that reflect the necessities of compromise: controlled, cunning, cooperative, attractive to the ladies, good with children, relaxed, tough, eloquent, skillful, knowledgeable and proficient in self-defense and hunting. Since positive feedback occurs between these more sophisticated social traits and breeding success, social evolution can proceed indefinitely without additional selective pressures from the environment. [Ibid.: 569]

Thus male traits are all positive, positively correlated with social and reproductive success, and genetically fixed long ago. Although Wilson does not discuss female traits, sociobiology holds that women are capable of prolonged maternal care. Apparently human evolution took place only in men.

Sociobiology is most faithful to the original paradigm elaborated by Herbert Spencer. Pieces of it have been elaborated by neospencerians. Thus Tiger and Fox have asserted that men have a male-bonding gene developed as a Pleistocene adaptation to group hunting. This is their explanation for the existence and necessary persistence of male dominance (Tiger 1969; Tiger and Fox 1971). Morris has asserted that families are based on men's sexual attraction to breasts and women's year-round sexual "receptivity." Fox (1972) has drawn on Levi-Strauss to assert that women are the sexual private property of men and that men play their power games with women as counters. This game is known as *kinship* and is the organizing principle of social life. Lorenz (1966) has postulated that humans are innately aggressive and that this trait accounts for much of the shape of social evolution. Ardrey (1961, 1966) has claimed that humanity has a territorial gene, which also explains much of the shape of human cultural interaction as hostile. And Herrnstein (1971) claims that the rich are rich because they are smarter genetically. What Wilson has done, as he acknowledges, is to put all of these assertions together into a new synthesis of sociobiology (1975: 551). None of these theories has been given any credence alone. Woven together, they are subject to the same criticism made of each of them individually: they do not fit the data; reality is not what it is asserted to be in these theories. Second, the causes of this alleged reality are not demonstrated; they are asserted and thus are not subject to refutation.

BACHOFEN

The reception and influence of J. J. Bachofen's *Das Mutterrecht* (1861) seems paradoxical. It was a social darwinist work held in high esteem by Engels (Engels 1891; Campbell 1967); it affirmed the superiority of patriarchy but inspired generations of very diverse feminist theories (Campbell 1967; Davis 1971; Diner 1965; Hartley 1914; Reed 1975; Montagu 1954; Firestone 1970; Miller 1970). The reasons lie partly in Bachofen's "discovery" that women created culture and that this early stage was ruled by women. Bachofen's stages of evolution from promiscuity to matriarchy to patriarchy were repeated with many variations by the nineteenth-century writers of universal history. To social darwinists and to Bachofen himself, each stage was superseded by a superior one, and history was progress. But to feminists, matriarchy was a golden age, while patriarchy represented a fall from cultural grace (Webster 1975).

There is another reason for Bachofen's appeal to feminist thought: his treatment of the allegedly innate characteristics of men and women. Spencer simply attributed a constellation of negative intellectual and emotional characteristics to women and a positive set of stereotypes to men. Although the bedrock of Bachofen's theory was also male and female innate characteristics, he was much more sophisticated in his treatment of stereotypes. The two sets he developed, in part from those of his own culture and in part from literary analysis of Greek mythology, have become cornerstones of a whole explanatory tradition.

The central contradiction in Bachofen's scheme is not simply between the innate characteristics of men and women. Rather each sex is a two-sided unity of opposites and thus is inherently contradictory: stereotypic woman as both mother and sensualist. The former is altruistic, chaste, and associated with "the tilled field" and culture; the latter is selfish, carnal, associated with "wild plant life," and the enemy of culture. Bachofen presents a similar stereotypic contradiction for men: the satyr and the transcendent empire builder. The former is the male counterpart to women's sensual side; the latter is a superior culture builder in that men can more fully transcend material, earthly concerns. Thus Bachofen's stereotypes are complex, literary archetypes and cultural themes handled as struggles between opposites, united in complex and ever-changing ways within each sex and within culture.

In Bachofen's treatment, stereotypically female traits—altruism and nurturance—are positive and have positive impacts on culture; women are culture heroes. The writing of innatist feminists elaborates on this theme but the conclusions are opposite those of Bachofen. Thus society did or will work better when womanly strengths are brought into public life (Montagu 1954; Kraditor 1971). This particular twist has been a minor one among anthropologists. Recently, however, structuralism has returned more directly to Bachofen's method of analyzing the interplay between stereotype or archetypal attributes of men and women.

Bachofen argues that the changing relationships of female and male essences are the dynamic force for human evolution. The initially dominant side of women's contradictory nature had at first salutory and culture-creating effects on moral and social development, while the initially dominant side of men's contradictory essence was retrograde.

At the lowest, darkest stage of human existence [mother-child love was] the only light in the moral darkness. [Father-child love required] a far higher degree of moral development than mother-love, that mysterious power which equally permeates all earthly creatures. . . . The relationship which stands at the origin of all culture, of every virtue, of every nobler aspect of existence, is that between mother and child; it operates in a world of violence as the divine principle of love, of union, of peace. Raising her young, the woman learns earlier than the man to extend her loving care beyond the limits of the ego to another creature, and to direct whatever gift of invention she possesses to the preservation and improvement of this other's existence. Woman at this stage is the repository of all culture, of all benevolence, of all devotion, of all concern for the living and grief for the dead. [Bachofen 1967: 79]

Without the requisite conditions for men to know fatherhood, and hence feel father love, their dominant side was lust. This is the part of Bachofen echoed in subsequent feminist writing. But Bachofen continued: "Having considered this lower stage of existence we shall now be able to recognize the true significance of the higher stage, and give the victory of the patriarchate its proper position in the history of mankind" (Ibid.: 109). How did patriarchy come about? The new conditions brought about by women's rule—the establishment of culture—allowed men's better or more spiritual side to flourish. As women's retrograde, sensual side chafed at the chaste world she had fashioned, men led them in the revolt against it and liberated the world from nature and sensuality to found transcendent, immaterial patriarchal society.

The stricter the law of maternity, the less woman was able to sustain the unnatural grandeur of her Amazonian life. Joyfully she welcomed this god whose combination of sensuous beauty and transcendent radiance made him doubly seductive. . . . One extreme followed the other, showing how hard it is, at all times, for woman to observe moderation.

. . . .

. . . with the transition to the paternal system occurs a change in fundamental principle; the older conception is wholly surpassed. An entirely new attitude makes itself felt. The mother's connection with the child is based on a material relationship, it is accessible to sense perception and remains always a natural truth. But the father as begetter presents an entirely different aspect. Standing in no visible relation to the child, he can never, even in the marital relation, cast off a certain fictive character. Belonging to the offspring only through the mediation of the mother, he always appears as the remoter potency. As promoting cause, he discloses an immateriality over against which the sheltering and nourishing mother appears as [matter]. [Ibid.: 100–01, 109]

This part of the story was ignored or reinterpreted in feminist histories (Diner 1965; Hartley 1914; Webster 1975).

At this point Bachofen introduced his second and ethnocentric theme, associating inherent limitations of women's sensuality and female culture with "backward" Asia and Africa, in contrast to Western male abilities to deny and transcend sensuality and establish "higher" and hierarchical civilization. This anticipates Spencer's social darwinism and was much in line with the ideas of this time.

This sensualization of existence coincides everywhere with the dissolution of political organization and the decline of political life. Intricate gradation gives way to democracy, and undifferentiated mass, the freedom and equality which distinguish natural life from ordered social life and pertain to the physical, material side of human nature.

The ancients were well aware of this connection; as they stated in no uncertain terms, they regarded carnal and political emancipation as inseparable twin brothers. The Dionysian religion represented the apotheosis of both Aphroditean pleasure and of universal brotherhood; hence it was readily accepted by the servile classes and encouraged by tyrants—by the Pisistratids, the Ptolemies, and Caesar—since it favored the democratic development on which their tyranny was based. . . .

But it was in Africa and Asia that the original matriarchy underwent the most thorough Dionysian transformation (Ibid.: 102–103).

Bachofen's message was at once imperialist, antidemocratic, and sexist. Asian and African cultures were inferior, that is to say matriarchal and democratic; the Roman empire was superior or highly stratified and patriarchal. Were it not for Rome's development of empire, the inferior would have destroyed their betters. Eternal vigilance is necessary.

For Bachofen, the maternal, material principle, defeated in the "Occident," nevertheless remains an eternal principle of life, within and without, and the future state of humanity depends on political policy for handling this enduring contradiction.

... mankind does not owe the triumph of this highest stage to the inner strength of the religious idea, but essentially to the political formation of Rome, which could modify but never wholly relinquish its fundamental ideas. This belief is eminently confirmed by the relation between the propagation of the Roman juridical principle and the growth of the Egyptian mother cult. Precisely when the subjection of the Orient was complete and the last Candace [Cleopatra] had fallen, the maternal principle, defeated in the political arena, started with redoubled strength on a new triumphant march, winning back from the Occident in the religious field what seemed irrevocably lost in the political sphere. . . . The new victories of the maternal principle over the revelation of purely spiritual paternity show how hard it has been for men, at all times and amid the most varied religious constellations, to overcome the inertia of material nature and to achieve the highest calling, the sublimation of earthly existence to the purity of the divine father principle. [Ibid.: 118–19]

Bachofen's mode of analysis is literary, both in the material he dealt with and in his treatment of it. He relied heavily on symbolic associations to elaborate contradictory essences within each sex and within the human cultural condition. For him these essences were explanatory principles:

Between the two extremes, the earth [woman] and the sun [man], the moon takes the middle position which the ancients designate as the borderline between the two worlds. The purest of tellurian bodies, the impurest of uranian luminaries, it becomes the image of the maternity which attains its highest purification in the Demetrian principle; as a heavenly earth it contrasts with the chthonian earth, just as the Demetrian matron contrasts with the hetaeric woman. Accordingly, conjugal mother right is always bound up with the religious pre-eminence of the moon over the sun. [Ibid.: 115]

STRUCTURALISM

Not until the 1960s did anthropology return to the methods Bachofen developed. Although Bachofen had no direct influence on structuralism, they share a central concern with the discovery of essential characteristics or elementary structures as building blocks or explanatory principles. But there are also very significant differences.

Bachofen believed that humanity evolved from a lower to a higher stage; its change was the product of a dialectical interplay between contradictory but immutable male and female natures. His theme is change through conflict of eternal essences, rooted in the different biological conditions of men and women. Structuralism is a child of two traditions—the search for essences and a functionalist denial of history and change, or at least denial of its importance for ascertaining these essences. Hence the dialectic is a frozen one in structuralism: structuralist oppositions persist forever, or more accurately, they are with us always. They are unlike Bachofen's contradictions, which are resolved eventually and lead in turn to new contradictions. In structuralism there is eternal strain between united opposites with no resolution possible save by assertion.

This difference can be illustrated in contrasting Levi-Strauss's approach to the origins of culture with Bachofen's. The latter saw it as a process caused by the interrelationship of contradictory male and female essences. Levi-Strauss (1969; 1971) searched instead for an essential attribute that distinguishes people from animals or, as he put it, culture from nature. Thus structural attempts are not historical reconstructions so much as they are a search for essential and defining qualities, logical building blocks out of which all that is human must be composed. It is in this respect that structuralism resembles Bachofen, who also sought to discover the essences of culture in opposition to nature.

For Levi-Strauss, the incest prohibition, which in one form or another is a human cognitive universal, marks the critical distinction between nature and culture. It is at the root of social organization in that it forces ties and alliances among families.

The prohibition of incest is in origin neither purely cultural nor purely natural, nor is it a composite mixture of elements from both nature and culture. It is the fundamental step because of which, by which, but above all in which the transition from nature to culture is accomplished. In one sense, it belongs to nature, for it is a general condition of culture. Consequently, we should not be surprised that its formal characteristic, universality, has been taken from nature. However, in another sense, it is already culture, exercising and imposing its rule on phenomena which initially are not subject to it. [1969:24]

The alternative was between biological families living in juxtaposition and endeavoring to remain closed, self-perpetuating units, over-ridden by their fears, hatreds and ignorances, and the systematic establishment, through the incest prohibition, of links of intermarriage between them, thus succeeding to build, out of the artificial bonds of affinity, a true human society, despite and even in contradiction with, the isolating influence of consanguinity. Therefore we may better understand how it came to be that, while we still do not know exactly what the family is, we are well aware of the prerequisites and the practical rules which define its conditions of perpetuation. [1971: 350]

Incest prohibitions take a variety of forms. Among most small-scale societies, however, instead of simply prohibiting marriage with certain people, it is more common to find specific categories of people who are expected to marry. Thus incest prohibitions are simultaneously marriage rules. And the essence of marriage rules, for Levi-Strauss, is that they are rules for the reciprocal exchange of women by men.

. . . to interpret kinship systems and marriage rules as embodying the rule of that very special kind of game which consists, for consanguineous groups of men, in exchanging women among themselves, that is building up new families with the pieces of earlier ones, which should be shattered for that purpose. [Ibid.: 355]

If the essence of culture lies in the reciprocity of marriage exchange, and if this reciprocity consists of the exchange of women by men, then in the structuralist perspective, the essence of culture and humanity is a product of male activity and male cognition.

In this tradition, the essence of social and cultural life proceeds from a fundamental opposition between male and female conditions of life—hence their parts in and shaping of the reproduction of humanity. Its appeal to feminists is similar to Bachofen's. Rubin says of Levi-Strauss's *The Elementary Structures of Kinship*:

It is a book in which kinship is explicitly conceived of as an imposition of cultural organization upon the facts of biological procreation. It is permeated with an awareness of the importance of sexuality in human society. It is a description of society which does not assume an abstract, genderless human subject. [1975: 170–71]

It has stimulated in the contemporary anthropology of women a search, which goes back to Bachofen, for basic cultural ideas and themes associated with men and women and their effects on the social roles played by each sex. They differ only to the extent that Bachofen stressed psychologically innate emotional characteristics, while structuralists stress cognitive essences innate not to people but to the human condition.

Bachofen stressed change from an inferior to a superior state of culture, propelled by the struggle of opposites. But the structural dialectic is frozen and timeless. Contemporary structuralists resemble functionalists in assuming that what is must always have been and must be based on a contrast in essential sexual functions. Thus Rosaldo explains a supposedly universal cultural theme, the unequal evaluations of men and women:

Put quite simply, men have no single commitment as enduring, time-consuming, and emotionally compelling—as close to seeming necessary and natural—as the relation of a woman to her infant child; and so men are free to form those broader associations that we call "society," universalistic systems of order, meaning, and commitment that link particular mother-child groups.... I suggest that the opposition between domestic and public orientations (an opposition that must, in part, derive from the nurturant capacities of women) provides the necessary framework for an examination of male and female roles in any society. Obvious as it may seem, its ramifications are enormous; it permits us to isolate those interrelated factors that make women universally the "second sex." [1974: 24–25]

Given this basic structure—male cultural transcendence and female domestic nature—Ortner shows, in a remarkably close parallel to Bachofen's emphasis on metaphorical imagery, how human cultural ideas associate women with lower nature and men with higher culture, thereby reinforcing an "efficient feedback system: various aspects of women's situation (physical, social, psychological) contribute to her being seen as closer to nature" (1974: 87).

For Bachofen, the male principle represented divine spirituality,

ascendance over nature in one of its aspects. Ortner presents the same
themes in almost the same language:

In other words, woman's body seems to doom her to mere reproduction of life;
the male, in contrast, lacking natural creative functions, must (or has the
opportunity to) assert his creativity externally, "artificially," through the
medium of technology and symbols. In so doing, he creates relatively lasting,
eternal, transcendent objects, while the woman creates only perishables—
human beings. [Ibid.: 75]

Like Bachofen, Ortner associates women with culture as well as with
nature. For Bachofen this meant that women created culture even as
they were rooted in nature. But for Ortner it means that women stand
in the middle and on both sides of a metaphorical divide rather than
facilitating a historical passage from a state of nature to the human
state of culture.

In short, we see again some sources of woman's appearing more intermediate
than man with respect to the nature/culture dichotomy. Her "natural"
association with the domestic context (motivated by her natural lactation
functions) tends to compound her potential for being viewed as closer to
nature, because of the animal-like nature of children, and because of the infra-
social connotation of the domestic group as against the rest of society. Yet at
the same time her socializing and cooking functions within the domestic context show her to be a powerful agent of the cultural process, constantly transforming raw natural resources into cultural products. Belonging to a culture,
yet appearing to have stronger and more direct connections with nature, she is
once again seen as situated between the two realms.

         .   .   .   .

First, of course, it answers my primary question of why woman is everywhere
seen as lower than man, for even if she is not seen as nature pure and simple,
she is still seen as achieving less transcendence of nature than man. Here
intermediate simply means "middle status" on a hierarchy of being from culture to nature. [Ibid.: 80, 84]

It is worth pointing out that Bachofen's handling of the culture-nature
relationship is the more sophisticated. Ortner presumes a universal
and eternal cultural cognition of its relationship with nature—a relationship of cultural dominance or domination over nature. Contemporary notions, as well as Bachofen's, postulate that the cognitive

systems are reflections (though not necessarily accurate or complete ones) of the kind of social order that obtains under specific conditions. Not all societies cognize their relations with nature as dominance or submission. Bachofen also postulates that this cognition varied: in the matriarchal stage, earthly and female symbols predominated over celestial and male ones.

Finally, the most interesting parallel with Bachofen lies in Ortner's explanations of the contrary stereotypes attributed to women.

> . . . we may envision culture in this case as a small clearing within the forest of the larger natural system. From this point of view, that which is intermediate between culture and nature is located on the continuous periphery of culture's clearing; and though it may appear to stand both above and below and beside culture, it is simply outside and around it. We can begin to understand then how a single system of cultural thought can often assign to woman completely polarized and apparently contradictory meanings, since extremes, as we say, meet. That she often represents both life and death is only the simplest example one could mention. . . .
>
> Thus we can account easily for both the subversive feminine symbols (witches, evil eye, menstrual pollution, castrating mothers) and the feminine symbols of transcendence (mother goddesses, merciful dispensers of salvation, female symbols of justice, and the strong presence of feminine symbolism in the realm of art, religion, ritual, and law. . . .
>
> . . . we are also in a better position to account for those cultural and historical "inversions" in which women are in some way or other symbolically aligned with culture and men with nature. [Ibid.: 85, 86]

Bachofen and Ortner are both working in the realm of symbolism, and both claim that this realm reflects similar things about male and female conditions of life. But there are three important differences. First, Bachofen sees symbolic evidence for a matriarchal stage in the myths he examines. This evidence took the form of descriptions of women on top, and predominance of symbols associated with women, or with women's alleged attributes, as dominant over male symbols and attributes: night over day, earth over sun, left over right, and so-forth (Bachofen 1967: 77). Whether these reflected social reality directly does not concern me, but it contradicts Ortner's claim that women are always seen as secondary because they are associated with nature, which in turn is always subordinate to culture. Bachofen suggests that women and nature were sometimes seen in myths as more valuable than men and culture.

The second and more important difference—that there was a battle going on—is that between Bachofen's contradictions ("carried to the extreme, every principle leads to the victory of its opposite," Ibid.: 93) and structuralist "oppositions." For the former, it is the contradictory essences of males and females that have been responsible for cultural change. For the structuralists, these stereotypic attributes are not real essences of human beings, but creations of culture—they only reinforce part of what is derived from biology. But the way they do so is consistently, universally, enduringly, and monumentally static. The stereotypes endure, and there are no forces for change in structuralism.

The structuralists give two different answers to change. Rosaldo argues that men need to participate equally with women in the domestic realm; Ortner argues that women need equal involvement with men in "projects of creativity and transcendence." But if sexist cultural themes (stereotypes) really stem from childbearing and if all the cultural variety known in the world's remaining cultures has had no effect in diminishing their potency, why should one expect domesticating men or making women more transcendent to have any effect? The only solution that follows the structuralist argument is for women to stop bearing children, a solution no one could argue for. The conclusion we are left with, though I suspect that the authors cited would disagree, is that no matter what women really do, no matter how transcendent they really are, reality will be effectively denied by the realm of cultural symbolism.

The essence of culture, then, as it pertains to women, is to select those themes and attributes that reinforce female subordination and to project them as the totality of femaleness and maleness. And so the concept of culture becomes the science of stereotyping; culture becomes the enemy of women; and we are led by this logic back to Bachofen where women really are rooted in nature, and hierarchy, or culture, is a male creation reflecting reality. There is not much to recommend this logic.

The third difference pertains to how men and women see themselves and what they purportedly represent. Bachofen has women resisting domination—as Amazons, as Demetrians, and even as sensualists. In contrast the structuralists have men create the world in their own image with total acquiescence by women. Compare Ortner's,

> woman's nearly universal unquestioning acceptance of her own devaluation . . . ; as a conscious human and member of culture, she has followed out the logic of culture's arguments and has reached culture's conclusion along with the male. [Ibid.: 76]

with Bachofen:

> The story recognizes the higher divinity of the paternal principle, but at the same time suggests that the heroic youth who strode swiftly across the stage before the astonished eyes of two worlds could not lastingly subject the feminine principle, which he was condemned to acknowledge at every step. [1967: 117]

In Bachofen there is at least room for a woman's liberation movement (even if he would disapprove of it). Structuralism excludes this possibility.

CONCLUSIONS

The key assumption of anthropology's social darwinist tradition applied to women is that baby makers cannot be decision makers. It claims that it is in the nature of culture that there be bifurcation into family and social spheres with the former subordinate to the latter, and women subordinate to men in the family and excluded from running society. Anthropology's general lack of a historical outlook has helped obscure its role in projecting what is a fairly recent bifurcation of family and society into a universal and naturally human condition. In this, anthropology has ethnocentrically adopted a basic premise of industrial capitalism. In the absence of a feminist challenge, as during the functionalist era, this pattern was assumed to be natural and inevitable. Every student imbibed it with her or his basic kinship charts. Only a few mavericks outside academe questioned it. However, when this pattern was challenged by an organized feminist movement, as it was in Spencer's time and has been in the last decade, anthropology reinforced its assumptions by insistence on one or another constellation of allegedly innate characteristics as requiring women's subordination. The blame lay with the victim: she was too weak physically, too stupid, too emotional, too rooted emotionally and cognitively in the world of motherhood, and the victim of her genes.

Beyond the prescriptively sexist arguments lay a more general darwinist view of society in which the woman question was only part of the totality. It viewed the human condition as a struggle for survival in which the weak are vanquished by the strong. Weak or less well adapted cultures are eliminated by fitter or better adapted ones, and less fit people are eliminated or subjugated by their betters. The view of a culture's "natural state" is that of a pecking order where the fittest, by virtue of their superiority, "naturally" claim wealth and political control over the less fit, either eliminating them in Spencer's scheme, outbreeding them in sociobiology's scheme, or taking their resources in Harris's scheme. Women fit into this intensely competitive and hierarchical milieu as the spoils of war and the means to perpetuate the fit. Who seeds their wombs is determined by the male struggle, a struggle in which the women do not directly participate. Thus hierarchy in sex as in class relationships is assumed to be rooted in nature. If that is the case, protesting economic, political, or sexual injustice is nonsense; inequality is a law of nature or culture. Radicals and feminists are urged to find happiness in complementarity, of master and slave, owner and worker, or husbandly authority and wifely submissiveness.

Men and women are asserted to have innate characteristics that lock them into the roles evolution destined for them. Men want to impregnate as many women as they can and to prevent other men from so doing. Women want protection from the struggle because they are too weak to be warlike actors; emotionally, women want only to bear and rear their own children.

Social darwinism postulates biology as the cause of a set of universal social patterns, but neither the causes nor the consequences have ever been demonstrated. First, the consequences: To portray nonclass forms of social organization as variations on a theme of hierarchical competitiveness (for wealth, power, or women) is a gross distortion of virtually all that anthropology has learned in the past century. The picture of male-female relations painted by social darwinism simply does not fit such data as there are on precapitalist forms of society. Since much of the sexist arguments' weight rests on alleging a universal pattern of male dominance and the incompatibility of motherhood with decision making, this point will be explored at length in the following chapter. The causes have been varied, as we have seen. But no one has looked for a genetic locus for anything behavioral, nor has it even been suggested by social darwinist biologists how one might do such a thing. Thus the form of the social darwinist argument is to assume a genetic, or otherwise unspecified biological, base for an assumed universal social pattern.

This approach is not scientific. Necessary to all scientific theories is the requirement of falsifiability. Social darwinism is not open to disproof in that a universal pattern of male-female relations is assumed and not subject to inquiry. The cause of this alleged pattern is derived from the consequence, not empirically but by "logic": if the pattern is a cultural universal, its causes must lie in biology (structuralism avoids the question by claiming that the cause is itself part of the human cultural condition), which is the species universal. But biology is not deemed worthy of investigation. Despite the lack of scientific method, social darwinism has been the dominant anthropological approach to the woman question. It is proof by reiteration and intimidation.

The real locus of sexual traits is not genetically eternal but historically specific, stemming from industrial capitalist ideology. In particular, it derives from the cult of the lady and from the bourgeois ideology that divides culture into a family sphere and a social sphere, a historically recent shift from a domestic to a social mode of production with the rise of industrial capital.

Why should anthropology, a discipline dedicated to transcending ethnocentrism, never transcend a crude version of it applied to women? Part of the answer lies in the fact that anthropology has never transcended its bourgeois ethnocentrism in general. It has viewed evolution fairly consistently through capitalist lenses, in its very definition of evolutionary progress (see, for example, Cohen's 1974 set of evolutionary trends; they do not apply to the poor half of the world or to the poorer half of "wealthy" nations; see also Sahlins's 1968 explication of evolution), and just as consistently accepted the inevitability of imperialist expansion (Gough 1968; Asad 1972). With respect to women, it has accepted the inevitability of the bourgeois order.

In periods of feminist activity, social darwinist answers and explanations have been challenged. The most enduring and productive explanations have been materialist, particularly marxist, ones. These show that there has been sexual egalitarianism and that psychobi-

ology cannot explain it or the cultural diversity and historical transformations in male-female relations. Instead they look to the ways in
which humanity has organized its social life, to ways of gaining a livelihood, the nature of property ownership, and relations of production
to explain both persistence and change in women's social position.

Thus marxism has been necessary for an understanding that will aid
in changing women's position. Social darwinism is necessary for
rejecting such a transformation, either because it is not desired or because it is inconceivable. Sexism has been the dominant reality and
organized opposition the subordinate one. Hence social darwinism
has dominated academic anthropology's approaches to women, while
marxist and more generally materialist approaches have been brought
to the discipline by radical and feminist movements. Without a feminist movement in the period between 1920 and the 1960s, academic
anthropology, with few exceptions (Mead 1935), simply asserted that
motherhood and equal rights were incompatible and passed lightly
over the issue. Recent feminist challenges, particularly materialist and
radical ones, force the question to be treated seriously and at length.
As we have seen, this has also called for the resurrection of the full
spencerian picture.

This new confrontation should not be surprising. The difference has
never been simply about the what and why of female-male relations in
other cultures and in other times; it is just as much argument and social
commentary about what these relations ought to be here and now. It
becomes clear, then, why social darwinism has been legitimate regardless of feminist activity. It is an expression of dominant capitalist
institutional practices, assumptions, and values on the one hand, and
on the other, it seems to mirror social reality as it is experienced in
daily life. It becomes clear, too, why organizational or materialist
explanations have become legitimate only in periods of feminist activity. These express tangible challenges to orthodoxy; feminists make
demands and behave in ways not predicted by conventional stereotypes. Because these movements have had some success in changing
institutional practices (women's control of property and wages and
their right to credit, to vote, and to abortions are examples) and beliefs,
they express as well the experience that the status quo is neither inevitable nor natural. On this issue as well as on others, social science
springs from and feeds into practical commitment and advocacy.

Chapter 2

THE CASE AGAINST UNIVERSAL SUBORDINATION

Social darwinism has rested for the last century on the premise that baby making is incompatible with culture making. Behind this is an assumption that babies and cultures have always been made in separate social spheres and that women could not be in two places at once. But the separation of reproduction from production, household from polity, has been a fairly recent development in European history, and the definition of women as wife-mother-dependent, circumscribed by a nuclear family sphere, is less than two hundred years old.

Many of the world's cultures did not sever family and kinship from production and polity. Indeed all preclass societies, and even many states, have been predicated on their unity in one or another form. It is quite likely that women have combined motherhood with production and the exercise of power, and indeed they have. Social darwinist assertions about what women do and do not, can and cannot do, can be refuted. Assertions about biological or psychological causes of social behavior are false, considering that the universal behaviors they purport to explain are not universal. A recent cross-cultural attempt comes to a similar conclusion:

We do not find a pattern of universal male dominance, but much variation from culture to culture in virtually all aspects of the position of women relative to men. Our findings do lead us to doubt that there are cultures in which women are totally dominant over men. . . . Rather, there is substantial variation from societies with very general male dominance to other societies in which broad equality and even some specific types of female dominance over men exist. . . .

The whole notion of assuming universal male dominance and then looking for universal explanations for that dubious assumption seems to us an unproductive enterprise. [Whyte 1978: 167–68]

Logically, explanation for why women's status is whatever it is ought to follow inquiry into what the position of women is or has been in various societies. The current feminist movement has stimulated and made respectable a vigorous anthropological inquiry into all aspects pertaining to women in many societies. The results of this renascence pose a fundamental challenge to the social darwinist tradition in anthropology and suggest that they have posed the woman question in an unscientific manner. Motherhood is indeed a cultural universal, but the nature and scope of other statuses, roles, and rights held by women are anything but universal. Some of the variety shows women as present in and the equals of men in areas of social life where women are not supposed to be. Thus social darwinism is inadequate to explain situations where women combine motherhood with relationships of economic and personal autonomy and political power. Consequently it is important to inquire into the specific and general conditions under which women have entered some or all of those relationships.

The search for a matriarchy or for a perfect egalitarianism, and the debates over whether each case fits the bill, have overshadowed analysis of conditions facilitating both equality and inequality. In fact, neither equality nor inequality has been much explored—the latter because it was presumed natural and hence required no explanation, the former because it was somehow aberrant, or an illusion, and hence also unworthy of explanation.

The goal of this chapter is to crack social darwinist lenses, to refute the axiom that motherhood and political power and economic and personal autonomy are incompatible. This task requires focusing on areas of life that have been central in sustaining the axiom: work, power, and cultural assessments of women and men. Indeed women have been significant producers in virtually all societies. In no way has motherhood diminished or been in contradiction with their economic importance. Women have also shared power and authority with men in the households and polities of many societies. Again, motherhood is not in contradiction to polity and power. And men and their activities have not always been more valued than women and their activities. A pecking order in general and with respect to gender is more a product of social darwinist thought than it is a widespread culture pattern.

MOTHERHOOD AND ECONOMIC AUTONOMY

A division of productive labor by age and sex is a defining characteristic of humanity that distinguishes us from other animals (Levi-Strauss 1971; Slocum 1975; Washburn and Lancaster 1968). While carrying, bearing, and nursing babies is certainly productive labor, no human society has defined this as the totality of women's labor.[1] Thus, in all societies, women combine the physical activities of childbearing with the physical activities of producing food and material objects. In human societies, physical activities are performed in the context of social relationships: childbearing and childrearing involve at least a relationship of motherhood, and production involves, most commonly, wifehood and sisterhood. What is striking about the productive activities assigned to women is their variety and importance in providing subsistence. Almost every productive task undertaken by humanity is assigned to women in one or another place. Yet "men's work" and "women's work" have been defined very differently by different societies. Thus a task such as milking cows may be defined as appropriate for men only in one place, while another society may regard it as properly done only by women, and still a third may be quite indifferent to which sex does it. This kind of variation, common to many tasks cross-culturally, indicates that tasks are not assigned to one or the other sex on the basis of any biological or psychological attributes or temperaments of men or women. Eskimo views on the sexual division of labor seem more accurate than American notions. They do not see the sexual division of labor as based on anything innate in men or women. If a family has no daughters, a son may help his mother in household work, and a family lacking sons may train a daughter to help her father in hunting. Orphans are said to know and perform the work of both sexes because of their unenviable position in the community (Briggs 1974: 270–71).

Women's contribution to subsistence has generally been major. In most food-collecting societies, women's gathering of vegetable food, fishing, and hunting of small game accounts for the bulk of the diet (Lee 1968: 46). While hunting is usually said to be men's responsibility, it is only the kind of hunting that involves projectile weapons and few people. When collective game drives are employed, women are integral participants (see chapter 4; Kaberry 1939: 18; Hart and Pilling 1960: 41–42; Jenness 1922: 149; Damas 1968: 13). Male hunting and female gathering are social norms—divisions of responsibility even more than of actual labor. Men very often gather vegetable food and, if circumstances make it convenient or necessary, women occasionally hunt large game, as among both the Ainu of Japan and the Eskimo of Alaska and Canada (Watanabe 1968: 74; Jenness 1922: 161).

Brown (1970a) has pointed out that women's productive responsibilities cannot include tasks that require high mobility and intense concentration because these are incompatible with child care. Yet child care is compatible with just about every economic task that has been tabulated. It has not prevented women from being breadwinners or from performing tasks requiring strength and stamina. Ironically child care responsibilities are probably less compatible with many productive activities under industrial capitalist conditions, with so-called labor-saving and strength-saving devices, than they are with preindustrial conditions.

Murdock (1937) tabulated the division of labor by sex in 224 societies for a large number of tasks. There were no tasks from which all societies in his sample excluded men, and women were excluded from two activities by all societies—hunting and metalworking. The first is not quite so ironclad as would appear from a table. As to the second, there is no apparent reason why women could not combine child care with metalworking. What is striking from Murdock's chart is the enormous range of economic activity women do perform and how the demands of child care do not create absolute barriers to economic activity of any type. Women's performance does not depend on anything intrinsic to the task itself, suggesting that performance depends rather on whether an activity can be organized in conjunction with childrearing demands. Judging from the tasks women perform, questions of strength or endurance are secondary. There are societies that assign women primary responsibility for mining and quarrying, stone work, lumbering, herding, clearing the land for agriculture, burden carrying, and grain grinding (Ibid.: 552).

The data suggest that it is not so much tasks themselves that require mobility and concentration as it is the way in which particular cultures organize them. Thus hunting and marketing both seem to require high mobility and intense concentration. But women organize their hunting so that it does not involve long-distance tracking and stalking. In much of Southeast Asia, West Africa, Mesoamerica, and the Caribbean, selling and trading are mainly in the hands of women; in much of South Asia, China, and the circum-Mediterranean area, the market is a male province. Trading generally involves absence from home and would seem difficult to combine with child care. Yet women do combine them. The way they do so suggests that particularly nursing mothers and those with young children more than those with older children stay together. Most women traders in Dakar are women thirty and older (Boserup 1970: 95). Nupe women on trading expeditions leave children of four or five at home (Nadel 1960: 411). Here there are indications of a conflict in that women are said to "refuse to have children, practicing abortion and using alleged contraceptives, in order to be free to choose this occupation. Again, the men are helpless; they can only brand this voluntary sterility as the gravest possible form of immorality" (Ibid.; see also Henderson 1972: 213). In some areas where women are heavily involved in market trading, the men take primary responsibility for peasant farming, as in Haiti (Mintz 1964), parts of Portugal (Riegelhaupt 1967), and Mesoamerica (Chiñas 1973). But in other areas women seem to combine trading with some or most responsibility for subsistence horticulture, as in parts of West Africa (Leis 1974; Mintz 1971; P. Ottenberg 1959) and Southeast Asia (Ward 1963; Boserup 1970).

Warfare is another activity that women seldom have responsibility for pursuing, but this is not always so. Among the Plains Ojibway of North America, "women have often achieved great fame as warriors" (Skinner 1916: 485). Sometimes wives accompanied their husbands to war, and if they acquitted themselves well, they gained war honors and the right to join in the warriors' dance (Ibid.: 456). In nineteenth-century Dahomey, the king had, as part of the standing army, an all-female fighting force of somewhere between four thousand and ten thousand, the famous Amazons, trained as professional soldiers; however, these women did not combine military service with childrearing (Herskovits 1938, vol. 2: 81–90). While it is often noted how difficult it is to combine mothering with the life of a warrior, it is seldom considered that fatherhood might also be incompatible with such a life. And, indeed, the Masai did not have men marry and found families until after they had retired from the warrior age grade. In this respect they were similar to other East African peoples (Forde 1963: 293).

These data indicate that the way a particular culture organizes its productive tasks is really a shorthand for a complex interplay of the productive forces available and the place of each particular activity in the totality of productive activities. It is important to note that women are part of the creators of those cultural organizations of tasks.

We have seen with respect to women's trading activities how they organize their reproductive lives to mesh with trading and how they pace their trading activities so that they can also rear children. To say that reproductive demands shape productive activities would be one-sided. An even clearer example of women's active role in making these activities compatible because women organize them to be so comes from the literature on collecting societies. It has been argued (Lee and DeVore: 248–49) that modern collector societies have populations that are considerably smaller than could be supported by the resources of their territory. Clearly something beside the food supply even in the generally harsh environments where gatherer-hunters are permitted to survive, is limiting the population. Lee and Howell (Lee 1972b; Kolata 1974) suggest that women's gathering activities combined with the conditions of raising children determine !Kung child spacing, number of children, and, thus !Kung population size. Birdsell (1968: 236) makes the same point for Australian collectors, though he argues that gatherer-hunter population size was not below the environment's carrying capacity. In both of these societies, women's gathering activities provided the bulk of the food supply. Women have to carry their infants and young children with them on their gathering expeditions. A mother can carry only one infant plus what she gathers and she is often not willing to nurse more than one child at a time. For Australia, Birdsell calculates that this means spacing children no fewer than three years apart. Lee and Howell give four years for the !Kung. Birdsell believes that the major solution to untimely pregnancies under nomadic conditions has been infanticide (see also Kaberry 1939: 107–08. Lee emphasizes the relationship between nursing and the suppression of ovulation on the one hand and the selection against women of high fertility on the other. If gatherer-hunter populations are below the carrying capacity of the land, then Birdsell's interpretation suggests that women adopt a family planning policy that fits reproduction to the demands of their productive activities rather than the other way around. In this case, motherhood is subordinated to the productive relation of food provider. Lee's interpretation, based on data from !Kung society where the land provides for the population, suggests even more strongly the importance of women's relationship to the food quest. It is reinforced by recent findings suggesting that fertility is regulated by the storage of estrogen in body fat. When women lose body fat, as Howell suggests !Kung do when combining nursing and the high energy activities of food collecting, then their store of estrogen, and hence their fertility, is reduced (Kolata 1974); thus reproductive biology is shaped by culturally determined productive activities. That !Kung women continue gathering, rather than retiring temporarily, attests to the cultural centrality of women's productive roles, as well as countering a simpleminded reproductive determinism.

In all save the ruling classes of class societies, women's productive role has been substantial both from the point of view of direct production of subsistence as well as participation in a wage labor force and from the point of view of variety of economic activities. Cross-culturally, women's work includes activities requiring strength, endurance, concentration, and entrepreneurial wit. Reference to any kind of biopsychological nature certainly explains nothing of this variety. Indeed were our own society not so sexist, it would be as silly to inquire into women's psychobiology as it would be to inquire into that of redheads to explain their social statuses. Today the argument that women are naturally dependent on men for their subsistence and material necessities sounds more hollow than it did a century ago. The reason is largely that women in the 1970s constitute almost half of the paid work force, and the majority of these women workers are wives and mothers. Thus even as a description of the culture that generated it, social darwinism is more capitalist ideal than capitalist reality, and less real now than ever before.

MOTHERHOOD, POWER, AND AUTHORITY

Women have combined motherhood with the exercise of political power and authority not quite so massively and universally as they have combined it with production, but it has been a rather commonplace and routine combination nonetheless. Indeed the highest woman political authority in the nineteenth-century city of Onitsha, counterpart of the highest male authority, was entitled *Omu* ("Mother"). In African modes of production, the combination of motherhood with power and authority was as logical as it has been antithetical to the industrial capitalist mode of production.

Although power and authority are critical aspects of women's place, it is important not to confuse them with some total notion of woman's status. Much of the literature takes one or another aspect of women's position and uses it as the basis for claiming dominance or subordination for women in this or that society. This exercise can lead to confusion. For example, Hopi women are sometimes said to be subordinate to men because women do not participate in important community religious affairs. Yet other writers stress Hopi women's ownership of land and their authority over their husbands in household affairs as evidence of female dominance. A similar dispute existed over preimperialist Southeast Asian societies. Some inferred matriarchy among the Khasi from women's control over property and wealth; others saw the key to dominance in male superiority in political and household authority and "disproved" the existence of matriarchy (Lowie 1961: 189–91).

The word *power* covers a variety of meanings, including the overt and socially recognized right to make decisions for others, commonly called *authority*. Most societies have positions of authority—chiefs, religious specialists, heads of households, and so forth. But authority may or may not include the ability to force others to obey. In many societies, the so-called authority figures have little beyond the powers of persuasion and exemplary action to back up their wishes. Power is not the same as authority; it is the ability to force others to obey. It may be legitimately exercised from a position of authority or on a personal basis, as in patronage, but it also includes behind-the-scenes, covert, and socially unrecognized abilities to make others comply and to manipulate them.

Institutionalized power rests ultimately on the possession of socially critical property, the means of production. Those who control these means have power over those who do not. Human societies have organized their political economies or ownership relations to productive means in one of three general ways:

1. *Communally.* The means of production are held in common and are equally accessible to all members of the society. All have equal power vis-à-vis the group, and hence the exercise of personal

power over the group is almost nonexistent. Real power as a coercive force, however, resides in group consensus because individuals are dependent on the group.

2. *States or classes.* In sharp contrast are societies where a small group or class owns and controls the productive property and has enormous power over those who depend on them for a livelihood.

3. *Corporate kin groups.* Somewhere between these two are societies in which productive property is held by groups of kinspeople. Every individual has access to at least some productive property by virtue of being born into one of these kin-based corporations. Here power exists to the extent that these corporations have unequal amounts of productive property and members within them have unequal access to their corporation's property.

Although the bases of power are sexually neutral, power itself is exercised with definite regard to sex in that men and women may have unequal or different kinds of access to kin-based property and to private property. Gender underlies but is not synonymous with either men's or women's relations to the means of production; each sex stands in a variety of relations to the means of production; and kinship relations—particularly those of sister and wife—are relations of production and, hence, relations of power.

In each of the three general kinds of human political economy, women, to varying degrees and in differing ways, are in relationships to productive means where they exercise power and authority over other people. Only in class societies are women of both ruled and ruling classes systematically excluded from equally shared power with men of their class.

The principal forms in which power and/or authority are exercised in each of these types of political economy differ.

1. In communal political economies, most commonly small-scale collecting societies, informal and diffuse mechanisms are the principal means by which power is exercised. Discussion, suggestion, teasing, and ridicule are used to arrive at consensus and to communicate it.

2. In corporate kin political economies, there is much more diversity in power and authority channels, including so-called big-men, solely achieved roles based on personal ability to create a following;

associations, age groups, and secret societies that often exercise power over particular domains of life; and socially designated authority positions based on position in kin groups, locality, or age groups, though these may or may not be positions of individual power.

3. In class societies, by far the predominant form for the exercise of both power and authority is that of official positions in the state hierarchy.

COMMUNAL POLITICAL ECONOMIES

The circumstances under which power and influence are exerted are as diffuse as the form. Roughly, though, they cover affairs of concern to the group: settlement of disputes, dealing with antisocial acts, external relations, movement of the group, and organization of both economic and religious collective activities.

Fairly widespread food sharing is a norm in all collecting societies and one that none can afford to honor in the breach. Since there is a sexual division of labor, men and women by and large appropriate different things. Women own the wild foods they catch or collect and can use or distribute them as they see fit. Phyllis Kaberry described Australian women as frequently cooking and eating on the spot much of the fish and vegetables they gathered. Groups of women and their young children who went out collecting together enjoyed and shared sociable meals while out in the bush (Kaberry 1939: 22). Patricia Draper (1975: 84) describes the same kind of control by !Kung women over the food they have gathered: "they also retain control over the food they have gathered after they return to the village. This is even more true of the vegetable food of women than of the meat brought in by the men." Almost invariably meat must be shared quite widely, but this is much less true of vegetable foods. In many collector societies, there is an additional set of restrictions as well. Once a man deposits his catch at his wife's hut, she has the right to distribute it as she wishes. Essentially men are giving food to the wife rather than bringing it home.

As a corollary, women in many collecting societies have, or share with men, the responsibility to enforce the social norms of sharing, which are so crucial to the community. The most common means of enforcing norms in general is probably gossip and private shaming. The following example from Eskimo society illustrates a more drastic measure employed by women—public humiliation used when a person persists in antisocial behavior.

There is yet another procedure established to see to it that riches are properly distributed, and that is another expression of the game being nobody's exclusive property. If, for instance, a hunter has been out alone and has caught a seal, and the other hunters in the settlement got no seal that day, parts of the animal must be given to the other families. This is called *payudarpok*, and responsibility for it rests completely on the women. No man debases himself [the author's bias] to worry about the provisions, once the game is killed and brought in.

Freuchen then goes on to describe the way in which women enforce the distribution of meat. Ivik was a good hunter, but his wife, Puto, was stingy, and her paltry distributions of meat were a subject of gossip. Being on the receiving end of somewhat generous *payudarpok* (in the hopes of shaming Puto) did not make her mend her ways, so more forceful methods were employed by Navarana, Freuchen's wife.

Then it was rumored that Ivik had caught a big seal, and there was great joy in the settlement. We were five families, all together, so we considered it a sure thing that we would have our fill of boiled meat that evening. After a while, we heard the dogs howl outside, reporting that somebody came visiting. It turned out to be Puto making her rounds and now bringing us our *payudarpok*. I quickly divined from Navarana's face that a veritable storm was coming up, for it was a wretched piece of three ribs and with the blubber carefully cut off. There were many people in our house, and it was such a ridiculous contribution that my wife broke out in righteous fury.

"Oh no," she said. "At long last something has happened that we can tell about when we journey out to visit people. The great Ivik has had game, and his wife now takes leave of almost the entire seal without thinking of her own."

There were some women visiting us, so Puto blushed from shame over these words.

"But please let me give you something in return."

Whereupon Navarana loaded Puto up with almost all the food stores of her husband's trading post, together with tobacco, needles, linen, and matches.

Puto reddened more and more from shame, and her eyes shifted helplessly from Navarana to the other women in the room. . . . She knew as well as anybody that this event would become a saga that would be told in the whole tribe from north to south. According to Eskimo thinking she had deserved much punishment for her avarice, and now she got it.

. . . .

She had broken the Eskimo's law, and Navarana was a lady who didn't permit that kind of thing to remain unpunished. She ran out after her, telling the other women to follow her. Everybody hurried outside where Navarana was standing, triumphantly raising in her hand the little piece of meat that Puto had *payudarpok*'d.

"Oh listen," she shouted after Puto, "wait a moment! Wait so that you can tell your husband something that I would wish him to know!" Involuntarily. Puto turned about and stood still. She was still crying. . . .

"Look I have a poor dog that is utterly gluttonous. At last, I have the chance to give it something—if not a meal, then at least enough to make its mouth water!"

And then she heaved the notorious piece of meat into the mouth of the nearest dog. [Freuchen 1961: 155–59]

Among gatherer-hunters in the least hierarchical societies known, some seem to have positions that anthropologists still refer to as *headman*. It is widely recognized that these were not positions of power or even of authority of broad scope, but they were statuses achieved by ability, and their holders accorded respect. Among the !Kung of Botswana, *headman* can be female and is often plural. A core of kinspeople are referred to collectively as "owners" of the band's land. More often than not, they include women, and a core of all-female owners appears more commonly than a core of all-male owners (Lee 1974).

CORPORATE KIN POLITICAL ECONOMIES

While the phrase *big man* came to anthropology from Melanesian societies, a more familiar analogy to Western readers may be that of the mafia godfather—a person who builds a dependent following by doing favors and distributing goods in exchange for loyalty and support in his or her endeavors. In many societies they are important modes of informal authority and influence by virtue both of their abilities and their personal followings. Two common bases for building personal followings are inherited family wealth and ability to command the labor and hence wealth produced by wives. While they do not appear so numerous as instances of women holding formal authority, there are societies where women can act as dispensers of patronage.

Among Nuer, *bull* is the term for people of wealth and prestige who can influence others, are called on to settle disputes, and have many followers. Gough's reanalysis of Nuer kinship (1971) suggests that there were significant inequalities among Nuer lineages as a result of nineteenth-century warfare and conquest. This brought about "an asymmetry in kinship relations such that both the men and the women in the conquering groups were advantageously placed in the business of owning and transmitting cattle, controlling land use and thus of building up a local following in each community from among the less advantaged and the captive" (Ibid.: 115–16).

The situation suggested is one where, in the context of political and economic inequality among lineages, those of the wealthy lineages act as individuals to bind people of the nonwealthy lineages to them as client-followers through ties of marriage and kinship. Men and women of the dominant lineages offer the patronage, while the nondominant majority manipulate marriage and kin ties to dispensers of patronage.

The genealogies collected by Evans-Pritchard (1945) show a female *bull*, and there is reason to believe that this was not a unique instance among the Nuer. Women of wealthy lineages could inherit cattle. If such a woman had no children, she could marry a wife of her own and become the social and legal father of children born to the wife, thereby becoming head of her own household. Among the Nuer, as among many other societies, the ultimate goal of wealth was to use it to build a following. Becoming head of one's own household is a first step to creating and attracting a following of kinspeople and affines.

As both Gough and Singer (1973) show, while the Nuer have a patrilineal ideology, its reality applies largely to the dominant lineages. For the rest of the population descent is actually not usually traced through men, nor is marriage often patrilocal. It appears too that the role of female husband was also open to women of nondominant lineages, though presumably without the power of patronage available to women of dominant lineages.

The Nuer are not unique; many other societies in Africa practice woman marriage (Krige 1974; Herskovits 1937; O'Brien 1972). Woman marriage is a political and social relationship, not a sexual one. The wife bears children by a male genitor chosen by herself or by her female husband. Although there are several forms of woman marriage, the one of interest here is that in which a woman marries another woman and takes on the status of female husband, head of the household founded by the marriage. She becomes the legal and social father of all children born to the wife and has control over the domestic services of the wife. In many of these societies, a female husband can also be married to a man and thus be simultaneously husband and wife.

Wealth is, in the eyes of traditionalists even today, not something to be sought after for its own sake. Influence and prestige lie not in the accumulation of wealth but in its consumption in the entertainment of kin and neighbors. The correct use of property in the form of cattle or money is to invest it in marriage, in building up human resources by establishing a "house" which will produce children and a following and secure the support of affines. [Krige 1974: 16]

Although this statement pertains to the Lovedu and to the social context of woman marriage in that society, it applies as well to woman marriage in other societies. Herskovits describes woman marriage in the precolonial kingdom of Dahomey as taking place among well-to-do women:

It is based directly upon the fact that women sometimes become independently wealthy. Such a woman, spoken of by the Dahomeans as a "free woman" in the sense of one who is economically independent though not necessarily sexually promiscuous, may continue to engage in wealth-creating enterprises after her own marriage. She may possess farms and palm-groves, and, if she wishes, may employ her resources to build up a compound of her own, whose "ancestress" she will be. To do this, it is necessary for her to obtain control of children who, when they are grown up, will be able to carry on the affairs of the compound and provide for its perpetuation. She therefore "marries" another woman. [1937: 338]

Among the Lovedu, wealthy women, particularly women who are successful diviners, have many wives. So too does the queen. It appears that the group of women most likely to have wives are themselves the wives of the queen (Krige 1974: 25). This is not to say that only wealthy or royal Lovedu women are female husbands. Indeed the status is potentially open to any Lovedu women (Ibid.: 15). It offers women the possibility of enhancing and extending their political authority, particularly as rulers of a village or district.

A successful woman trader in Onitsha Ibo society might repay the bridewealth her husband had given for her, thereby divorcing him and insuring her independence. She might become a female husband, founding her own house, or return to her natal kin group. "Certainly separation must have been common; villages expect to have a core of daughters in residence and to provide them with houses. Trade in village marketplaces appears to be organized by its daughters" (Henderson 1972: 235).

Woman marriage seems to function as an avenue for women to exercise social influence and patronage. It is found in African societies where inheritance and succession pass through the male line and where women can acquire property through their own efforts and/or through inheritance in default of a male heir. In this context, woman marriage allows women access to the social status of household head, which seems to be necessary for the translation of private wealth into social standing.

Woman marriage is not the only way in which women can achieve significant social or political standing. Leadership and the creation of a following in some West African women's groups seems to be largely by personal initiative and success in the accumulation of wealth (Hoffer 1972: 159–62). Among Mende and Sherbro peoples in Sierra Leone, "before the colonial era there was no tidy structure of chiefs and chiefdoms. There were famous warriors who commanded a following, and other notable persons who extended their influence through force of character, marriage alliances, and exchanges of gifts and favors" (Ibid.: 154).

The positions of household and descent group heads were important ones because they conferred management of the group's land and other property and provided a basis for building community influence. Among both Mende and Sherbro, women can be appointed to these positions. Little (1967: 164–65) reports that women, particularly in important families, can be given these positions, noting that in recent years this status has made them eligible for political office as well. For Sherbro, in one community, a capital town of a chiefdom,

Hoffer (1972: 154) noted that twenty-three of the thirty-nine house-hold heads in 1970 were women. Among both groups, women held chiefships prior to colonialism and continue to do so.

Associations, age groups, and secret societies also provide the context for demonstration of an individual's abilities in a peer group and the context for organization of manifold types of undertaking, opinion shaping, and social reinforcement. Such groups—for women as well as for men—may also have a formal and important role in the political arena.

Women's societies were widespread on the North American plains. Cheyenne men had several military societies responsible for hunting and warfare organization; women had a variety of societies centering around quilling, rawhide painting, tentcutting, and other activities. The men's societies included all men and were not hierarchically ranked: the women's were selective in membership and were ranked. Among the Hidatsa, both men and women had their own hierarchies of associations closely related to each other and responsible for per-forming certain socially important ceremonies (Lowie 1961: 294, 305). In Kenya, there seems to have existed a women's council, in some ways perhaps parallel to the men's councils, which constituted basic village and regional political authorities in Gikuyu society (Ken-yatta 1965: 108; Middleton and Kershaw 1965), but there is almost no information attesting to the activities and power of these groups.

In West Africa, women's organizations were particularly strong in societies with strong corporate kinship groups. Sometimes associated with women's role as market traders, sometimes independent of it, these organizations were central parts of many West African socie-ties' power and authority systems.

Among the Mende and Sherbro in Sierra Leone (Hoffer 1972), most women are initiated into the Bundu society, a secret decentral-ized society with authority over certain aspects of their life. It has a counterpart in the men's Poro society. These two are a religious coun-terbalance to the authority of the secular chiefs and work together. Bundu seems to function to insure the proper treatment of women by massing the women to confront offenders. They may fine or otherwise punish those who offend their wives or intrude on Bundu ceremonies, secrets, or medicines. Hoffer states that one chief was deposed for such an intrusion and cites the instance of Bundu punishing another chief who abused his wife.

In precolonial Igbo society of Onitsha, Nigeria (Henderson 1972: 309–13), women had their own organization, the Women of Onitsha, made up of all women who had ever been married. This organization, with its internal ranking of titles, an *Omu* and her councillors, had a parallel men's organization. It also provided something of a counterbalance for a king's secular rule. In certain respects, the women's leader was a counterforce to the king; she was surrounded by many of the same trappings, her palace was a sanctuary for those fleeing the king, she outranked the king's chiefs, and her ability to mobilize women made her a major power.

The title *Omu* has been conventionally translated as "queen." But, as Okonjo has pointed out, this is a serious distortion of its meaning: "In fact, she did not derive her status in any way from an attachment or relationship to a king. The word *omu* itself means 'mother,' being derived from *nne omumu* or *omunwa*, 'she who bears children'" (1976: 48). In two areas women were paramount authorities: certain kinds of ritual purification and affairs pertaining to the market. Women, especially the *Omu* and her council, were prophets of the community, warning through dreams of danger that was to befall it. They were responsible for rituals for cleansing the town of evil and were in direct charge of the market. They held public meetings to establish who could sell what goods and at what prices. They had their own court to settle market conflicts, and they received regular tribute from women traders. Just as they were responsible for the spiritual well-being of the town, so too were they for the market, and they could close it when they held ceremonies.

Some literature describes collective action being taken by women in various parts of West Africa when their interests are threatened. Sometimes it is related to or seems to be through the use of women's organization (Leith-Ross 1965; Perham 1962; Hoffer 1972). In other instances (Ardener 1973) no organization is mentioned. Women's solidarity is also manifested around both personal and political incidents. An example of the former are the Bundu women who punish men who mistreat their wives. In other parts of Africa, women take collective action against men (or women) who insult women by making sexual slurs or by physical mistreatment. The offense is seen as one against all women and demands proper punishment of the offender. Characteristic tactics include grabbing the culprit, singing obscene songs ridiculing him, exposing their genitals, urinating and defecating on him, and fining him (Ardener 1973; Edgerton and Conant 1964). Somewhat similar to these practices is Malinowski's somewhat incredulous description of gang rape (coupled with most of the above indignities) of any man who stumbles upon a women's collective work group in the Trobriand Islands (1929: 273–79).

In the political arena, Shirley Ardener has described a woman's uprising among the Kom in Cameroon. While it was provoked by an oppressive colonial agricultural policy, the form utilized was a precolonial pattern of female militance, called *anlu*.

Anlu is started off by a woman who doubles up in an awful position and gives out a high pitched shrill, breaking it by beating on the lips with the four fingers. Any woman recognizing the sound does the same and leaves whatever she is doing and runs in the direction of the first sound. The crowd quickly swells and soon there is a wild dance to the tune of impromptu stanzas informing the people of what offence has been committed, spelling it out in such a manner as to raise emotions and cause action. The history of the offender is brought out in a telling gossip. Appeal is made to the dead ancestors of the offender to join in with the "Anlu." Then the team leaves for the bush to return at the appointed time, usually before actual dawn, donned in vines, bits of men's clothing and with painted faces, to carry out the full ritual. All wear and carry the garden-egg type of fruit which is supposed to cause "drying up" in any person who is hit with it. The women pour into the compound of the offender singing and dancing, and, it being early in the morning, there would be enough excreta and urine to turn the compound and houses into a public latrine. No person looks human in that wild crowd, nor do their actions suggest sane thinking. Vulgar parts of the body are exhibited as the chant rises in weird depth. [Quoted in Ardener 1973: 428]

In 1958, a colonial agricultural assistant tried to enforce a regulation requiring that women ridge their farms horizontally along the hills instead of vertically. Ardener affirms that it is much more difficult to ridge horizontally than vertically, and women refused to obey the government order. Several grievances came together: the agricultural assistant's uprooting crops; a sanitary inspector's destroying allegedly bad food and liquor in the market; chiefly negligence in allowing cattle to wander on women's gardens; and a visit from the head of the government party associated with these so-called modernizing policies that jeopardized the women's food supply. The women began the *anlu* at a meeting by cursing and stoning a councillor who advocated fining the women and inviting the head of the modernizing party to visit. They set up their counterdemonstration farm, marched on the market, forcing the few men who had set up to close down, closed down the Catholic school and forced the transfer of some unpopular teachers, and set up their own courts in opposition to the regular courts, which were considering fining the women. The demonstrations culminated in a march of two thousand women to the police station at Bamenda, forty miles away, while some four thousand women sat at the market until they should return. The *anlu* was successful in preventing any further interference with women's affairs (Ibid.: 428–31).

Perhaps the most widespread and well-known women's uprising occurred in 1929 among the Igbo of Nigeria. Although the accounts (Perham 1962; Leith-Ross 1965, from Perham) are from a British colonial perspective, they, as well as subsequent studies (Okonjo 1976; Van Allen 1976; Gailey 1970; Onwuteaka 1965), show clearly that the Aba riots, as they were called, were directed against a whole variety of colonial practices from taxation, "native" courts and officials, to "the way in which the [European] firms were cutting out their position as retailers and middle-women" (Leith-Ross 1965: 29). These rebellions involved tens of thousands of women in towns in Igbo and Ibibio country, marching on colonial offices, burning European stores, courts, and a Barclays Bank, breaking open prisons and releasing prisoners, and cutting telegraph wires. Although the women could have killed many officials easily, they did not. The British called out the army and police and created irregular forces, "among whom the Boy Scouts worked hard on the side of law and order" (Ibid.: 26). The British army and police killed some fifty women and wounded another fifty.

The line between chiefs, or positions of social authority, and patrons is not always a hard and fast one, as the nature of Mende chiefship indicates. Yet in political economies based on corporate kinship organization, women often fill positions of social authority, as well as acting as patrons.

Iroquois society may have typified the pattern of male and female leadership positions prevailing in precolumbian eastern North America. Although it had formal authority positions, these were achieved rather than inherited ones. Moreover, as in much of the eastern woodlands, people in authority had little power to contravene the wishes of those they represented. Among the Iroquois there was a clear-cut division and balance of authority between the sexes. Men were the chiefs, but they were nominated by the women, who could impeach them. Women were organized under their own formal leaders, the matrons, who were elected to represent all women. The matrons organized agricultural labor, supervised household management, and acted as the ultimate controllers over decisions of war and peace by their power to allocate or withhold food from both war parties and council deliberations (Brown 1970b).

In South Africa, the Lovedu were probably similar to the Iroquois in the limited power available to chiefs, but they differed in how authority positions were allocated. Inheritance played a greater role and sexual differentiation was much less pronounced. The highest authority was a woman, the queen, who controlled the medicines for making rain. Under her were chiefs of districts of the country, and these were both men and women. Often in districts where the titular chief was a man, he was actually sharing authority with his mother or sister, the latter having formal authority over her brother's household.

CLASS SOCIETIES

Female rulers have been fairly commonplace in European history, but this status has not been related to the exercise of power by women as a gender or even as a gender of the ruling class. Similar situations obtained in states elsewhere in the world.

The pattern of sharing the highest authority positions between a mother and son, brother and sister, or brother, sister, and mother was common in precolonial Africa. It was exemplified in the kingdoms of Lunda, Bemba, Ganda, Ankole, Swazi, Bamileke, and Ashanti (Lebeuf 1971). In Polynesia, in the most stratified societies such as Tonga, Tahiti, and sometimes Hawaii, the eldest child, regardless of sex, succeeded to the highest chiefship (Goldman 1970: 554–55). All these are highly stratified societies, where authority carries power with it and where inheritance predominates over achievement in succession to office.

In the kingdom of Nupe in northern Nigeria, women had access to both inherited and achieved political positions. A few royal women, close female relatives of the king, held high rank, entitling them to positions of great influence at court. "They took part in the king's council, they could join in the war with their own troops of slaves and serfs, they held fiefs and owned land. Theirs was the position of 'kings over the women of Nupe' " (Nadel 1942: 147).

Among commoners in the Nupe capital, the women market traders elected one of their own as leader of the women. In addition to supervising market affairs, she settled disputes among women, offered advice, and organized collective women's work for the king. In precolonial days she also held a royal fief and levied tax on marketed produce. Every village also had its own "head of the women" elected by the married women of that village (Ibid.: 148).

HUSBANDS AND WIVES

Power and authority are important aspects of relationships between spouses in all kinds of political economy. It is important to stress that the focus here is on power relationships within families and that these relationships say nothing about the range of things over which families—or particular social relations within them—have power and authority. In communal and kin corporate political economies, the range of family-based power is much greater than it is among nonruling classes of states. Families themselves and head(s) of them have a very truncated range of authority in class societies.

Regarding a wife's power or authority with respect to her husband, it is probably fair to say that where neither the husband nor the wife is dependent on the other for the means to livelihood, the norm for domestic relationships is egalitarian. Inegalitarian norms seem based on control of those means by one or the other spouse (Sacks 1974). Almost uniformly in communal political economies marriage is described as egalitarian. Jenness's description of Copper Eskimo marriage is typical: "Marriage involves no subjection on the part of the woman. All important matters, such as the migrating to another settlement, are discussed between them before any decision is taken. Both within and without the house she behaves as the equal of the men" (1922: 162). This should not be surprising given the absence of any differential access to the means of production on the part of men or women. Combined with the complementarity of men's and women's work, husband and wife are economic equals. By and large, any power exerted in a marital relationship under these circumstances derives more from force of personality and proximity of kinfolk than anything else. Consider, for example, marital infidelity and sexual jealousy.

These exist among gatherer-hunters, as well as other types of societies. While they often lead to marital discord and divorce among gatherer-hunters, there is not the double standard here. Kaberry (1939: 142–53) reports husband beating as well as wife beating, women as well as men walking out of a marriage they no longer want, and neither men nor women being at a particular disadvantage in divorce. One instance of husband beating is worth quoting to lay to rest the old notion that men's strength gives them dominance:

There was the instance of Barudjil [wife] and Wanbierin [husband] who were tribal brother and sister. They were a most devoted couple when I arrived, yet they quarrelled five months later, and she accused him of going with another woman who lived twenty miles away.

Barudjil, in the heat of the argument, picked up his [Wanbierin's] boomerang, banged him, then grabbed a tomahawk to enforce her point and pummelled him with the blunt edge on his arms and shoulders, till the situation became dangerous, and an old man wrested it from her. Wanbierin rolled up his swag and departed, hurling obscenities and an occasional boomerang at her, which she avoided easily. . . . After a temporary reconciliation she again made the same accusation of infidelity, and left him for good. Two months later, she had found another husband, and Wanbierin was living with the other girl. [Ibid.: 144]

In kin corporate societies it is most common to find one of the spouses living on the estate of the other spouse's corporate group. The in-marrying party generally was under the authority of the spouse, spouse's mother, and members of the spouse's corporate group.

Iroquois marriage involved husbands' living on their wives' estate. In Iroquois society and perhaps in most of the other eastern woodland Indian societies of the United States, women held the rights to the cultivated land and were the distributors of all food, "one of the major forms of wealth for the tribe" (Brown 1970b: 164). The household unit was the longhouse, the core of which was a group of matrilineally related women with their in-marrying husbands. As Judith K. Brown has shown, Iroquois women definitely controlled the affairs of the longhouse; they arranged their children's marriages, could initiate and effect divorce as easily as a husband, kept the children after divorce, and were in charge of receiving and dispensing all food, including that brought in by the men.

Nuer society of southern Sudan was based on a subsistence combination of cattle, agriculture, and fishing. Ideally wives lived on the estate of their husbands' group. Nuer ideology says that inheritance of livestock and land descends through the male line to males and that marriage is marked by the husband's lineage's giving a large number of cattle to the wife's family. This transfer of cattle marks the husband's and his family's claim on all children the wife bears, on her domestic services, and legal rights over her person. In a sense this is the mirror image of husband-wife relations among the Iroquois. But most Nuer marriages do not follow this ideal, which is only one of many types of socially accepted union between a man and a woman. Many unions, particularly those of the nonwealthy, do not involve the transfer of cattle and, in these, women "are under the legal guardianship of no man in respect of their work and domestic services. Often, in fact, they own cattle and always they are separate legal personalities" (Gough 1971: 109). In fact, it seems reasonable to infer, as Gough does (Ibid.), that almost half the Nuer women of childbearing age lived in unions that gave them legal autonomy. A frequent pattern among non-wealthy Nuer is for the woman's family to transfer cattle to the man's lineage. In return, the husband lives in his wife's village, and it appears that she and her family gain rights to the husband's domestic services (Singer 1973: 87).

In class societies, or states, women can also have considerable power over husbands based on their control over productive means, though states seem more prone to deny women's authority. In Europe, women as well as men do inherit and own land (Friedl 1967; Silverman 1967; Goody 1976). In Vasilika, Greece (Friedl 1967), both men and women bring their own land to the marital household, giving women a position of real and legitimate power in the family regarding decision making. Indeed people in Vasilika assume that when a man has no land to bring to the marriage, his wife makes all the household decisions. Such a man has no public prestige. In contrast to equality within the household, the public sphere is an exclusively male one, re-plete with public deference of women to men, male monopoly of public power positions, and the need for men to act as representatives of the households to the larger society.

Aswad (1967), writing of women's power in a landowning lineage of a village on the Turkey-Syrian border, points out similar contradic-tions. Under certain circumstances, women can inherit and control property, but they cannot engage in any important supravillage relationships. And, as Aswad points out, with the extension of city control, cash cropping and mechanized farming, these are becoming increasingly important for the exercise of power.

Silverman presents essentially the same situation for Italian villagers of property-owning families. Women own property, are economically active outside the household, and "some income-earning village women have an important area of decision-making almost completely independent of their husband" (1967: 137). Yet formally they have no political role in the public sector.

Nadel, writing of the Nupe emirate in northern Nigeria, argues that in colonial and precolonial times, women were often successful itinerant traders and, as such, were often economically wealthier than their peasant husbands. Husbands were often in debt to their wives, and wives often took responsibility for affairs men believed were the proper responsibility of husbands. While husbands resented this position, there was little they could do about their wives' behavior since wealth carries power (1960: 411).

THE VALUE OF WOMEN

This is a terribly elusive question, because we are concerned with how people in other societies rank each sex relative to the other in some vague and comprehensive sense. More specifically, do all societies value men's economic tasks, and perhaps therefore men, more highly, than women's activities and women? The affirmative answer seems to be implicit in the near absence of women from ethnographic writings, theories that ignore women as actors, and has also been explicitly argued (Mead 1949; Rosaldo 1974).

"The hunters" was suggested as the title for this book simply because it sounds more interesting than "Woman's Work," "The Gleaners," or "The Foragers." But in only a few instances (the Eskimos particularly) is the hunting of animals as productive as the gathering of seeds, roots, fruits, nuts, and berries. Neither men nor women, however, in any society, find their interest much aroused by a description of domestic tasks. "Women's work is never done" goes the saying, and woman's work is also dull, repetitive, unromantic, and usually unremarked." [Service 1966: 10]

This is a fair statement of the Western male bias through which anthropology has viewed women's work in other societies. But it is not a fair statement of how other societies perceive male and female tasks in general or even with specific reference to hunting.

There is much ethnocentrism built into the assumption that all cultures rank economic activities. It is fair to say that Western capitalist ideology ranks such activities. For example, nonmanual labor is ranked more highly than manual labor, and a manager is paid more than a laborer. Capitalism shares this particular dichotomy with many preindustrial states, some of which make more or less elaborate hierarchies, but by no means is this a general characteristic of all societies. It might be more accurate to say that inegalitarian societies, particularly class societies, have inegalitarian ideas about how tasks are valued, while societies where power is widely shared do not rank economic tasks (Sacks 1976). Even within class societies, various strata or classes may lack any systematic hierarchy of the kinds of work they perform. For example, Friedl (1967) reports that in Vasilika, a Greek peasant community, neither men's nor women's work has any prestige. Both are regarded as "distasteful" but necessary, and either sex will do the work of the other with no shame attached.

Several other examples illustrate the ethnocentrism of the insistence that all societies share a single and hierarchical notion of the relative valuation of men's and women's work—or of men and women. In writing about her fieldwork among Eskimo in the central and eastern Arctic, Jean Briggs has tackled this question directly. Here, men and women agree that the most exciting times center around men's activities: hunting and its associated feasting, men's trips to the trading post and the goods they bring back, and visits to and from other camps. Women enjoy the stories of hunting and trading and sometimes express some envy of men's greater opportunities for exciting activities. But they are aware of the attendant hardships and dangers.

One elderly man remarked in a regretful tone that in the old days, women used to help men hunt a great deal more than they do now. And when I asked why they no longer do so, he said: "They don't want to." . . . On the one hand, differential prestige does not inevitably follow from differences in skill. . . . Men and women each have their own realm, as we have seen, and prestige accrues to excellence in each.

. . . .

Moreover, the skills of women are as indispensable to survival as are those of men, and they are so perceived by men. . . . The question, "Which is better (or more important), a good hunter or a good seamstress?" is meaningless in Eskimo; both are indispensable.

. . . .

Differential prestige does not necessarily follow from the existence of different spheres of decision making either. I have asked Eskimos, both men and women, whether men are considered to have more intelligence or better judgment than women, and I am consistently told no: men have better judgment concerning things they have been taught and women have better judgment concerning things *they* have been taught.

. . . .

I have never heard a man derogate women in general or marriage in general. [Briggs 1974: 286–88]

While Eskimo men and women agree that the most exciting activities are men's, this does not mean that men's work is more important, nor does it imply greater overall value of men.

Other patterns exist. Men and women may differ from each other as to what they find important. Among the Akwe-Shavante of central Brazil, both men and women agree that meat is the most highly esteemed food, but only the men are interested in endlessly discussing the details and technicalities of hunting (Maybury-Lewis 1974: 35). And Kaberry reports the following for Australian gatherer-hunters in arguing against the thesis that men's skilled crafts are "the first link in the chain that ultimately leads to the apotheosis of the male in the community" (1939: 164):

In the Kimberleys there is little specialization and little economic competition, but some men enjoy respect as craftsmen and were esteemed by their own sex. The women's admiration was more utilitarian and went to the successful hunter. Similarly, as far as I could ascertain, the men did not especially commend the women's work, though the women themselves would be generous in their praise of a well-designed and woven dilly-bag. Workmanship as a rule was appreciated by those who were practitioners. [Ibid.: 165]

In other places, women and men may hold conflicting ideas as to what is proper or socially legitimate behavior. Among the Mpondo of South Africa, men viewed their own extramarital sexual affairs as proper, but those of women they deemed improper. Women, on the other hand, saw extramarital affairs as proper for both sexes. Among the Mundurucu of central Brazil, women and men had different ideas about who was head of the household:

> Through their wives or mothers, the men are considered to belong to one or another household, and the males frequently refer to a house as being under the direction of the senior male. Thus, if the senior couple in a house are named José and Maria, following Brazilian usage, the men will refer to the dwelling as "José's house." The women, however, look upon this as just one more male pretension and will be quite emphatic in saying that the house is Maria's. After all, they point out, it is Maria who lives in it and directs its activities, and not José, who just comes there for sex and water [men live in a village men's house]. Faced with this objection, most of the male informants back off and admit that the house probably is the woman's, but qualify the concession by saying that the distinction is not very important. [Murphy and Murphy 1974: 116]

In trying to figure out how or whether a society symbolizes something as amorphous as total relative worth of men and women, we face great problems. We cannot simply assume that such a concept exists in all or most societies. While to the best of my knowledge no ethnographer has asked, "Who is worth more, men or women?" many anthropologists have translated symbolic statements and forms of behavior into answers to this question.

Deference behavior is a common example. When a woman kneels to greet her husband, for example, this is taken as a sign of wifely submissiveness. But without information on the power and authority of husbands and wives, this is an unwarranted conclusion. We would not assume the United States to be a matriarchy because men were expected to pay deference to women by holding doors, chairs, and coats, lighting cigarettes, kissing hands, and walking on the curb side. Moreover men who practiced these customs did not see themselves as submissive to women in any cosmic sense. These customs were as much expressions of proper masculine behavior as was sitting and waiting for a woman to cook and serve dinner unassisted. The following can summarize American male deference behavior toward women: "To observe these manners which are expressive of a female superiority is not regarded as impairing a man's independence in any way; to omit them would be an impairment of his masculinity." Actually the sexes have been changed in this quotation. The original is a Burmese woman's interpretation of the meaning of deference behavior by women toward men in Burma (Khaing 1963: 116). My purpose is to argue that shows of deference by themselves tell us very little: a pedestal can be high, but it can also confine whichever sex is on it—in other cultures as in our own.

Sometimes what appears to be a clear and general symbolic statement of men being worth more than women turns out on inspection to be something else. For example, in eighteenth century North America, the Iroquois claimed to have reduced the Delaware Indians to the status of women by conquest. The Delaware were prohibited from waging war, selling their land, and entering into political relations with other societies, particularly European ones. But the Iroquois interpretation is inconsistent with the position of women in the political life in their own and in Delaware society. In both societies women were recognized as the political equals of men. Miller (1974) has resolved this apparent contradiction by showing that the key ingredients seem to be as follows. First, in both Iroquois and Delaware society, the relevant division of the spheres of authority between the sexes seemed to be that women were associated with internal affairs and men with external relations. These activities were not hierarchically ranked. Second, the Delaware, who lived on the coast, and not the inland Iroquois, bore the brunt of European expansion in the east. The Delaware undertook several migrations for the express purpose of avoiding having to deal with the Europeans. Before the Europeans came on the scene, the Iroquois and Delaware were often in conflict; and the Delaware were the stronger of the two. By becoming "women," the Delaware were not claiming subordination to the Iroquois but were declaring neutrality in the myriad conflicts taking place with the advent of the Europeans. To the Iroquois fell all the burdens of alliances and conflicts with the oft-warring Europeans. Third, the Iroquois statements of "male"/Iroquois dominance over "female"/Delaware were more the influence of Iroquois contact with Europeans—or, I suggest, the product of symbolic language appropriate to dealing with the Europeans, given the great differences in Indian and European allocation of authority between men and women.

These examples indicate that all societies—or women in all societies, or even men in all societies—do not value men and male activities more than women and women's activities. Many nonclass societies have no problem in seeing differentiation without having to translate it into differential worth. Industrial capitalist ideology has little, if any, place for such ways of seeing. Its ways of ordering the universe center on a social darwinist pecking order in general and with regard to women and men in such a pecking order. Consequently this strait jacket has hindered even those anthropologists who would see in feminist ways (Rosaldo 1974; Mead 1935).

CONCLUSIONS

Biology in social darwinist explanations is more an anthropomorphization of industrial capitalist social relations projected on the animal world than it is about the biology of the human species or either of its sexes. Women have borne children and taken on the social relations of motherhood everywhere. The biological process is the same among the Igbo, the Mpondo, the !Kung, and the industrial capitalists, but motherhood is not. What social darwinism presumes is biological in capitalist motherhood clearly comes from somewhere besides biology.

First, biologizing explanations do not fit the facts. Women, and mainly mothers at that, have been significant producers of food, clothing, and shelter almost universally. They have combined this work with child care as universally. Indeed one ought to emphasize a corollary to Brown's (1970) oft-cited point that women's tasks need be compatible with child care: men's tasks are largely determined by what women do not do. Moreover mothers and female nonmothers have wielded power and authority over children, husbands, brothers, villagers and subjects. Industrial capitalism may deny mothers' authority over their children, but many more places have built on and elaborated such relationships, such that one is mother-head of a family or kin group (Tanner 1974) or mother-head of her people (Hoffer 1972; Okonjo 1976). In addition, many nonclass societies lack a first and a second sex and lack the distinctions between gender-related important work and menial work. Indeed Friedl's discussion of Greece suggests that peasants in a capitalist country may have accepted this particular bit of ideology less wholeheartedly than the anthropological and academic community has. Thus, on three points— production, power, and worth—social darwinism is empirically invalid.

Second, these explanations are methodologically and logically deficient. For social darwinism to explain the data presented in this chapter, it would need to refine and amplify its approach. Such an endeavor must be either ad hoc or point the way to a fundamentally different approach. Either such data are interpreted as exceptions that prove the rule of male dominance or their presence and absence are accounted for by reference to particular social conditions. The latter course requires scuttling innatism as an explanatory principle.

Let me illustrate. Two varieties of ad hoc explanation argue that women in power are exceptions that prove the rule. The first claims that even where women hold power, they are subordinate to men in other, somehow more significant ways. Ever since Engels (1891), the Iroquois have figured prominently in debates over women. He insisted that women were at least the equals of men in power and authority, basing his conclusions on women's control of longhouse management and on their role as producers and political decision makers. Subsequent arguments against Iroquois egalitarianism or female rule have stressed that the council was all male and that a sexual double standard obtained. The latter was manifested by beating wives for extramarital affairs, whereas men, presumably, were not punished. These counters imply that a council seat is more significant than other forms of exercising authority and that freedom to engage in extramarital affairs could not possibly be denied to power holders; hence women could not have held much authority. This line of argument suggests that reexamination of apparent equality would reveal more "important" aspects of social life where men had dominance over women, and the rule would then be confirmed.

The second type of argument claims that, where women hold authority, it is because exceptional circumstances face the society; under normal ones, men rule. Thus Spencer believed that polyandry and matrilocality were inferior types of organization, the products of inferior and exceptional environments. Iroquois women's political prominence has been explained similarly as a product of unique circumstances requiring the men to be away for long periods of warfare.

Both these lines of argument share an ad hoc approach to instances of women in power. The first manifests it in defining or conceptualizing equality in a slippery way: whatever women lack is the critical marker. The second utilizes ad hoc reasoning to explain the conditions that underlie men's and women's social positions: if the data do not fit the theory, an unusual circumstance has overridden biology. There is no investigation of similar circumstances to see whether they produce similar results, nor is there any definition or conceptualization of what constitutes a normal circumstance. Thus the premise and conclusions shared by social darwinism are that women, in some necessarily unformulated way, are always subordinate to men. It is a theory that cannot be disproved by contradictory data.

NOTE

1. There is a large marxist literature on what constitutes productive labor. For a useful summary see Fee 1976.

Chapter 3

SISTERS, WIVES, AND MODE OF PRODUCTION I

The search for women's overall or essential position long ago or far away is an outcome of the confrontation between social darwinist anthropology and the feminist and socialist movements over sexism here and now. Thus far, I have concentrated on showing how social darwinism has seen in the past what it advocates for the present: continuation of the sexist social order. Its methodology has ignored egalitarian orders and egalitarian aspects of social life or has interpreted them through capitalist lenses. These highly selected data were the basis for their argument that it was natural and inevitable for women and men to be separate and unequal and to be associated with separate and unequal spheres of social life.

Marxist feminist thought advocates equality and has also sought to discover in the past what it seeks for the present. It has developed methodologies for understanding how to create egalitarian social orders and explaining what prevents the present social order from being egalitarian. In contrast to social darwinism, however, marxist feminist advocacy has generated questions, concepts, and theories that explain past and present cultural diversity and change. The first part of this chapter sketches the ways in which marxist feminist advocacy can generate sound science, while that of social darwinism cannot. The second part discusses some contradictions between marxist feminist questions and some of the concepts and methodologies used in answering them. The third part attempts to resolve the problem by suggesting a conceptual and methodological shift. The purpose of this chapter is to introduce a marxist way of seeing women. Subsequent chapters will apply it to analysis of precapitalist African social orders by way of arguing that it is a fuller and more useful way of seeing. It is more useful because it illuminates the kinds of productive relationships which, in a general way, underlie contemporary feminist visions of equality and reveals seeds and sources of such relationships in contemporary capitalist social orders.

ADVOCACY AND SCIENCE

Engels's *The Origin of the Family, Private Property and the State* is still the basic marxist feminist statement, and most contemporary marxist feminists have not departed conceptually from it.[1] In their stances on industrial capitalism, their visions of the future, and their analyses of the past, the contrast between Engels and the social darwinists of his time, particularly Herbert Spencer, could not have been greater. Where Spencer assumed a primordial state of war and interpersonal hostility, Engels emphasized the way in which people organized their relations of production and gave almost no credence to assumptions about hostility and aggression. For Spencer, female-male relations and family form were selected under pressure of battle; for Engels, they developed from the group's organization for reproduction and property relations. For Engels, natural selection played a very limited role in human history; for all intents and purposes, it had no effect in shaping the existing forms of family and society. Spencer attributed progress and even sexual temperament to natural selection. Spencer and Engels both saw a division between family and society under capitalism. To Spencer, this was something to preserve; it suited men, women and the future of the species. To Engels, this division was oppressive and degrading to women, and the private ownership of property upon which it was based was at least as oppressive to men and women of the propertyless classes.

Where Spencer saw the evolution of the bourgeois wife devoted to a family sphere as great progress, Engels saw it as the end product of a process of domestication and subjugation of women: "Today in the great majority of cases, the man has to be the earner, the breadwinner of the family, at least among the propertied classes, and this gives him a dominating position which requires no special legal privileges. In the family, he is the bourgeois; the wife represents the proletariat (Engels 1891: 121). Spencer approved of the bourgeois family and strongly resisted women's entry into politics and society. Engels looked simultaneously forward to the proletarian family and backward to pairing marriage and communal society for equality. Among the proletariat,

all the foundations of classical monogamy are removed. Here, there is a complete absence of all property, for the safeguarding and inheritance of which monogamy and male dominance were established. Therefore, there is no stimulus whatever here to assert male domination. What is more, the means, too, are absent; bourgeois law, which protects this domination, exists only for the propertied classes and their dealings with the proletariat. It costs money, and therefore, owing to the worker's poverty, has no validity in his attitude toward his wife. Personal and social relations of quite a different sort are the decisive factor here. Moreover, since large-scale industry has transferred the woman from the house to the labour market and the factory, and makes her, often enough, the bread winner of the family, the last remnants of male domination in the proletarian home have lost all foundation—except, perhaps, for some of the brutality towards women which became firmly rooted with the establishment of monogamy. Thus, the proletarian family is no longer monogamous in the strict sense, even in cases of the most passionate love and strictest faithfulness of the two parties, and despite all spiritual and worldly benedictions which may have been received. The two eternal adjuncts of monogamy—hetaerism and adultery—therefore, play an almost negligible role here; the woman has regained, in fact, the right of separation, and when the man and woman cannot get along they prefer to part. In short, proletarian marriage is monogamous in the etymological sense of the word, but by no means in the historical sense. [Ibid.: 117–18]

Proletarian marriage then is more egalitarian than its official bourgeois counterpart, largely because proletarian women are not confined to private work for a propertied male. But Engels was aware that social production by proletarian women in capitalist society was in contradiction with family responsibilities and marital equality.

When she fulfills her duties in the private service of her family, she remains excluded from public production and cannot earn anything; and when she wishes to take part in public industry and earn her living independently, she is not in a position to fulfill her family duties.... The modern individual family is based on the open or disguised enslavement of the woman. [Ibid.: 120–21]

Based on his analysis of the past and present, Engels predicted the possibility of an egalitarian future and its necessary conditions.

We are now approaching a social revolution in which the hitherto existing economic foundations of monogamy will disappear. Monogamy arose out of the concentration of considerable wealth in the hands of one person—and that a man—and out of the desire to bequeath the wealth to this man's children. . . . The impending social revolution, however, by transforming at least the far greater part of permanent, inheritable wealth—the means of production—into social property will reduce all the anxiety about inheritance. . . . This revolution will create the conditions for the development of egalitarian and "individual sex love" between men and women. [Ibid.: 123]

Engels described what he saw as a historical process by which women were transformed from free and equal productive members of society to subordinate and dependent wives and wards. The growth of male-owned private property, with the family as the institution appropriating and perpetuating it, was the cause of this transformation. Engels contrasted a generalized state of primitive communism and kin corporations with the beginnings of family-based property and the subsequent rise of class society. In the former stage, productive resources were owned communally by the tribe or clan. The grouping of husband, wife, and dependent children, which Malinowski called the "individual family," existed for Engels in daily life (his pairing marriage). But it was neither a productive nor a property-owning unit; it was not even a unit for consumption purposes. Hence, for Engels, the family did not exist as an economic unit at this stage. It had not precipitated out of the larger household or clan, which was the basic economic unit of society. It was the clan, or gens, based on kinship and residence in a common territory that was the context of women's and men's life and labor. Equal membership and equal participation in the work and property of this corporate group gave women and men economic and social equality.

Where the spencerians advocated unequal complementarity as natural egalitarianism, Engels's vision of social equality was one of equal rights. Equal rights is a demand, a construct created by more than a century of feminist practice and bourgeois resistance to that practice. Feminism created itself as a social movement first by sensing and then by analyzing those social connections among different domains of social life for women under capitalism. It has developed a theory, albeit imperfect, for comprehending the position of women in our own society as an integrated but internally contradictory and oppressively logical system. The system has a name—*sexism*—which I will use to denote the particular forms of sexual inequality and oppression characteristic of the capitalist mode of production. *Patriarchy* seems better reserved for all those sexual oppressions and inequalities not specific to capitalism (Eisenstein 1977). I intend *patriarchy* to be a vague term, because we do not know much about precapitalist forms of inequality and equality, and hence about the precapitalist roots and genesis of sexism. Without that knowledge, it is difficult to know what it will take to uproot not only the sexism specific to capitalist society but also those forms of patriarchy not specific to capitalism. Thus, profeminists and antifeminists, bourgeois and socialist feminists have all been drawn to study the past—or more accurately, its attempted reconstruction.

Marxist feminists have a hyphenated heritage. As heirs to and participants in marxist understandings of the capitalist mode of production, we seek to integrate it with our understanding of sexism and to unify and deepen our analysis. We have some understanding of the origins, development, and interrelatedness of the many dimensions of social life that define women's place. Thus, for example, assigning women to home and children, associating women with emotional characteristics appropriate to this sphere and inappropriate to the sphere of capitalist productive relations, and separating domestic from social spheres have been traced historically and analyzed as economic, political, and social processes (Rowbotham 1972; Zaretsky 1976; Lerner 1969; Sacks 1976b).

When we ask about precapitalist patriarchy and roots of sexism, there is much less to go on regarding conceptualizing both patriarchy and precapitalist modes of production themselves. Let me deal first with patriarchy and how as a concept it is and is not the same as sexism. The linkages among all those aspects of women's place that allow us to see sexism as an institutionalized system in a capitalist mode of production were discovered in the context of struggles for concrete demands. And these demands, in turn, make up the hidden criteria of egalitarianism. In other words, anthropologists and feminists alike measure the position of women in other societies by the yardstick of our own demands: Did women elsewhere have the rights feminists demanded of capitalist society? If they did, this was cause for feminist optimism; if not, it lent weight to pessimism. In one sense, these demands have covered virtually everything, but in another sense we can be more specific and group them into four enduring and widely agreed upon points.

1. *Economic autonomy.* In the nineteenth century, this meant a woman's right to inherit property, to receive her own wages, and to be paid more than a pittance. In the twentieth century, it means ending credit discrimination, receiving equal pay for equal work, ending occupational segregation, and the right to more than a pittance in pay.

2. *Equal access to power and authority.* This has always been central to suffrage, access to decision-making positions and political office, and in challenges to a legal code that has defined wives as children and wards of their husbands.

3. *A single sexual standard.* In the nineteenth century, this tended to mean premarital and extramarital chastity for both sexes (Gordon 1977). More recently, it has meant demands for women's right to greater sexual expression and to control over our own reproductive lives.

4. Ending invidious stereotypes of women as inferior beings doing inferior things.

Analysis of sexism as a system of inequality has been projected onto analysis of women's roles in other societies. Asking whether women are ever the social equals of men has presumed that women's status is discrete, that its parts are the same as in capitalist society, and that they are interrelated in the same way. Thus inquiries into the question have an element of essentialism to them; an often cursory and incomplete examination of one aspect of women's roles is assumed to have the same meaning with respect to the totality of male-female relations that it would have in our own society. This assumption is unwarranted because comparable analyses of precapitalist forms of social organization are almost nonexistent. It has had the consequence of making it virtually impossible to begin comparative analysis of sex roles even on those dimensions that are so important for feminist and antifeminist arguments alike. Consequently it is an open question as to what the various patterns of women's roles are, as well as what gives rise to the variety.

We need to conceptualize the shapes of equality and patriarchy and to explain the conditions underlying women's and men's relative social positions. This work requires a notion of equality applicable to situations where women and men are expected to play different social roles, as well as to situations where they play the same ones. It cannot presume that differences always imply dominance and subordination; it must provide room to explore the question. It must also be multi-dimensional so that it can distinguish different areas of social life and assess women's position relative to men's in each of them. Thus instances of women's wielding socially legitimate authority do not by themselves prove that these societies are egalitarian. They show only that many cultures have allocated these kinds of roles to women and have survived to tell the tale. But authority is hardly the only dimension of social life that needs to be considered. We need to be able to deal with how a society is sexist or egalitarian, as well as how sexist or egalitarian it is. Thus marxism must have room for a variety of possibilities from full equality, through equality in some, but not all, domains of social life, to complete inequality. Finally it must deal with the reasons why a society is sexist or egalitarian. Conditions that underlie all these possibilities must be framed so that they are applicable to societies at different levels of political and economic organization and thus allow comparison among them.

The marxist tradition is unique in seeking to explain both equality and inequality of the sexes. It allows posing the question the way the real world suggests it be posed: What kinds of cultural organization foster egalitarian relations between women and men? And, more specifically, what kinds of organization foster such relations in those areas of life where people today seek change: income, decision making and power, marriage, personal autonomy, and sexuality?

PROBLEMS IN MARXIST ANALYSIS

The shapes of patriarchy and equality cannot be explored apart from an analysis of their social contexts. Such an endeavor raises many questions about precapitalist modes of production that have nothing to do with women specifically but that have a great deal to do with creating a marxist perspective that includes women as well as men. In developing such analyses, we need to resolve two contradictions in Engels's approach. First, Engels asks about origins, about history and change, but his work is really not a history at all. It is evolution, a logical arrangement of static descriptions of a variety of social systems (or modes of production) frozen in time and truncated in space. This makes for problems in analyzing causality in precapitalist systems and forces us to confront the possibilities and drawbacks of attempting to answer questions about process or genesis and development with extant, static ethnography. Second, changing productive relationships—patterns of ownership—are most of Engels's explanation for women's place. Modes of production—as particular constellations of land, livestock, tools, their ownership, and people's work organization—is quite undeveloped as an explanatory concept, but it is a necessary one. Elsewhere (Sacks 1974) I have indicated the importance of work organization (an aspect of productive forces) as well as productive relations for understanding women's place, but I did not attempt to analyze their relationship. To deal with that relationship involves employing mode of production as a central analytic concept for understanding women's places. I now think that is a necessary endeavor. There is a growing literature, mainly by Althusserians, on precapitalist modes of production. With the exception of Engels's *Origin of the Family*, however, marxist attention to modes of production has been fairly rigorously separated from attention to women's place (Molyneux 1977). Althusserian approaches to modes of production face the same problem Engels faced: they speak to history and change, but their concepts are quite static and ahistorical. This is particularly true with their conceptualizations of women, which are through bourgeois lenses, as essentially mothers and wives.

Engels's analysis was an ordering of static ethnographic descriptions and historical materials from a variety of social systems at particular points in their histories. Thus, nineteenth-century Australian gatherer-hunters, eighteenth-century Iroquois, ancient Hebrews, Germans, and Greeks, and imperial Romans were all arranged in order. The logic behind this ordering was an evolutionary one, shared with Spencer, that some forms of organization are more primitive than others in the sense that they originated prior to them and were necessary conditions for the development of later forms. Something of that logic is confirmed by archeological evidence: wheels appeared earlier than automobiles, agriculture precedes cities and class society, and so forth. But evolutionary thought also presumes a notion of abstract history, a summing of human history without reference to particular groups of people at particular points in their historical developments. Indeed the neoevolutionists called it "general evolution" in contrast to "specific evolution" or the real histories of real groups of people

(Sahlins and Service 1960). But evolutionists have not done real history. Consequently the bulk of evolutionary thought has pertained to abstract history. It is, in fact, an attempt to answer questions about origin and development in the absence of historical materials, or data that deal with particular processes of origin and development in real time and space.

Consequently evolutionary explanations tend to be teleological (O'Laughlin 1977): if a practice or organization exists, it must have been intended or must be a manifestation of a particular developmental logic. For example, agriculture was believed developed—and spread—because it was more efficient than food collecting. The logic in this example is that evolution's motivating force is toward more efficient forms of production. Spencer's motivating force was improvement of the species by a competition insuring survival of the fittest. There have been no end of such unseen hands. It is not surprising that teleology fills the gaps, considering that explanations are demanded even when there are no data upon which to base them. By and large, Engels avoided unseen hands, yet they emerged at crucial points in his argument: in the overthrow of matriarchy, matrilineal inheritance, and collective ownership of productive means. Why would men insist on bequeathing livestock to their sons instead of to their sister's sons? After all, the latter were of their own gens while the former were not. We need to assume that something in men chafed at matrilineal inheritance. We also need to assume that something in men (or livestock) chafed at collectively owning livestock. In any event, it is not clear what Engels believed was the cause of this major change in productive relations. In part, this is because Engels had no information about real and specific historical transformations from which to build an explanation.

In contrast, a fundamental principle of marxist analysis is that the laws of development and change are learned from specific histories, developments, and changes and that there are no unseen hands or principles guiding human evolution. It also sees change as produced by forces internal to the social system itself. In other words, causes are not external to and independent of social organization. Inevitable population growth, ecological conditions, or God's will are not explanations of war, poverty, sexism, or any other social question. Thus since we start from the point that the causes of women's subordination or equality are internal to social systems, it is necessary to analyze women's roles in the same way—in their historical and social contexts.

Mode of production has been a critical concept for such analysis. A mode of production is a particular constellation of *means* of production (the tools and equipment appropriated from the natural world or constructed from its products for purposes of producing subsistence and material needs), of the *forces* of production (the means together with the ways people organize themselves to use them, their organization as producers), and the *relations* of production (denoting how people stand in relation to productive means and therefore to each other). Thus the organization of work itself—for example, of people together with tools they use for the purpose of clearing a field in a particular society—is a productive force. But the organization of ownership—for example, the fact that the field and its fruits belong to some of those individuals while the rest have access to productive means only through these owners—describes a productive relationship.

Marx formulated this concept in historical analysis and came to understand the capitalist mode of production by analyzing its genesis and development, its process of differentiation from its predecessors. His analyses of preceding modes of production—slave, Asiatic, and even feudal—were not consistently historical. In particular, his discussion of the so-called Asiatic mode was more evolutionary and functionalist than historical (Marx 1964). Anderson (1974) suggests that much of the controversy surrounding it can be traced to the fact that Marx did not look at process of development here but instead accepted the prevailing bourgeois contrast between capitalist and noncapitalist states and attempted to find the shared essentials to define the latter type. This method has proved to be most elusive indeed. Recent efforts by marxist anthropologists to delineate preclass modes of production share the same fate (Meillassoux 1972, 1973; Terray 1972; Marie 1976; Hindess and Hirst 1975; Taylor 1976; see Law 1978 for a review of recent works).

I think that at least some of the ambiguities and problems of application stem from the fact that most anthropologists are working from static descriptions or, at best, from histories of transformation of precapitalist modes of productions under capitalist impact. Our access to the genesis and development of precapitalist modes of production themselves is or has been limited. Anthropological data speak to precapitalist and nonclass organizations, but virtually all fieldwork has been done while these societies were being transformed by capitalism. Seldom have ethnographers analyzed the process. More often they have sought to reconstruct a precapitalist past or to add (or subtract) the present to (from) the reconstructed past. In either event one or two static analyses result. Those analyses of precapitalist orders, together with oral and written histories, provide about the only information there is on nonclass social organizations and on women in such organizations. There is no clear historical analysis for the times and places when patriarchy (or social class) first came into being. Our best approximation is a small glimpse of societies that lack them.

Here then is part of the problem. We necessarily work with static data and try to apply concepts developed from historical data. Moreover the concept of mode of production speaks best to questions of developmental dynamics, to processes of differentiation. Can it serve to distinguish or to classify in a useful way static slices of temporal and spatial history? I think it can.

The other part of the problem pertains to what questions can and cannot be answered with anthropological data. I do not think that we can answer questions about what originally caused the subordination of women. The question of origins—be it conceived of as a single essence (which I do not think is the case) or as particular forms of equality or patriarchy—is historical and cannot be answered without analysis of real historical processes. Some histories—the geneses of preclass patterns—are, with extant data, opaque to social history inquiry.

But the situation is not all bleak. Deficient as it is, ethnography does show patterns of male and female roles that are very different from our own and that ought to (but do not) prevent facile generalizations about women's universal and uniform subordination. I think, however, that ethnography allows us to do more than nip at the heels of ethnocentric generalizations. It allows us to speak to material conditions (not origins) of various shapes of equality and patriarchy. Comparative analysis of people's organization at a particular point in time can direct our attention to conditions under which particular types of change may take place by highlighting relationships among various shapes of women's place and various political economics. Looking backward, comparative analysis allows us to make nonteleological guesses at the possible developments of contradictory forces that may have precipitated change. It will not tell us what really happened, but as historical material is sought, comparative analysis may generate the hunches for its analysis. Looking forward, comparative analysis can shed light on barriers to equality that are not specific to capitalism and that are being and will continue to be confronted on the road to socialism. Historical analysis speaks to birthings and developments of new forms from old roots in new relationships. Static comparisons let us see something of the roots. But it takes historical analysis to tell us what these roots create in their struggle—and how they do it.

We can also turn the question around: What barriers to overcoming sexism are presented by ignoring ethnography? Marxism has given us histories of capitalism—of its various origins from feudal class societies in Europe, its imposition on the rest of the world, and the resultant transformations and class struggles. But we have almost no comparable preclass historical analyses for Europe (see Muller 1977) or anywhere else. With respect to women, feminist history is providing a richer understanding of changes in the forms of women's oppression, but the experiences of class society are really not adequate to saying very much about a society of no oppression. Nor do the particular histories we have allow us to think creatively about forms of oppression in kin-organized societies, about the relationship of kin to class to women's places. Ethnography raises sharply—more sharply than the historical analyses we have—the question of what prevented women's subordination and what prevents our equality. Historical and comparative analyses complement each other.

A growing body of work on precapitalist modes of production by marxist anthropologists, mainly from an Althusserian perspective, has been important in raising questions about change and process and in attempting to develop the concept of productive mode as an analytic tool. Much of this work deals with African modes of production, generally societies with patrilocal residence and patrilineal descent groups (Meillassoux 1972, 1973, 1975; Rey 1975; Terray 1972; O'Laughlin 1974; Marie 1976). The case studies in the following chapters are also of African modes of production. With the exception of the Mbuti, the societies are patrilineally and patrilocally organized. While the previous analyses centered on West African societies, the case studies here focus on East and South African organizations, thus providing comparative perspective within the framework of African modes of production. While my thinking owes a great deal to these efforts, I believe that Althusserian notions of a "base"/"superstructure" division and of "social formations" being made up of several modes of production are static and ahistorical. There is a third area of disagreement with these studies, and that lies in the way they conceptualize women within the framework of social darwinist categories (though they are not social darwinists).

In my view productive relations, and hence mode of production, is a concept at once economic and political. Economy is always political, and relations of production are about people's relations to each other by their respective relations to the means of production. Thus I disagree with the Althusserian division of the social universe into three parts—economy, politics, and culture—or economic "base" and political-cultural "superstructure." Thus, the glossary in Althusser's *Reading Capital* states:

Formation, Social (Formation sociale). A concept denoting "society" [so-called L.A.]. The concrete complex whole comprising economic practice, political practice, and ideological practice (g.v.) at a certain place and state of development. Historical materialism is the science of social formations. [1970: 313]

And Hindess and Hirst:

Marxism has traditionally conceived of social formation as a definite social unity organised into three distinct levels (economic, political, cultural) in which are combined modes of production in a definite hierarchy of determination. [1977: 49]

Marxism has traditionally done no such thing, although Althusser apparently has. Such a view has more in common with Leslie White and the American neoevolutionism of 1960 than it does with the Marx of 1860. And they are very different materialisms from each other. The former is ahistorical and static; the latter is historic and dynamic-dialectical. Somewhat similar is Meillassoux's insistence that the means of social control do not always have economic roots: "Our own investigation does not lead to the conclusion that there is a single element whose evolution could be used to characterise different stages of economic development: the means of social control have varied through time and they have not always rested on control of the means of production" (1972: 98). This suggests that Meillassoux would disagree that control over the means of production, most likely in non-class modes of production, is at the base of political power however it is allocated. I think for him mode of production does not necessarily say anything about the allocation of political power.

A second point of disagreement has to do with what the Althusserians imply by *social formation* and what is implied by *society*. The latter word in anthropological literature implies units frozen in time and isolated in space. While this is not an accurate reflection of people's organizational reality, it does at least describe accurately the material anthropologists have helped shape and have at their disposal for preclass organizations. For these reasons I will use it. It at least reminds me of the limitations of my analyses. The phrase *social formation*, on the other hand, carries implications that I think are just as static (but circuitously so) and that are also cumbersome and inaccurate. In the Althusserian view, social formations are somehow outcomes of differing combinations of various modes of production, several of which are asserted to coexist in a single social formation. A social formation is also frozen in time and isolated in space. As O'Laughlin (1977) has argued with respect to Meillassoux, what appears at any given historical moment to be a combination of several productive modes is really the appearance given by the process of uneven development of one productive mode. Her focus is on the capitalist mode of production, but her argument is historical and pertains to preclass history as well. Groups of organized people were never isolated or static. Isolated stasis is an artifact of our cameras.

Beyond this, the problem with Althusserian usage of social formation is that it is a cumbersome, particularist label and not a comparative concept. Every historical group of people at a particular point in time is a unique social formation. In this the concept is like the conventional usage of "Mbuti society." And that is how I intend to use the word *society*: to refer, for example, to the people called Mbuti in the literature, described at a particular point in their history. To speak of a "Mbuti social formation" promises more but confuses because it does not deliver. Althusserian modes of production seem to be categories of more than one; their social formations are not.

SISTERS AND WIVES IN NONCLASS MODES OF PRODUCTION

Two nonclass modes of production seem adequate for analyzing nonclass societies. I think of them as *communal* and *kin corporate*.

As pigeonholes, they sort in ways not all that different from either marxist or evolutionary schemes. The former roughly encompasses foraging societies or bands; the latter, the evolutionists' tribes and chiefdoms and Meillassoux's (1972, 1975) domestic mode of production. But I hope they are more than new labels on old pigeonholes; I hope they let us see and explain men's and women's places. No doubt many more than two modes of production could be created from what we know from ethnography about human social organization. But I arrived at these two by focusing on women's roles in the ethnographic literature. Perhaps it will be clearer to derive modes of production as they emerged from looking at women. While that is hardly a conventional exposition—usually modes are described and presented and then women are fitted in or added on or left out—I find it the clearest.

In nonclass societies, people relate to each other as relatives, as opposed to members of a class or subclass or occupation, as in class societies. Siskind (1978) has said that kinship in these societies is relations of production. By this, I take it that the term *sister*, for example, has, at the base of its meaning a description of how that person stands in relation to the means of production and therefore to other people in the same and different relations to these means.

I have been struck by the counterpoint between sister and wife in a number of preclass or protoclass African societies with corporate patrilineages—for example, the Lovedu, Mpondo, and Igbo. I have also been impressed with the obliteration of the sister relationship in class societies by the relationship of wife, as in Buganda. Further, in foraging bands, I do not see either wives or sisters clearly, as among Mbuti. Wife and sister have similar contrastive meanings in a variety of patrilineal societies with reference to a woman's relations to productive means, to other adults, to power, and to their own sexuality. I do not think I do much violence to the data by interpreting *sister* in situations of corporate patrilineages to mean one who is an owner, a decision maker among others of the corporation, and a person who controls her own sexuality. By contrast, a wife is a subordinate in much the way Engels asserted for the family based on private property.

To emphasize the wife-sister relations of production differs from emphasizing women's relations of production. I think we have accepted the social darwinist assumption that women as a gender have a single and essential relation to the means of production. Consequently we have tended to reduce everything to what is believed to be the essential relationship: the wife relationship. I am simply suggesting that women (and men), especially in nonclass societies, have several essential and contrasting productive relationships. To believe that one sees a single essence in women's relations to the means of production, I think, is to take a capitalist view. Capitalist ideology holds that men as a gender belong in the economy, roughly the sphere of capitalist productive relations (as workers or owners), while women as a gender belong in the home, where they maintain and reproduce the working class and have very different relations from men to the means of production. We know that this ideology is not reality; the gender woman is both housewife and 45 percent of the work force. But that ideology insists that the housewife role is the essence of woman's relations to the means of production. There is no reason to presume that the capitalist equation of one gender–one relation to the means of production is any truer in other modes of production than it is in capitalism itself.

There are two implications of seeing kinship as productive relations to which I do not want to commit myself. First, if wife and sister are productive relations, then so too are all sorts of other kinship terms—aunt, cross cousin, male of a senior generation not of my lineage, and so on. To see them as productive relations suggests that there is far more than one constellation of productive relations in societies having corporate lineages and also in communal societies. Ought this not suggest that there are many more than two modes of production? I do not think so, as I will try to show by looking at uniformities below the surface variation in the productive modes themselves.

There is a second implication. Is not the focus on sister and wife a suggestion that this is somehow a key or fundamental set of relationships? The answer is yes and no. Yes, in that this particular contrast provided me with a key to integrating two inquiries that always seemed to be at loggerheads. When marxists focus on precapitalist (or even capitalist) modes of production, they consign women to a domestic sphere and append both as an afterthought or forget about them altogether. Alternatively women are seen as victims or social objects, and such objectification is said to be necessary for social functioning (Meillassoux 1972). Modes are male, but they do not have to be that way. If mode of production is a socially illuminating concept, then it surely can illuminate women's social places. The center of a sister-wife contrast lies in the fact that it illuminates women's productive relations more fully than I think they have been. On the other hand, I am not prepared to say that this contrast is more basic than any other, even for women. I simply have not adequately explored mother-daughter as a relationship, in relation to age, or as dimensions of a wife-sister constellation. Nor do I want to assert any primacy of wife-sister over class relationships. Indeed that would do tremendous violence to the complexity of the interrelationships between class and sex.

COMMUNAL MODE OF PRODUCTION

While kinship terms in the communal mode of production tend to emphasize generation (Marshall 1957), they also divide the world into categories of people whom one may and may not marry. Thus for every individual, the opposite sex contains two categories—brothers and sisters, who are not marriageable; and those men and women who are potential spouses. The distinction between sister and wife, and brother and husband, exists in the communal mode of production. Marriage joins the families of spouses together, and affinal ties are of considerable importance for determining productive groups, both actual and potential.

The means of production are restricted to tools, individually owned and often individually fashioned. Land is a resource rather than a productive means. Human labor power is not applied to transform it in order to make it produce. Rather its products are directly appropriated. Yet there are some very limited relations of ownership—or restricted access—to some natural resources: !Kung waterholes and mongongo nut groves are associated with particular camps; Mbuti and !Kung wild honey is individually claimed by its finder (Solway 1976; Marshall 1976: 370). But by and large the means to subsist, both the means of production and the natural resources, are equally accessible to all. Tools are generally fashioned for individual use, though many subsistence techniques require cooperation among several people. Often production involves groups necessitated not by technology but by the goal of production, as in hunts among Mbuti or Great Basin Shoshoneans. Other times cooperation is generated by the constellation of tasks undertaken. For example, gathering is seldom undertaken as an isolated task; it is more often done with infant and child care; and the combination seems to necessitate cooperation. In any case, pro-

ductive groups may or may not be divided by sex, but their lines of cooperation are more or less coincident with the residential group (such
as band or camp) and not with the family. Nor is consumption mainly
a family affair. The complexity involved in the wide distribution of
meat is often noted (and described, Marshall 1976; see chapter 4 for
Mbuti). Meat is given to individuals of both sexes by virtue of their
specific relation to the giver. It is not given to families, nor do families
have a common pot (Marshall 1976: 363, 370). I suspect that vegetable distribution follows similar principles, but on a much smaller
scale. Women give to small children and to other women, often in the
gathering process, which is linked directly to consumption prior to returning to camp (Kaberry 1939: 22, 33; see also James Woodburn's
film, *The Hadza*). And while children are not responsible for food
collecting, they generally gather increasing amounts of their food as
they grow older.

   All people have the same relationship to the means of production,
and hence they stand to each other as equal members of a community
of "owners."[2] The productive difference between men and women is
not that they stand in different relations of production to each other;
after all both appropriate from nature, transform the fruits, and own
them (be they food or tool). To insist that because they act on different
aspects of nature and make or own different particulars, they then
stand in different relations to productive means seems like insisting
that workers in an auto plant and those in a sausage factory stand in
different relations to productive means. That logic would lead to a
proliferation of classes along lines similar to categories in the occupational census. In addition it would see men and women as different
classes, hence reducing sex to class with respect to economic questions. Yet there are differences in the productive responsibilities wom-
en and men are assigned. I think, though, that these differences are at
the level of productive forces—how they organize their work and who
does what. If we see it this way, then the problem of whether a sex division of labor must imply social inequality evaporates. And indeed this
was what Engels insisted at one point (1891: 79).

   !Kung spouses call and refer to each other by terms that translate as
man and *woman* (Marshall 1957: 16), terms whose significance is
that of adulthood. To marry and rear children is to be an adult; to
marry is to be responsible for production (Solway 1976; Shostack
1976). Mbuti similarly equate marriage, adulthood, and productive

responsibility. But in both cases, the linkage is not that of production for or with a spouse. Rather it is a more generalized one, and I visualize it in this way. To make babies is to create the next generation of people (in a more inclusive group sense), and that commitment represents a commitment to productive responsibility in the sense of daily maintenance. Marriage involves entry into an adult relationship vis-à-vis the larger social group; one's relationship as a spouse of a particular individual is secondary.

In addition and more fundamentally, affinal relationships are productive relationships that transcend particular camps and establish a community of "owners" encompassing "the whole people." That is, while members of a particular camp or band have the right to resources associated with that residential group's area, the actual composition of any band may change greatly from one season to the next (Lee 1972a, 1972c). People may visit or live with bands among whom they have kin or affines and thus claim membership and use rights over that group's resources. Since all people can trace some kind of relationship with virtually every other person, ownership—or rights of unimpeded use—relations exist among the whole people. Thus affinity and blood kinship together establish the right of any individual and family to use the resources virtually anywhere in that society's territory. Hence "the !Kung" or "the Mbuti" are a community of "owners." However, they are also a community of producers, and ties of kinship and affinity are also forces of production. To visit for more than a few days requires undertaking productive responsibility—joining others in gathering or hunting. It requires actually relating to the means of production.

Both Mbuti and !Kung express preferences for brother-sister exchange marriages and for interband marriages. In the former situation, the husband of one woman will be the brother of the other woman, while the latter's husband is the first woman's brother. In the second situation, for example, band A sends a man to marry a woman from band B, while band B sends a woman to marry a man from band A. Postmarital residence may vary: In some cases men leave their bands or families; in others women move out. It is important to stress that such exchange marriages are not exchanges of women. But Levi-Strauss (1969, 1971) and Meillassoux (1972) have interpreted virtually all such exchanges to be exchanges of women that establish affinal ties between the two groups. In their view, women are objects cementing alliances (see Singer 1973 for refutation). Such an interpretation has no basis at all in the communal mode of production, where husbands and wives are man and woman—adults, producers. In patrilocal and patrilineal organizations, the husband-wife relationship changes, and marriage does involve "giving" women of one's own group to men of another group. But that is not the case in this mode of production nor is it an accurate description of women in other nonclass society modes of production.

KIN CORPORATE MODE OF PRODUCTION

The most striking aspect of this productive mode is the productive relations: people are all members of a corporation with collective ownership of the main means of production and, in one or another sense, are thus political decision makers with respect to the basis of their group's economic well-being. Thus women and men within a corporation stand in the same relations to the means of production, basically summed up as the relations of brother and sister. This is not to deny variations in productive relations. Some have been pointed out time and again by social anthropologists—particularly differences between societies where all corporation members have equal access to the productive means and thus to decision making and those where these are unequally distributed within the corporation (Fried 1967; Kirchhoff 1959; Suttles 1960).

Means of production differ significantly from those of collecting societies. Agricultural land is the principal productive means. Human labor has been invested in its transformation, and its fruitfulness lasts for varying lengths of time. Kin corporations are a productive mode of food producers, as has been noted often (Meillassoux 1972; Sahlins 1968). And yet there is tremendous variation in productive means among nonclass food producers, even if one were simply to focus on principal means of production and ignore different combinations of subsistence strategies. Among horticulturalists, for example, there are complex interrelationships among how different means are combined. Thus land use (how long a plot is used, fallow periods, and therefore total land requirements) is related to crop complex (grains and/or roots), and to tools for working that land (digging sticks, axes, hoes) in a variety of ways (Boserup 1965; Smith 1972; David Harris 1972). And these variations in productive means relate to the forces of production—how people organize themselves, together with the land, tools, and seeds, to perform the tasks that produce their subsistence. Thus ecologists have commented on the relationships of human labor time to land use (intensive, extensive cultivation) and to tools and human organization (Boserup 1965). Moreover it is important whether land retains use value for three years, say, or three generations, because people's relations to that land and hence to each other differ greatly in the two cases.

Are there any uniformities in productive means and forces underlying this variability? If not, then it is more accurate to speak of kin corporate relations of production than of a mode of production. I think that there are uniformities in productive means and forces or, more accurately, in how these interrelate with productive relations. These uniformities are my reasons for calling it a mode of production. As in the communal mode, the productive means can be worked by one or a few people for the most part. Some tasks may require all or most group members of the appropriate age(s) or sex(es) within the corporation: clearing the land in Onitsha Igbo patrilineages (Henderson 1972), protecting livestock from attack among Mpondo, taking cattle to dry season water among the eastern Nuer (Evans-Pritchard 1940), and cultivating among Iroquois matrilineages (Brown 1970b) are all examples. In these instances, productive forces tend to synchronize with productive relations. But other productive tasks may require some subset of the appropriate age or sex—such as boys or girls of a house, two brothers, a husband and wife—for their performance. In these cases productive forces tend not to be synchronous with productive relations. In speaking of productive tasks requiring different combinations of people for their performance, I do not mean that a particular combination is somehow determined by something in the task itself. All eidence suggests that different peoples organize the particulars of similar tasks differently. The reasons they do so are beyond the scope of this inquiry

The point to be emphasized here is that variety in task organization is a uniformity in kin corporation modes of production; that the productive means are amenable to this variety, being simple and usable for the most part by individuals; and that the relations of production are uniform and corporate. The defining dynamic of this mode of production then seems to rest in a contradiction between corporate relations of production and both corporate and subcorporate forces of production.[3] Kin corporations are both owning and producing groups. But they are not groups for all (and sometimes most) productive tasks, nor do they own all (or most) of what is produced, on corporate means of production.

It is in this contradictory relationship within the productive forces (between producer-owners and producer-nonowners) and between them and the productive relations (of producer-owners and nonproducer-owners) that I see the dynamics of the kin corporate mode of production. I intend this mode of production to apply to the vast majority of nonclass societies described in the ethnographic literature, so it clearly encompasses a wide variety of particular organizations. I see this variety as having two sources. First, some of it rests on varieties in the subsistence bases, their combinations, and the particulars of task organization. Second, some of the variety may be a manifestation of particular patterns and stages of devleopment of the contradictory relationships that define the corporate mode of production. The second source suggests an approach to why fission of kin corporations occurs with great regularity. That is, we need not see fission as a product of "crowding," or a natural desire to be the one's own boss, or of an ecological imperative such as too little land. Rather it may be a possible development of contradictions between individual-household-corporate subgroup centrality in production and corporate ownership of productive means. This contradiction may be expressed in conflict over particular products—say between producer-owners of the means of production and nonproducer-owners of the means of production. I have in mind the tensions and complexities surrounding cattle in eastern and southern African societies with kin corporate modes of production and mixed livestock and horticultural subsistence bases. The cattle graze on lands claimed by the corporation as a whole and are protected in part by that same group; yet day-to-day care and responsibility is provided by a subgroup of a household. But the claims on the cattle themselves and on some of their products extend beyond those primarily responsible for their care. Thus Nuer cattle for bridewealth are often legitimately claimed by lineage members not directly involved in producing those cattle. The particular rationales of a person's claim on another's cattle rests on the fact that they are both co-owners of the means of production. Or conflict may arise over use of the means of production—for example, in access to garden plots where they are allocated each year.

We are also able to guess at processes of developing inequalities within kin corporations. Should a subcorporate group increase in importance as a productive group, uneven success among those subcorporate groups can lead to unequal distribution of the means of production themselves. As the production of grain, for example, involves the kin corporation in allocating plots according to the labor resources available for subcorporate tasks, plots will be of unequal sizes. If frequent reallocation does not happen—perhaps because crops are perennials (trees), swidden is short fallow, and land is scarce—the means of production may remain corporately owned but in practice be controlled by subgroups. Over time, productive relations change such that land-shy members stand in different relation to the productive means than land-rich members.[4]

These discussions of fission and of developing inequality are ahistorical and evolutionary because they describe processes without reference to real social changes in time and space. They are guesses suggested by what I see as the central dynamic of a kin corporate mode of production. They fit particular points in the histories of real societies. They are not substitutes for the study of history but hypotheses to approach such study.

Where men and women in the communal mode of production had the same relations to the means of production, only siblings share this relationship in the corporate mode. Spouses stand in different relations to productive means. Moreover the forces of production—in particular, the organization of men's and women's work—often reinforce the differences between spouses' productive relationships and undercuts the shared relationship between brothers and sisters. However, the organization of work can also reinforce sibling-shared productive relationships and undercut the spouse relationship of production. The point is that there is some variability in this mode of production. Nevertheless sibling and spouse relations are in contradiction, and women's and men's work organization may reinforce one or both sides of these contradictory productive relationships.

In patrilineal and patrilocal corporations, marriage means somewhat different things for men and women. I suspect that matrilineal and matrilocal corporations present a mirror image (despite conventional kinship wisdom that they do not) and that there are still more variations that depend on the ways residence is combined with membership criteria, but I have not examined these dimensions.[5] The following discussion is based on patrilineal and patrilocal corporations because those are what I have examined.

Wives gain access to the means of production through their husbands. Husbands exert differential control over their wives', labor, and/or labor's products. Thus while husbands may clear land for their wives, wives may have to cultivate a plot belonging to their husbands and work their own plot. Produce from the former may belong exclusively to the husband for use as he chooses, while produce of the wife's plot may be specifically for family use. Alternatively husbands may claim grain from a wife's field, but wives may not distribute the products of their labor to nonmembers of the husband's group without explicit permission. Thus the husband's corporation, especially its sisters and brothers and the husband's mother, controls the productivity of its wives.

Yet every wife is also a sister and, as such, has claim to productive means, to their fruits, or to the labor of brother's wives. These rights, like those of a brother, come into being only upon marriage and adulthood. Unlike brothers, though, sisters in a patrilocal organization are often in a poor position to exercise these rights when they are married. Sisters need not stay married to hold their rights, and divorced sisters living at home or on extended visits are common.

In a corporate mode of production, a woman's adult life cycle alternates between two productive relationships. Wifehood involves working for and bearing children for the husband's group. It is generally a woman's dominant productive relationship in her young adult years. In these years she is more a daughter or junior member of her own corporation. Her brothers are also juniors. As a woman's children and those of her brothers grow up, both brother and sister become more involved as corporation decision makers. A woman's change of status in her own group is paralleled by a shift in her relationship to her husband's corporation. The latter shift is from wife to mother (of adult children).

Motherhood relates a woman to her husband's group's means of production independently of any relationship to her husband. Children depend on their mother for access to productive means. She is the person who maintains and allocates land and livestock assigned by her husband to her home. As children enter productive adulthood with the means of production from their father's lineage, their mother becomes a nonlineage member with control over their access to productive means. As such "mother" is a different relationship to lineage means of production than is "wife." Mothers' influence is reinforced by their position as sisters within their own lineage. Thus in a woman's life cycle, her relations to the means of production of both her own and her husband's lineage change. Young married women in their own lineage and in their husband's are subordinates, specifically daughters and wives in productive relations. With age, they become controllers of labor and productive means—as sisters who control brothers' children's lineage affairs and as mothers who control their own children and their children's productive means.

For men, some of these changes have been remarked upon—in particular, the shift from junior to senior or elder, and the relationship of husband to wife—with respect to expropriation of labor and/or surplus product (Meillassoux 1972; O'Laughlin 1974; Terray 1972). But the relationship of a brother to a sister has received almost no attention. I believe that this omission has contributed to the one-sided view of women as subordinate in marxist discussions of modes of production. Thus these discussions emphasize that a woman's lineage gives her labor power in the production of subsistence and maintenance as well as her labor power to bear and rear children to her husband's lineage. Control over this is said to be transferred from a woman's own to her husband's lineage. In return, the husband's lineage provides bridewealth goods (not to the wife but to her lineage), which will allow them to find a wife to do for them what their sister does for her husband's linege. At the point of a woman's marriage, this may indeed be an accurate description of what obtains; women may indeed not control or claim bridewealth or their own children. But this double alienation in youth is often transformed into a delayed claim on both one's own lineage and that of one's husband. Sisters have a claim on a brother's products or labor. Perhaps more importantly, they also have a claim on the labor of junior members of their own lineage. Often this is phrased as a return for their having provided their brother with the wherewithal to marry and have children. Thus brothers' claims to their own children's labor are shared with the claims of their sisters and the children's mother. It is the particular constellation of a woman's productive relationships that determines her place in the society. And the relative importance of each of these productive relationships for men and for women is determined by specific conditions of social life in a given society—in particular on how work is organized for each sex.

Hence the organization of work is necessary to understanding the relative importance of each constellation of productive relationships. Work organization differs from society to society, but I do not think the variety is totally random.[6] Men's productive tasks are performed alone or in conjunction with several or many other men of a man's own lineage. Men's task groups are commonly groups of corporate brothers. Women's work is performed alone or in conjunction with other wives, women of neither the corporation that appropriates the product nor of a woman's own group. Mixed sex work groups typically combine men of the corporation and its wives. Men work with those with whom they share the same relations to the means of production. A man's task group may be synonymous with the owning group, or it may be part of it. Lines of conflict or fission tend to be within the lineage rather than overlap and cross lineage bounds. Women work together with other wives of the lineage, and lines of conflict between "workers" and "owners" unite the lineage and divide it from its wives. To the extent that tasks assigned to women are performed by wives and mothers (as opposed to sisters) working as a collectivity, the forces of production associated with women are in contradiction with lineage productive relations. Production by nonmembers is expropriated by members. Rather than standing in an individual relationship to a husband, wives stand in a collective relationship to the husband's lineage. In this collectivity, wives assert some of the prerogatives of the sister relationship in their roles as wives, making the contradiction manifest. If the forces of production isolate wives—or prevent them from being active sisters in their own lineage—then the autonomous woman's place stemming from sister relations is difficult to develop.

One final point needs to be stressed. The contradiction between women's relationship to their own lineage means of production and to their husbands' is not resolved in patrilocal corporations. By the same token, the contradictory relationships of husband and brother in matrilocal corporations are unresolved; and the contradiction between sister and wife is also part of a contradiction within each lineage between producers (or members of a specific work team) and owners. Producers may be wives and some lineage brothers; owners may be a much larger group of lineage brothers or a few lineage brothers (or sisters) who do not participate in the work team. These then are the contradictions a kin corporate mode of production lives with. Finally, one would expect to find a plethora of ideological assertions that deny or attempt to resolve them by reducing contradictory relationships to sexual dichotomies, as in myths about male or female rule. But I think it is important not to mistake such attempts for statements about real relationships of men and women.

CONCLUSION

In these two nonclass modes of production, the productive relations of men and women differ. In the communal mode, the dominant productive relationship is that of adult woman (or adult man), a member of a community of producer-owners. The distinction between potential spouse and sibling does not mark contrasting productive relationships.[7] That is, sisters and wives both have the same relations to productive means and resources. This is not the case in the kin corporate mode of production where there are several communities of owner-producers linked by relations of affinity. Here sisters and wives are two different productive relationships. In patrilineal and patrilocal situations, the former are owners and not producers, and the latter are producers and not owners. Yet every woman embodies these two different relationships. That the contrast exists stems from corporate control of productive means. How it is manifested—that is, how women combine them—depends on the organization of productive forces. The central point here is that in nonclass productive modes—even in patrilineal, patrilocal corporations, often conceived of as necessarily patriarchal—the existence of a corporate owning group allows for a range of relationships, some of which are sexually egalitarian.

Class societies, or more accurately, the processes by which ruling classes established themselves, involved the breakup of corporate owning groups and their replacement by class ownership of productive means (Adams 1966). There is no clear point of division between classes and nonclass societies with respect to amount of productive means under corporate kin group control compared to that under ruling class control. However, African history reveals many processes of class formation and something of the processes by which ruling classes broke up corporate kin groups. We are thus able to discuss the geneses of modes of production in class societies in historical context.

The case study of nineteenth-century Buganda (chapter 8) will discuss one process of class formation and breakup of kin corporations. I will compare Buganda's developmental process with that of Dahomey in West Africa (in chapter 9). To the extent that ruling classes broke up or subverted patrikin groups as owning and producing corporations, they radically altered women's place. I will suggest that class societies, to the extent that they developed from patricorporations, transformed women from sister and wife to daughter and wife, making them perennial subordinates. The final chapters will explore some of the processes by which these transformations have occurred and will allow us to discuss the relationship between sex and class.

NOTES

1. For reexaminations of Engels's work, see Leacock 1972; Sacks 1974; Gough 1975; Rubin 1975; Lane 1976; and Aaby 1977.

2. Fried (1975: 55) argues that *ownership*, even communal, is an inappropriate and ethnocentric term in description of collectors' relationships to basic resources. I agree but am uncomfortable with substituting *users* or *appropriators* here.

3. This is not the same as Sahlins's (1972) insistence on a contradiction between households as productive units and lineages as exchange groups.

4. Inherent in kin corporations is the possibility of private control of the means of production. One can even find such seeds in the communal mode of production in the individual ownership of the tools produced by an individual. The common denominator is that productive activity, the transformation of nature, involves appropriation and ownership. But reduction to a common denominator makes a mockery of history (or what we know of it). It reads the present onto the past, confuses an acorn with the oak, and hence prevents understanding either or their relationship. Individual tool ownership is not a homunculus of capitalist productive relationships.

5. I suspect that much of what is described as kin corporate, particularly the wife-sister and husband-brother constellation of relationships, can apply with appropriate modifications to a variety of corporate matrilineal situations. Schlegel's (1972) study deals with the brother-husband half of this constellation as it affects women, but investigation of the reciprocal seems to have been precluded by the research design. Such a study remains to be done.

6. A discussion of what causes particular types of work organization, such as one on the causes of the division of labor itself, is beyond the scope of this inquiry; I will not try to explain the work organizations that exist.

7. I regard the discussion of the communal mode of production as theoretically incomplete, because it does not suggest any organizational tensions, or internal social contradictions, that might generate change in this mode of production under particular historical conditions. This gap stems from the nature of the ethnographic literature I have examined on African collecting societies. However, an approach that may resolve the problem may be embedded in three recent papers. Rosaldo and Collier (Forth-

coming) suggest that collecting societies and what they call "hunter-horticulturalist" societies share a basic organizational similarity despite differences in subsistence bases, and are best discussed as a single type of organization. Knight (1978) and Siskind (1978) view the dual, or bifurcate, organizations of lowland South American horticultural and collecting societies as representing a basic social structure. Given this view, Siskind's discussion of kinship as productive relations suggests that historical and organizational examination of bifurcate organizations may be a promising direction for theoretical elaboration of a communal mode of production. Indeed, Siskind's own work (1973) is an apt place to begin because of its combination of historical and structural analysis.

Chapter 4
MBUTI

Mbuti Pygmies of Zaïre have a communal mode of production. Although they are almost certainly the original inhabitants of the forest, such little of their history as is known is one of economic symbiosis with later-arriving horticultural peoples. These relationships have been described as clientage; and indeed the productive relations described ethnographically between Mbuti and their patrons make this seem accurate. Yet among the particular groups studied ethnographically, clientship was not the predominant productive relationship. Rather intergroup exchange appears to have been principally through trade relationships of individual collectors with individual patrons, with these relationships themselves shaped by communal collecting productive forces and relationships. There are no pure communal modes of production in Africa; instead there are varying histories of symbiosis between collectors and producers, or peoples with communal and those with kin corporate (or state) modes of production.[1] The Mbuti live in the Ituri forest in the northeastern part of Zaïre, just south of Sudan and west of Uganda. The forest is also populated by Mangbetu and Lese peoples, speakers of Central Sudanic languages, Forest Bira, and other related Bantu-speaking peoples. The Mbuti have adopted the language of the particular group with whom they associate. All save Mbuti practice shifting cultivation as their subsistence base and live in settled villages cleared in the primary forest. The Mbuti are nomadic hunters and gatherers in a symbiotic relationship with the villagers.

The history of this part of Zaïre is yet to be written. Prior to the nineteenth century, the Ituri forest appears to have been isolated from the forces of class formation and trade that were in motion over much of the continent. Pygmy gatherer-hunters are believed to have been the original inhabitants of the forest. Early on, the forest borders began to be penetrated in the west by peoples speaking Eastern Nigritic languages, in the east and south by Bantu speakers, and in the east by speakers of Central Sudanic languages. The Mangbetu, Central Sudanic speakers in the northern part of the Ituri, developed a plantain horticulture, supplemented with goat raising. They exchanged iron and vegetables with Pygmies for meat.

Traders from Khartoum had penetrated Mangbetu lands by the 1860s and opened up an ivory trade with Mangbetu chiefs. From Schweinfurth's descriptions, latter nineteenth-century Mangbetu appear to have been fairly hierarchical chiefdoms, with royal ivory monopolies. Apparently this stratification at least partly preceded the ivory trade as the Mangbetu armies, led by a king's daughter, routed the first Khartoum army, with the first firearms, to enter their lands (Schweinfurth 1873, vol. 2: 83–85, 95–96).[2] Subsequently the ivory trade was pursued under Mangbetu control. Schweinfurth (Ibid.: 124) noted of the Pygmies in this connection that, "their services [in killing elephants] in this way were asserted to contribute very largely to the resources of the ivory traders."[3] In addition, Schweinfurth mentions that Pygmy clients of a Mangbetu chief also served as warriors against the Momvoo (Lese?) and were noted as fighters (Ibid.: 131–32).[4]

The Mamvu, also Central Sudanic speakers, lived to the southeast of the Mangbetu. To the southwest of them were the Babwa, a Bantu-speaking people, also with a long agricultural adaptation to the forest environment (Birmingham 1975: 325–29). During the nineteenth century, some repercussions of the ivory trade, from Khartoum and from the Swahili-Arab traders on the east coast, likely penetrated the Ituri (Birmingham 1975: 254; Slade 1962: 91–105). So too may have the slave and forced labor raids of their successors, the Congo Free State and the Belgian Congo (Ibid.; Bourne 1903: 192–93).

This chapter concerns Mbuti whose ties were primarily to Bira shifting horticulturalists and who hunted by setting up a large semicircle of nets and driving the game into them, where the male hunters speared them.[5] Although Turnbull's fieldwork and hence this analysis focuses on the forest foraging context, it is necessary to make some mention of the net hunters' orientation to the horticulturalists as well.

The relationship between villager and Mbuti is complicated and changing. I will be concerned only with the later period of Belgian colonialism (1951–1958). The villages, accessible to effective colonial pressure, were forced to meet heavy Belgian demands for road labor and cotton growing, in addition to having to produce their own subsistence. Some sort of exchange and clientage relationship between villagers and Mbuti existed prior to Belgian rule. With the imposition of colonial demands, villagers' needs for Mbuti labor increased. Apparently in the past as well as in the present, villagers relied on Mbuti to supply them with meat and building materials from the forest. In the economic sphere, colonialism heightened village needs for Mbuti goods and services.

While colonialism impinged directly on Bira, the Mbuti were only beginning to be affected in the mid-twentieth century. Although they were induced to make gardens and to engage in wage labor, the forest still supplied them with ample food. The Epulu band could and did go for periods of three to six months without any reliance on village foods (Turnbull 1965a: 148). There were other bands less reliant than the Epulu on village life (Turnbull 1962: 243, 248). Unfortunately it is not known how much time they spent in the forest as compared with the village. Sometimes the entire band was together, in one or the other place, but at other times it divided between the two.

Mbuti depended on Bira to supply them with metal knives, axes, and machetes. In the twentieth century these were capitalist manufactures, but prior to that time, at least elsewhere in the forest, metal was smelted locally by horticultural peoples and exchanged with collectors. While they lived in a Bira village, Mbuti depended on village foods. It appears that Mbuti retained much of the decision making about their visits to villages. Bira chiefs complained that Mbuti often disappeared when asked to work on the cotton harvest. Moreover Turnbull's information suggests that Mbuti often received more goods from their patrons than the latter received, in goods and services, from the Mbuti (Ibid.: 240–59; 1965a: 39–43, 81–83, 148–50, 325). Yet Mbuti women pounded and threshed grain and carried goods to markets and men built houses and performed all heavy work. Turnbull does not say that Mbuti did roadwork or harvested cotton, but they did set up gardens near the village and thus must have been directly in contact with colonial forces (1962: 23, 31–32). In addition, Mbuti moved to a village as an escape from dissension and when bands fell below (or above) a size able to hunt effectively.

Mbuti and Bira had different ideologies about their relationship.

Bira emphasized patron-client ties (*kpara*) between a patrilineal band
and a patrilineal village. In both the chief was the senior member of the
patriline and had authority over others of the group. The two patrilineages were seen as in permanent association. Bira initiated Mbuti boys
with their own sons at the *nkumbi* ceremony, thereby controlling
Mbuti access to adulthood. In addition, individual Bira and Mbuti
stood in patrilineal hereditary patron-client relations. Bira sought to
increase their number of clients by arranging marriages, thereby gaining the services of an Mbuti wife and children. Funerals too were part
of extending clientship after death. Initiation added a dimension of
mutual aid (*kare*) to individual patron-client relations when a Bira
patron had his son circumcised together with his Mbuti client's son.
Two boys circumcised together owed each other permanent reciprocal aid. Bira viewed inherited clientage together with their control of
Mbuti life cycle ceremonies and their threats of witchcraft and sorcery
as sanctions of patron-client relations.

Mbuti accepted these relationships but appear to have acted more
upon ties of clientage between individuals than those between groups.
Mbuti productive relations in the forest made for a collecting organization different from Bira perceptions. Mbuti bands were cognatic
rather than patrilineal, lacked chiefs or headmen with any authority,
and had fluid membership during and over the years. Thus with
respect to village relations of production, individual clientage relations and participation in the forest organization of a band were often
likely to be out of phase. It was quite likely that an individual or group
whose *kpara* lived in one village would be in a forest territory claimed
by another village. Mbuti would make alliances with individuals in the
new village and temporarily or permanently drop the old (without
negotiating with either set of villagers), much to the annoyance of the
original *kpara* (Turnbull 1965a: 47–48). Thus while a band might
accept clientage to a particular village, the particular individuals involved in particular patron-client relations were likely to be more fluid
than village expectations.

Clientage is not an egalitarian relationship but nevertheless is predicated on a certain amount of political and economic autonomy between the parties. Mbuti asserted their autonomy in claiming to "eat
the village," meaning that they were out to gain from the relationship,
and in claiming that they maintained only relationships that suited

them. Villagers did compete for clients and did complain of being cheated by Mbuti. But it is also clear that stable long-term relationships existed. Turnbull shows two separate groups of patrilineal descendants in three- and four-generation stable clientship to village patrilineages (1965a: 47–48, 322). It may be that colonial demands on Bira, together with increased availability of metal goods by the mid-twentieth century, were tipping the balance in favor of Mbuti. Unfortunately there is no historical information on the question.

The nature of Mbuti behavior as clients emphasized the individual nature of the relationship in general and the autonomy of Mbuti women in particular. In the collecting organization, the band with its men and women was a productive team. In the village, nuclear families or individuals within them acted independently of each other. Husbands and wives sometimes separated, attaching themselves to different patrons in the same or different villages.

SUBSISTENCE BASE AND DIVISION OF LABOR

Game, wild plants, and cultivated vegetables made up Mbuti subsistence. Honey in season was of major importance. The division of labor was based on age and sex. Married men were responsible for hunting, and married women were responsible for gathering wild vegetable food, slow game, and grubs. Together with older girls they acted as beaters for the band net hunt. Men also gathered significant amounts of vegetables. Honey in trees was collected by men; that near the ground could be collected by women. Women neither hunted nor climbed trees. Men made their hunting equipment, though women made the twine for the hunting nets. Often too, mothers made nets for a son, and men and women frequently cooperated in making twine for nets: "Net-making is a major and constant activity calling for cooperation between men and women" (Turnbull 1965b: 197, 212). Women made baskets and huts and prepared the food. Men made bark cloths, an even more time-consuming task than net making (Ibid.: 197; 1965a: 151, 166).

In production, age overshadowed sex. Younger married people and some of the older unmarried youths (boys and girls) were the major food collectors and craft producers. Older people looked after the children, did most of the cooking, and made twine. Boys and girls carried water and gathered firewood (Turnbull 1965a: 115). Bands contained four age groups: children, youths, married adults, and elders, with the married adults as the principal producers.

FORCES OF PRODUCTION

The net hunt, involving both men and women in both hunting and gathering, was the major productive event and took place about every five in seven days. Youths and adults participated, while small children were left in camp and watched by older men and women and some of the older children. The hunt often took no more than half a day; the rest of the time was spent in cooking, craft activities, and socializing (Ibid.: 119). Each married man had his own net (a few bachelors who were skilled hunters had their own nets too). These nets, a hundred to three hundred feet long, were strung end to end to form a large semicircle. Between seven and thirty nets made for an efficient game drive. Too large a circle made it difficult to control the game; too small a circle resulted in premature scaring and escape of the game. These considerations set the size of a band at somewhere between seven and thirty families—the average being about seventeen (Turnbull 1965b: 202; 1965: 327). Generally the best hunters were stationed in the center of the circle, and older boys guarded the ends of the arc. Women acted as beaters and gathered wild plants and slow game during the hunt.

The adult men and women of the band were the major productive forces as gathering and hunting were combined in a single event requiring a mixed sex collective for their execution. "Each net is utterly dependent on the others, as is each beater, and it is the cooperative aspect of the age group that is emphasized rather than the distinctness of each family" (Turnbull 1965a: 120). Other subsidiary productive activities were often performed in groups. Women's gathering within and without the hunt context was often done in small groups; women generally cooperated in hut building; honey gathering was done cooperatively by groups of men, though women went along to make sure they got some of the honey (Ibid.: 93, 102; Turnbull 1965b: 210).

RELATIONS OF PRODUCTION

Collectively the territorially defined band owned major productive resources to which all members had equal access. First-use rights to honey and bark cloth trees, though, were claimed by individual men, and a man's home band was likely to be where he had claims to such trees (Turnbull 1965a: 93–94). Residence in a band was at base membership in it. This at once entitled residents to access to resources and obligated them to participate in food collecting. Actual band composition and size fluctuated from month to month and seasonally. About once a month, bands moved camp in search of new food sources. These were generally times when its composition changed as visitors arrived and some members left to visit. Size of band, interpersonal conflict, desire to meet marriageable people, type and quality of hunting and gathering, or desire for village foods were effective causes for moving.

Bands were tied together by these interfamily visits and by the obligation of the visitors' band to reciprocate to any member of the hosts' band in the future (Ibid.: 221–22). The basis for such visits stemmed largely from affinal ties. Mbuti preferred band exogamy as a means of establishing a wide network of social relations. Turnbull also claims that postmarital residence was mainly patrilocal, but his table of band composition and marriages does not bear out the practice of either as a band phenomenon (though there were discernible patrilocal clusters, Ibid.: table 4).

Kinship terms of address and reference extended to all band members. The five terms—glossed as grandparent, mother, father, sibling, and child—stress relative age within the band context and sum up at once the forces and relations of production. All members of a band are kin and hence part of the community of owners of productive resources. As we have seen, the community divided productive responsibility by age group. In the same way specific areas of political responsibility were also allocated to different age groups as groups of siblings. There were no individual authority positions; decision making was by consensus. Although wisdom and ability were recognized and influential, "any tendency toward charismatic leadership is countered by ridicule" (Ibid.: 179).

As in productive organization, the nuclear family was unimportant politically. Young married couples as the producers were primarily responsible for economic decisions: where and when to hunt, whether and when to go to the village. This group was also responsible for bearing children and raising them until they were about four years old; after that they became the responsibility of the band, particularly its elders, to a greater extent (Ibid.: 113). Youths, together with elders, bore most responsibility for the education and care of the children, who spent most of their time in a play area adjacent to the camp. Questions of betrothal and marriage were the concern of the youths, though in cases where the adults objected strenuously, the elders made the final decision (Ibid.: 114–15). In the sense of their being the economic support of the band, the younger married people were the dominant age group in the band (they participated most heavily in discussion). They determined most strongly the composition of the band and the relations of band to village. They were also the most quarrelsome. Mbuti emphasized the need to air grievances, since unaired injuries could fester and destroy the cooperation necessary for food collecting. Thus interpersonal disputes were soon brought to the attention of the band, generally by the disputants themselves shouting and fighting or by a third party. Once the quarrel was out in the open, even though there was no formal adjudication process, elders took major responsibility for mediation because they were immune to being molested (Ibid.: 127). Thus kinship terms are about relationships to productive means and forces, as well as being about particular domains of political responsibility and rights. It needs to be stressed that age prevailed over sex in the division of political influence; both women and men of a given age group participated alike and together in whatever decision making their group was responsible for.

While motherhood and fatherhood are central relationships of adulthood, those of husband and wife are not. It seems that parenthood is part of adulthood, the other part of which is productive responsibility to and for others of the band. And parental responsibility is conceptualized in a way analogous to productive responsibility in that adults have a responsibility to care for the children of the band. Although there is a general category of sibling and no general category of spouse or potential spouse, Mbuti did distinguish those who could and could not marry. Blood relatives of mothers' and fathers' mothers could not marry or have extramarital sexual relationships, though premarital sex relationships were not a serious breach of the rules (Ibid.: 111–12). The minimal elaboration of spousehood stemmed from the fact that the organization of productive forces and relations was at the band and not a family level with respect to both food and children. The only activity families seem to have done together was to shift residence to another band or to the village.

MODE OF PRODUCTION AND GENDER

The social personalities of men and women stemmed from the organization of productive forces in the context of the communal mode of production. People were defined more by age than by sex, for that was how production was organized. Thus Mbuti saw personalities and responsibilities associated with youth, adulthood, and elderhood rather than with gender. But gender was also a social attribute. Men and women produced and owned different things; sexually women's childbearing was recognized differently from men's reproductive maturity. Although men and women did different specific things, the fact that their work was organized in the same way and that they stood in the same relationship to the band's means of production sustained a genderless standard of economic, political, and personal autonomy and equality.

Each sex owned and disposed of the fruits of its labor. Men allocated honey, barkcloth, and game and distributed game at the hunting site. Women built and owned the houses, distributed all food that came into the house, and managed gifts and exchanges outside of it (Ibid.: 160, 271). For a woman to dismantle a house was tantamount to a threat of divorce and was used by them in marital fights (Turnbull 1962: 133–34). Personal property was lent out freely and was inherited by sons from fathers and daughters from mothers (Turnbull 1965a: 116; 1965b: 229–30). Men and women also formed independent clientship relations with villagers. Husbands and wives even visit patrons in different villages.

Men and women within the same age grouping shared equally in the collective authority allocated to that age group with respect to both band and family matters. Family concerns were few compared with those of the band, but infants and young children were primarily the responsibility of the mother. In divorce, the women took the children. Boys who were old enough were said to return to their father's band, while daughters remained with their mother. "The authority of the mother over her children is fully equal to that of the father, and this is one of the most frequent sources of quarrel" (Ibid.: 212, 221).

Decision making and dispute settlement within the band involved both sexes. Married women and men had an equal voice concerning hunting decisions. Male youths and elders decided when to hold a *molimo* ceremony; girls and women elders made decisions concern-

ing the *elima* ceremony. It is often hard to see how conflicts were
brought to the attention of the band. Frequently one or a few individuals played a prominent role in defusing or settling them. Turnbull's
case material (Ibid.: 185–215) includes thirteen disputes in which the
sex of the person(s) who more or less formally brought the conflict to
the attention of the band, and/or the persons who played a dominant
role in settlement or defusing, is clear. Nine involved men and seven
involved women; in three disputes both men and women played major
roles. There was no clear differentiation along issue lines. Women as
well as men spoke from mid-camp, thereby claiming the attention of
the band, on hunting questions and on whether to move to the village;
their opinions carried the band. Men and women both set forth and settled domestic quarrels. Two cases were cited where male youths attempted to usurp the position of a leading hunter in his absence
through their kinship with him. In these cases, a male elder in one and
two male adults bordering on elderhood in the other put the offenders
in their place. Concerning relations with the village or with other
bands, women were again prominent in decision making. In marriage
between a boy and girl of different bands, elders of both bands, male
and female, mediated any objections to the marriage that might arise
from either band (Ibid.: 218–19). Adult men likened decisions about
village visits to hunting, as distinct from gathering and regarded these
as their province when the whole band was involved with the village.
Kare ties involved men only. But Mbuti women also had their own patrons. Although Mbuti male adults regarded the village as their
province, women were said to be better hunters of the villagers and to
participate equally with men in decisions pertaining to a move to the
village (Ibid.: 179, 210).

Mbuti did little ritual or ceremonial elaboration of their social relations. When a woman joined a new band on marriage, the young married women of the band she entered sang *elima* (girls' initiation) songs
to incorporate her into the women's age group of her new band (Turnbull 1965b: 221). There was no equivalent activity for in-marrying
men. There were only two ceremonies with any great social or supernatural significance among the Mbuti. The *molimo*, held when a death
of a highly regarded individual threatened the band's solidarity, was as
likely to be performed for a woman as for a man. The two *molimos*
Turnbull witnessed and described were for women. The other major
ceremonial event was the *elima*, a puberty ceremony for girls. A

molimo could last from one to three months; an *elima* continued for a month or two. The former was a men's ceremony, from which, with one significant exception, women were excluded. The *elima* was primarily an affair of women, but male youths were an important part of any *elima*.

An *elima*, held when one or more girls had her first menstrual period, was a public announcement of a girl's readiness for motherhood and a time for celebration. The ceremony involved the girls of an age group of the band and emphasized band over family relations. Older girls of the band acted as instructors. A married woman, the "mother of the *elima*," provided a hut for housing the girls and was the main teacher. The teaching was about sex and motherhood. The "father of the *elima*" was a married man whose main task was to break up fights among youths who gathered around the *elima* hut. An *elima* was a time of sexual experimentation, mainly with youths of the band. These sex relations were also a social recognition of boys' manhood in that boys had to make public entrance to the *elima* hut and run a gauntlet of women armed with sticks and stones. The ceremony also widened girls' social horizons, particularly with respect to marriage partners as they traveled in a group to neighboring bands looking for possible spouses (Turnbull 1960; 1962: chap. 10; 1965a: 70–73, 132–41; Putnam 1954: 216–17).

The *molimo* was a festival affirming life and band solidarity. The determining factors for holding one were the feelings for the deceased, circumstances of death, state of interpersonal friction within the band, and the quality of hunting. If the band were in bad straits, it was likely to hold a *molimo*. Since an individual must take responsibility for ensuring that food and firewood are supplied from every household, no one was likely to undertake the job unless there was consensus in favor of holding a *molimo*. Here all males (except children) were under strong obligation to participate in singing *molimo* songs and dancing throughout the night, every night, for the duration of the *molimo*. The elders did most of the singing, and the youths did most of the dancing. Women and children had to stay in their huts when the singing began. They were never supposed to see the *molimo* trumpet. The stated purpose of the *molimo* was to please the forest with song.

A legend holds that women used to own the *molimo* but that men stole it from them. After the *molimo* had been going for some time, women joined in the dancing for a few nights. An old woman would attack the *molimo* fire and scatter it; the men would regenerate it. She also tied up the men with vines (phrased as tying up the *molimo*). To obtain their release, the men had to give her a few gifts. During this dance other women were present and engaged in singing of their own. A young woman joined the older one in some of the dancing. Turnbull was told that the rather complicated dance performed by these women was learned in the *elima*. At least one theme of this dance was the struggle between men to preserve their *molimo*, and women to destroy it (Turnbull 1960b; 1962: 18–45, 146–68; 1965a: 74–80, 260–67).

Raymond and Leibowitz (1974) discuss the legend of the *molimo* as well as similar ones in other collecting societies about the overthrow of women's power by men. They argue convincingly that such stories are not legitimations of male dominance as they are commonly interpreted in functionalist analysis; rather they are attempts to resolve a set of contradictions perhaps peculiar to collecting societies. The contradiction is one where adult men and women have the same relation to the means of production, but the division of labor requires both male-female cooperation in productive tasks and male direction of critical parts of the process. In the Mbuti case, the men, behind the nets, need to direct the timing of the beaters and the organization of the drive lest the game escape or they be injured. Yet, as with other collectors, men had no basis for directing women. It is this contradiction which they see the *molimo* legend as attempting to solve by assertion. This may also be an explanation for a battle-of-the-sexes theme running through Mbuti culture—in a recreational tug of war between women and men and in the gauntlet of women that men must run to enter the *elima* hut.

Both men and women had a single standard for social and sexual behavior. Both sexes joined in the same social activities and did so on a basis of equality (Turnbull 1965a: 170–72). Premarital and extramarital sexual relations were common and condoned, though premarital pregnancy was not; there is no mention of what happened to whom in such an event (Ibid.: 129, 138; 1965b: 221). Of extramarital sex relations, Anne Putnam (1954: 213) was told that "no one ever raised any objections to affairs unless the injured husband or wife found out about it."

Women, but not their husbands, were expected to not have sexual relations while they were nursing. (This was to prevent consecutive pregnancies.) Even this restriction was loose: "Immediately following childbirth is a rather vague period, sometimes stated as days, some-times more grandiosely as years, when intercourse is forbidden." Turnbull noted three cases; in two the period of abstinence was about a year and in the third there was no abstinence (1965a: 122–23).

To have children was desired and expected. Together with food collecting, parenting was an integral part of adulthood. A childless woman was viewed as "the most unfortunate of beings" (Ibid.: 129), suggesting motherhood as a central part of a woman's identity. There are no indications that a childless woman was despised or mistreated, and adoption by childless women occurred (Turnbull 1965b: 214). Sterility was not seen as the fault of one sex exclusively; childless couples were likely to engage in mutual accusations. One of the most important hunters in the Epulu band had only one child, though he had three wives (serially). People believed he was not the genitor and pitied him for his sterility. On one occasion he was ridiculed for it.

In general husband-wife relations were egalitarian. However, even though wives fought back, wife beating existed. Polygyny occurred occasionally, each wife having her own hut. Although the ideal was co-wife harmony, there was plenty of friction in the Epulu polygynous household arising from the husband's obvious preference for one wife to the exclusion of the other two. One of them openly had affairs with other men. The overt conflicts were mainly of wives against the husband (Ibid.: 222; Turnbull 1965a: 207–10; 1962: 121–24). Ending marriage was simple. A couple was not considered married until the woman became pregnant or until they lived together for over a year. Childlessness often led to divorce, which was effected whenever one party, generally the woman, left (Putnam 1948: 337). After children were born divorce was said to be rare (Turnbull 1965a: 140, 274–75).

CONCLUSIONS

In Mbuti society, the band, and perhaps all bands linked by ties of kinship and affinity, formed a community of owners of productive means. Productive and reproductive responsibilities divided along age more than sex lines, with married adulthood marked by parenthood and productive responsibility. Marriage and children were social responsibilities, and young people were encouraged, and sometimes pressured, by their elders to marry and take up responsibilities for band life. The central food collecting task joined women and men of the band in a single endeavor. Both sexes then related to the means of production as adult-parent-producer-owner. As members of a community of such owner-producers, they shared equally in band decision making and in decision making about their own marital, personal, and sexual lives, including establishing ties of clientage with Bira villagers.

NOTES

1. Such historical materials as exist for symbiosis involving collecting peoples, mainly with respect to the !Kung San of Botswana and Namibia, suggest much variation in the importance of clientage relations in shaping productive modes among collecting peoples (Wilson and Thompson 1969: 155–56; Lee 1976). There is a recent and extensive ethnographic literature on the !Kung, principally in the works of Lorna Marshall (1957, 1959, 1960, 1976), and Elizabeth Marshall Thomas (1959) for !Kung in the Nyae Nyae area of the Kalahari, and in the works of Richard Lee (1967, 1968, 1972) and his associates (Draper 1975; Lee and DeVore 1976) for the Dobe area. Unfortunately and despite the richness of some of the data, I encountered gaps and other problems in analyzing the data on kinship, political economy and women, areas central to my analysis. Thus the !Kung could not be included in analysis of a communal mode of production here.

2. "The achievements of his daughter Nalengbe, a sister of the present king, are still fresh in the memory of all who were present at the engagement; eye-witnesses gave me detailed accounts of the exploits of this veritable Amazon, whom I have mentioned before and related how, in full armour, with shield and lance, and girded with the rokko apron of a man, she had with the utmost bravery led on the Monbutto troops, who then for the first time came in contact with firearms; and how her exertions were attended with a complete success, the adventurous Aboo Guroon being repulsed with considerable loss, and forced to relinquish altogether his design of entering the country" (Schweinfurth 1873, vol. 2: 95).

3. The same method of individuals killing elephants by running underneath and stabbing them in the belly with a spear is also described for the twentieth century by Turnbull (1965a: 164).

4. Turnbull's recent statement, made in connection with Mbuti troops being used by the government of Zaïre to help put down a rebellion in Shaba province, that the Mbuti have no history of war, is not accurate (quoted in *Newsweek*, May 2, 1977, p. 60).

5. Data are from Colin Turnbull's work, which is based on field study of a single band, the Epulu, with some comparative material from other bands in the same area.

Chapter 5

LOVEDU

By mid-twentieth century the Lovedu of the northeast Transvaal, like most other black South Africans, had to migrate for wage work in order to survive (E. Krige 1975: 236). Their transformation to marginal proletarians from swidden horticulturists controlling their own means of production began with missionary, settler, and state expropriation of their land in the 1890s and with the imposition of cash taxes on the Lovedu after annexation in 1894 (Krige and Krige 1943: 313–14).

By the 1930s, when ethnographers were describing their culture, taxation and male labor migration had begun to have a significant impact, such that roughly half of the adult males between ages twenty and forty-nine were absent from Lovedu, working primarily and reluctantly to pay their taxes (Ibid.: 59, 323). The Lovedu lost some 75 percent of their land to European farms after 1890, and by the 1930s the land was overcrowded with over three-quarters of the total area under cultivation (Ibid.: 13, 20). Under these circumstances Lovedu adopted the Shangana Tonga practice of cultivating the valley floors instead of confining themselves to the hill slopes. Labor migration encouraged the use of plows to make up for the shortage of workers, but plow use destroyed the protective borders of the fields, led to a decrease in the variety of crops planted (particularly legumes, which were cultivated by women), and to the breaking down of stone contour walls, which Lovedu had long used to prevent soil erosion. Not only was the soil depleted as a consequence, but the runoff from the hills silted up and destroyed many riverside gardens. Shortage of fallow land reduced grazing areas and destroyed wild plants, which were important nutritionally as relishes and fruits. Hence malnutrition in-

creased, and with it has the incidence of tuberculosis, bilharzia, tape-
worm, dysentery, and malaria (Ibid.: 36–38, 325–26). As self-sub-
sistence became more difficult, Lovedu have become more enmeshed
in wage labor and increasingly impoverished, dependent on purchased
cornmeal as their staple food (1975: 236).

Little social history has been written about the Lovedu so we do not
know what kinds of changes may have been taking place over the three
preconquest centuries they lived in the lowveld of the Transvaal. Historically and culturally, Lovedu came into being as a fusion of Sotho
peoples, with a ruling group that traced its origins to the Rozwi kingdom of present-day Zimbabwe. By the nineteenth century a hetero-
geneous society of Lovedu, various Sotho groups, and some Shangana
Tonga were tied together by their allegiance to Mujaji, the Lovedu rain
queen. There are no first-hand preconquest descriptions of Lovedu,
but there is a rich body of ethnographic description dating mainly from
the 1930s, in the works of E. J. and J. K. Krige. Despite the fact that it
leaves the Lovedu in historical limbo, their work describes a variation
of Sotho patrilineal and patrilocal kin corporations in which brother
and sister relations of production were reinforced by the forces of agricultural production such that women's place appears to have been
mainly sister's place. The fact that Lovedu political economy stressed
sisterly relations to such an extraordinary degree makes it important
to examine.

Lovedu organization in the nineteenth and twentieth centuries
seems to have stemmed from and shared much with that of other
Sotho-speaking peoples. While Sotho and the neighboring Nguni peoples by the nineteenth century had similar subsistence bases—cattle,
agriculture, and some hunting—and both were organized into corporate patrilineages, there is some indication of differing historical trajec-
tories. Unlike Nguni, Sotho peoples have a long history of smelting
iron and mining and working copper, which dates prior to 1000 A.D.
They were also involved in longstanding and far-flung trade networks
of metal, leather, and ivory goods. There is some indication that this
pattern held in Lovedu as well, and it is likely that metalworking and
trade were important sources of cattle for Sotho groups. Although the
routes and the organization of trade are largely unknown, Wilson
notes that chiefs controlled trade by the nineteenth century (Wilson
and Thompson 1969: 143–52; Marks and Gray 1975: 417–19).

From an examination of Sotho rituals Wilson notes a second contrast with Nguni.

One can hardly escape the conclusion that the ancient Sotho rituals reflect the life of a people for whom hunting was more important than cattle-keeping, and some of whom, in the distant past recognized the smelting of iron as their major resource. [Wilson and Thompson 1969: 162]

She suggests an ancient Sotho subsistence base of hunting, horticulture, and iron smelting, with livestock added later. This is contrasted with the early centrality of cattle for Nguni.

Contrasts in nineteenth-century Nguni and Sotho marriage patterns may have stemmed from these early subsistence contrasts, Wilson notes. Unlike Nguni, Sotho marriages involved bridewealth of few cattle, which were not returned in the event of divorce. Some Sotho also lived with the wife's mother's family until a child was born and also stressed husband's bride service for the wife's parents. These practices are more like those of collecting societies than herding ones (Ibid.: 163). To this one might add the contrast between Sotho and Nguni marriage patterns. While Nguni prohibited cousin marriage, for Sotho some type of cousin marriage was a preferred form: "the principle is accepted among all the Sotho that the girl 'born to be your wife' is the daughter of a kinsman. She will be your great wife whomever else you marry, and the higher the status of the family the more rigidly cousin marriages are insisted upon" (Ibid.: 159). Cross-cousin marriages emphasize and maintain affinal ties among lineages. But parallel cousin marriages, particularly of brothers' children, emphasize the exclusiveness of the lineage and are indeed found among pastoralists. Both Middle Eastern pastoralists and the Sotho-speaking Tswana, who are heavily dependent on cattle, practice this type of preferred marriage. We have seen the emphasis in collecting societies on brother-sister exchange or cross-cousin marriage. It is tempting (though speculative) to view the various patterns of Sotho cousin marriage as developing from a collecting pattern and appropriate to the different subsistence strategies and relations of production of Sotho societies. Thus the Lovedu pattern of marriage between the children of cattle-linked brother and sister will be seen in the context of a predominantly horticultural society in which sisters are most significant actors in patrilineage affairs.

It is in the context of general Sotho history that we need locate Lovedu as they existed in the nineteenth century, prior to about 1890 when they came under white rule. Information comes almost exclusively from the works of Eileen Jensen Krige and J. D. Krige, who did fieldwork among the Lovedu between 1928 and 1939 and again after 1964. They attempted to specify preconquest patterns, both those that persisted and those that were described to them. Their writings, together with brief mention of other lowveld social organizations, suggest that much of the Lovedu organizational pattern, including brother-sister relations, woman marriage, and woman officials, was a shared one among the Sotho peoples of the lowveld (E. Krige 1938; Krige and Krige 1943: 301–14; Jacques 1939) as well as among the neighboring Venda (Stayt 1931; Lestrade 1930a, 1930b; Junod 1920; Gottschling 1905; O'Brien 1977).

By the nineteenth century the Lovedu were united under Mujaji, the rain queen, and her royal group, which made up perhaps 10 percent of the population. People lived in patrilineal homesteads under the political leadership of local leaders who were male and female, royal and nonroyal. The bases and scope of their authority seem to have been quite limited. Subsistence came principally from horticulture and gathering wild plant foods and secondarily from small livestock. Cattle were scarce and largely tied up in bridewealth commitments. The means of production were owned by patrilineal corporations. While the queen and perhaps local leaders controlled more cattle, these were not significant productive means. Subsistence labor was locally organized along kinship and neighborhood lines; chiefs (local leaders) did not control or organize significant economic activities. Instead the organization of work and ownership of productive means was localized, the former in a neighborhood of related kinspeople and the latter in patrilineal households. Although there is no direct information, it is reasonable to suggest that the economic basis for the unity of Lovedu under queen and royal group most likely lay, as with other Sotho groups (Wilson and Thompson 1969: 152), in their control of trade, particularly the cattle and metal goods used in marriages and obtained largely from trade or as gifts to the queen for rain. A trade route between Delagoa Bay and Shona country across the Limpopo River passed through the eastern part of the Lovedu mountains, a route that had been used by the Tonga of Mozambique for centuries prior to 1800. We know that Lovedu orphans and sisterless men without access to bridewealth cattle or hoes contracted to a trading expedition to carry salt or iron ore from Vendaland or other "far countries" to the north to local smiths. In return they received marriage hoes or cattle. "It used to be said that 'the great road helps bachelors (who have no sisters) to mary the sisters of young men' " (Krige and Krige 1943: 57; E. Krige 1964: 173; 1975: 254; Wilson and Thompson 1969: 151, 164).

As among other Sotho, ironworking, leatherwork, and woodworking were highly developed crafts in Lovedu. They were performed by men, but of their preconquest importance on external trade there is no indication (Krige and Krige 1943: 47). Nor is there any indication of the organization or scope of Lovedu trade relations.

The major events of nineteenth-century Transvaal history were, at first, the widespread wars, social upheavals, and displacements of large numbers of African peoples in the wake of the Zulu revolution (Omer-Cooper 1969). The first half of the century saw the incorporation of many small groups of refugees into Lovedu, largely under their own leaders. The second eventuality was Boer expansion, warfare, and expropriation of African people's land, a process that hastened after discovery of diamonds and gold to ultimate white rule over the Transvaal. Occupying the latter half of the century but not impinging on the lowveld directly before 1880, this process was marked in Lovedu by their loss of sovereignty in 1894 (Krige and Krige 1943: 314). But Lovedu, by its geographic location seems to have been sheltered from bearing the direct force of these two processes. They were isolated in the Lovedu Mountains, foothills of the Drakensberg, surrounded by a tsetse fly belt to the east and north along the Limpopo, with the escarpment on their west and south. In addition to their seclusion, the Lovedu had few cattle, the plunderable wealth that was the economic base of many neighboring peoples. The lack of cattle together with their geographical isolation may help account for peaceful conditions in Lovedu.

It is difficult to locate the Lovedu political economy I describe in history. There exist chronologies of groups arriving and departing, the paths of their migrations, and accounts of their rulers (Krige and Krige 1943: 5–12, 303–07; E. Krige 1938; Kruger 1936). But of changes in livelihood, productive relations, authority of rulers and warfare, there is virtually nothing, or at best, tantalizingly contradictory fragments. In addition, although the Kriges' work describes in some detail the structure of formal political organization as it existed prior to conquest, it does not present anything near an adequate picture of its functioning.

Until the end of the eighteenth century, Lovedu was ruled by kings. In the midst of conflicts over succession, the last king chose his daughter to rule, and women have ruled since that time. In this the Lovedu were not unique. The nineteenth century saw a number of female rulers among neighboring and related lowveld Sotho groups (Krige and Krige 1943: 10; O'Brien 1977).

Though Mujaji, the rain queen, and her councillors formally ruled from a capital village, Lovedu was more a federation of local groups, called districts by the Kriges, each under a headperson or chief. Over the nineteenth century, though earlier as well, settlers who came in groups under their own chiefs tended to be given a locality by the queen in which to settle, and their chiefs were given headship of what then became a district. Other districts were ruled by members of the Lovedu royal lineage. Agnates tended to be the core, though not the majority, of a district and to be patrilineally related to the district chief. Within districts people were linked largely by ties of kinship or affinity to the chiefs, making for a complex web of bilateral kinship operating within districts, together with affinal ties linking people of different districts (Krige and Krige 1943: 178–80).

Settlements of perhaps forty to eighty buildings were scattered through the districts. With patrilocal residence, these tended to contain the homesteads of close agnates. In the twentieth century, under conditions of land scarcity, these settlements were quite stable over time. "Over a period of thirty years [1931–1961] most of the larger homesteads known to me have remained in the same place or been rebuilt a few hundred yards from the old site after the death of the head" (E. Krige 1964: 159). That households or minimal lineages tended to be spatially stable in the nineteenth century also is suggested by the contiguous distribution pattern of patrilineal groups, as well as by patrilineal inheritance of garden lands.

It is difficult to assess the nineteenth-century demographic picture since late nineteenth- and twentieth-century land expropriation and accompanying disasters made for significant changes. In the 1930s there were some forty thousand Lovedu; about thirty-three thousand lived on a reserve of 150 square miles. The drought, locust plague, rinderpest epidemic and ensuing famine of 1894–1896 were responsible for the loss of about one-third of the Lovedu population. Prior to expropriation Mujaji effectively reigned over some 600 square miles, and sporadically and less effectively over an additional 400 square miles. In the 1930s districts were small—between .5 and 9 square miles, and most were under 1 square mile. They were larger prior to European occupation and were subdivided to accommodate those whose land was taken (Krige and Krige 1943: 178). In the 1930s there were some 140 districts. As districts fissioned or were split by the queen, the number of districts in the nineteenth century may have been smaller. But on the basis of some sixty thousand Lovedu over 600 square miles, the average district size would have been about 4 square miles and with a population of some 430. In 1930 districts averaged two hundred fifty people, and in 1975 E. Krige noted that sizes ranged from under a hundred to over two thousand people (1975: 236). Lovedu political units then were likely small.

MODE OF PRODUCTION

In the nineteenth century Lovedu were predominantly shifting hoe agriculturalists, cultivating the hill slopes with the aid of stone contour walls. They planted maize, millet, eleusine, and sorghum together with a variety of beans, groundnuts and pumpkins. Gathering of wild plants was an important subsidiary subsistence activity. Cattle and goats contributed as well, though the former were few and largely tied up in bridewealth payments (Krige and Krige 1943: 42–45). Vegetable food provided by far the bulk of the diet, and Lovedu put forth claims to status and hospitality not by slaughtering cattle but by offering beer.

In the sexual division of labor, men were responsible for clearing land, house building, smelting, leather work, woodwork, basketmaking, and livestock tending. Women's responsibilities centered on legume cultivation, gathering, cooking, beer brewing, pottery, and child care. Both sexes hoed, weeded, and reaped the grain crops. In polygynous households, each wife had responsibility for her own grain field and for helping the husband cultivate his field. Women were not prohibited contact with cattle or from herding, but cattle were generally herded by armed men because of the dangers of raiding and animals. Expropriation of ore sources by Europeans, decimation of the forests, and the expansion of manufactured goods in the twentieth century all but destroyed Lovedu craft production. There is no information on its organization in the nineteenth century.

Uncultivated land was available to all residents of a district for gathering wood and grazing. Cultivated land belonged to the man who cleared it and was inherited patrilineally by men. Livestock were individually owned and patrilineally inherited. With the exception of the royal group, Lovedu corporate patrilineages were localized and small-scale units whose principal estate lay in the gardens and livestock of their members. The work force for agricultural tasks, as well as for building, brewing, tanning large skins, and for other activities, was drawn largely from the bilateral kindred who made up a neighborhood.

Kin and affines of a neighborhood tended to have "all or some of their fields in large blocks (*demo*)." Those whose fields were together cooperated in clearing, hoeing, weeding, reaping, and protecting the fields. The Kriges describe a cooperative group, the *khilebe*, which seemed to overlap substantially or perhaps be identical with the cooperation involved in *demo* cultivation. The *khilebe* was made up of close relatives from the neighborhood. Collectively they hoed, weeded, and reaped the fields of each member in turn. These fields are said to be close together, but to what extent they were in a single *demo* is not clear. Members of the *khilebe* provided their own food; no beer was given for the work; and the produce belonged to the owner of the field. These groups had a stable membership over time (Krige and Krige 1943: 40, 52).

A larger cooperative group, the *lejema*, was called into being, mainly for agricultural work but also for house building and tanning large skins. *Lejema* was basically work with a beer feast supplied by the person for whom the work was done. Some people came from a fair distance, but neighboring kinspeople and affines made up the bulk of the workers. Most large tasks, but light ones as well, were performed by *lejema*. So too were tasks that could be done individually. The purpose was to combine generosity and sociability.

The group of local patrilineal kin, together with one's mother's relatives, was called a *moloko* (E. Krige 1964: 158). Unlike a local patrilineage, this bilateral kindred had a name and appears to have been the principal task group of Lovedu. Thus we can reckon them as the main human productive forces of the society.

Productive means, however, were held by localized patrilineages. These were descent groups of paired uterine brothers and sisters who

corporately owned land and livestock and shared decision-making au-
thrity and judicial and ritual responsibility for its affairs and its children. In addition, both shared control over the labor and marriages of
children born to that group. One important aspect of a sister's rights in
this group was her right to a daughter to "cook for" her, either as a
daughter-in-law and wife to her son or as her own wife.

Spatially, however, brothers and sisters lived in separate households during their adult lives. Marriage was patrilocal, necessitating
sisters to go and live as wives of their father's sister's son. As a wife a
woman bore children for her husband's patrilineage and was under his
authority to some extent, but she worked for and under her father's sister, who was also a senior member of her own lineage. Over 60 percent
of all men married a mother's brother's daughter in 1936 (E. Krige
1964: 186). Where horizontally shared authority characterized relations of production between brothers and sisters, wives were under the
authority of their mother-in-law, who was also a senior woman of their
lineage. In a similar way sons and husbands were in some senses under
their father's judicial authority.

Lovedu brother-sister relations of production together with the
place of obligatory cross-cousin marriage in it, leads one to expect that
marriages took place within a small area because women had to be at
once political and economic decision makers in their own house and
wives in the house of their husbands. That does indeed seem to have
been the case. Neighborhoods were typically composed of a number
of local lineages, or extended households, linked by ties of marriage,
as *vamakhulu* (people who provide bridegrooms) and *vadakulu* (people who provide brides). These terms applied to own and classificatory grandchildren.

Although at one point E. Krige (1975: 237–38) insisted that the
Lovedu did not have corporate descent groups and exogamy, this lack
clearly did not apply to a local level. Here the corporate lineage was a
shallow co-resident group of three or four generations, "brothers' sons
of one father" who "share even the head of a locust" (Krige and Krige
1943: 98). Marriage within this group was, for nonroyal Lovedu, considered incest. These groups shared common property and were
further identified by a name, generally that of a father or grandfather.

Although the precise relationships between the cores of uterine
brother and sister and the larger local patrilines were complex and not
clearly delineated in the ethnography, the latter, or extended house-

holds, were composed of several such cores stemming from the constituent houses of the lineage. Corporateness was manifest in occasional linking of nonuterine brothers and sisters, from different houses, such that the cattle of a sister's marriage might be used for a half or classificatory brother; or where a classificatory brother might marry a classificatory father's sister's daughter (E. Krige 1975: 245, 247; 1964: 169, 170, 183, appendix 1).

The patterns of affinity bear out a picture of neighborhoods as composed of linked lineages. The productive force of neighborhood was also the kindred, *moloko*. Thus E. Krige (1964: 188), in tracing the ties of thirteen homesteads making up a neighborhood, shows four households of the crocodile totem, which had been a single household until the death of the patriarch, also the district chief. These were affines to two fraternally related porcupine totem households and two fraternally related pig totem households. Two other households were linked by marriage to pig and porcupine. The three unrelated households were Tonga, with whom intermarriage was discouraged.

The picture that emerges is of a neighborhood, or district, having at its core a local lineage, itself made up of agnatically linked houses. These were often the patrilineages of district chiefs, to which were attached other patrilineages by ties of affinity. These ties were repeated each generation since sisters had a claim on their brother's daughter to marry their son.

Although district chiefs were conceived of as owners of the land and as chiefs, their ownership rights were limited to allocating unowned land to new settlers for cultivation and in having residents of the district cultivate a garden and build their huts. Chiefs may have had a preponderance of livestock, but there is no direct indication of clientage relations between them and their followers, unless affinal relations can be so construed. District chiefs played no discernible role in organizing production beyond the minimal labor that residents of their districts gave to a garden.

Chiefly ownership of the land was marked mainly in gifts of perishables—an annual harvest gift of beer and wild foods. In their capacity as organizers of girls' puberty rites for the district and (in the case of some chiefs) of national male initiation schools, chiefs received a goat from the families of each initiate, but this was the only form of storable wealth received (Krige and Krige 1943: 180–84). "The society is remarkably egalitarian and there is no concentration of wealth in the hands of the ruling group. . . . Nor does property as in Western society, command the services of others to any appreciable extent" (E. Krige 1964: 157, 161).

Dispute settlement was diffused among the populace, with self-help and reconciliation as prominent forms. Each chief had a court (*khoro*) and the queen had hers, but neither courts nor chiefs had any power to exact compliance with their decisions. Blood feud was an acceptable way of settling homicide. Indeed homicide could not be handled at the queen's court, which was a kind of court of last appeal. The only offense that was cast as a public crime, one against society, was sorcery. Offenders were tried in the queen's court by poison ordeal and then killed.

Indications are that chiefs wielded little actual power or authority over their people. District organization seems to have been one of linked local lineage segments, with that of the chief as central, standing perhaps as "wife receiver" to other family groups of the neighborhood and district. Vis-à-vis the queen, chiefs stood in a structurally intermediary position between their people and the queen, particularly in her capacity to give or withhold the rains. Chiefs owned the drums necessary for dancing parties to beg the queen for rain (Krige and Krige 1943: 180–84).

At the center of the formal political structure were the queen and her councillors. They performed the national rain ceremonies, which were of utmost importance in the welfare of all Lovedu. Without the queen's power, there could be no rain. Ritual secrecy surrounded the queen and her rain medicines. She was not directly accessible to people, could not leave the capital, and could be approached only through her relatives and district heads. The rain medicines were the strongest sanction to the political authority of the queen and her relatives. Should she be displeased with people's behavior, she might withhold the rains (Ibid.: 220, 271).

Each queen chose her own councillors from among her relatives in the capital, generally those related through the previous queen or through the ruling queen's biological mother. Their role, beyond acting in dispute cases brought to the queen's court, is unclear. In addition to councillors, there was another group of advisers drawn from among the queen's relatives, who were also important district chiefs. They chose who would raise the next queen, and they acted generally in matters concerning succession. The queen's court was presided over by the most influential councillor, ideally a brother. Like other courts, this had no special power to compel obedience to its decisions beyond the power to try, and execute, sorcerers.

The whole question of warfare is unanswered. E. Krige maintains there was never an army (1975: 249). Internecine fighting existed in feuds and over succession to the throne, and some fighting took place to acquire cattle.

The queen acted as chief of the subdistrict of the capital and as such commanded the same goods and services as other chiefs. In addition, each district provided beer tribute and labor for the queen. Building, roadwork, and cultivation were organized for men and women on an age-grade basis by district. As with chiefs, the amount of work was not major. Planting was done by men and women, as well as by initiated boys and girls. Work was performed in groups, in unison, to the accompaniment of songs. One of the two fields planted for the queen was done by women and perhaps men; this took one morning's work per year. The other field was planted with nuts, by women only; this probably took about the same amount of time (E. Krige 1931: 221-22, 226). In the 1930s, and possibly also in precolonial times, the youngest age set of the capital district, boys and girls, weeded the queen's fields. All other work was done by men of all ages organized collectively and by district. Beer tribute was carried to the queen by women and girls. Although the queen had over one hundred wives who did regular women's work, the vast majority of these women stayed in the capital only a short time. The brunt of the work, and it was hard work, fell on those who remained in the queen's household (E. Krige 1932: 349; Krige and Krige 1943: 18).

Lovedu conceptualized tribute and service to queen and chiefs as fulfilling normal kinship obligations to one's affines. A husband's family was obligated to aid his wife's people, and they in turn gave a son-in-law a yearly gift of grain and beer. But the wife's family provided "something bigger than cattle," and no request they made ought be denied (E. Krige 1964: 164). The queen provided land, rain, and supernatural protection against enemies. The beer tribute, carried by a large party from each district, was consumed by those who brought it, in the same manner as gifts of beer from a parent-in-law to a son-in-law (Krige and Krige 1954: 58).

E. Krige has argued that Lovedu was integrated principally by the affinal links among families established by marriage of women to a father's sister's son. These links operated to join the families of district chiefs to the queen and to each other as well. Chiefs gave a daughter as wife to the queen (*vatanoni*). This gift was often initiated by way of begging for something, such as cattle, rain, or a chiefship from the queen. The practice of pledging a daughter had wider application as a way of requesting a favor. The queen in turn allocated these wives to other district chiefs and to her own male relatives in the capital. The gift of a wife to the queen established a tie with the giver's family, which, following the Lovedu marriage rules, was repeated over the generations, thus placing the district chief's family in a permanent relationship of wife giver (*vamakhulu*) to the queen as wife receiver (*vaduhulu*). The queen's reallocation of most of these wives established relations of affinity between the agnates of the wife and the husband but not between the queen and the husband's family because the queen's action was likened to allocation of widows—where no bridewealth was given (E. Krige 1975: 251).

Leach (1961) argued that this practice reinforced a ranking system in Lovedu. Because wife receivers outranked wife givers, the queen maintained supremacy over the chiefs. The queen's politics of reallocation also established rank ordering among chiefs, which was perpetuated by repetitions of these affinal ties each generation. A similar argument could be made for the relationship of chiefs with their affines if chiefs' families received wives from other lineages in the district, but here information is lacking. However, E. Krige (1964, 1975) has explicitly denied Leach's analysis linking Lovedu political and economic ranking to marriage. The most germane aspect of her argument is that if such rank inequality is to have any meaning, it must reflect inequality in political economy, and this she maintains was absent in Lovedu. In addition, gifts to the queen, like gifts to a son-in-law, were consumed largely by the bearers and/or reciprocated with a feast provided by the receiver: that is, affinal exchanges were balanced. And yet the initiation of an affinal relationship with the queen seems to have entailed adopting a client role, in giving a daughter to beg for a favor. What this meant in terms of power cannot be ascertained. It does seem clear, though, that Leach was wrong in seeing reallocation of wives by the queen as establishing or perpetuating a ranking among chiefs. Those ties proceeded through the queen, and her reallocation seems to have differed over the generations (E. Krige 1975: 250). This is consistent with the Lovedu history of numerous small territorial groups in loose federation through their ties to Mujaji.

The cultural elaboration of the centrality of brother-sister relations is sharpest in the history of the Lovedu royal line. Here the theme is phrased alternately as father-daughter incest and brother-sister incest underwriting their success. It was the latter that established the Lovedu when a daughter of the Rozwi king became pregnant by her brother and fled with her son. Father-daughter incest legitimized the transition from kings to queens and the good fortune it brought (Krige and Krige 1943: 5–11). The ruling core of Lovedu was the brothers and sisters of the royal line: the queen's unofficial husbands were lineage brothers; her confidential advisers and councillors were related through the previous queen or through the biological mother of the present queen; and the wife of Mujaji II chosen to bear Mujaji III was a sister to Mujaji II (Ibid.: 171–74).

To illustrate the stress on brotherhood and sisterhood, even when a marriage relationship was involved, it was the intralineage ties that were emphasized. For her councillors, Mujaji III chose kin who were related through Leakhali (her own physiological mother, who was also "sister" and head wife to Mujaji II), through Mujaji II, through Mujaji I (also a mother of Mujaji II), or through brothers of Mujaji I, for example, Malegudu. Descendants of Malegudu were lineage brothers to the queen and the queen's unofficial husbands were chosen from this line. In addition, queens were expected to learn their rainmaking secrets from their mother's brother. The case of Leakhali again illustrates. She headed a village, had several wives, and lived independently. Together with her brother, she opposed the influence of a lover of Mujaji II. For this, Leakhali and her brother were forced into exile. There the future Mujaji III learned the rainmaking secrets from her mother's brother, thus preserving the custom that heirs be taught by a mother's brother (Ibid.: 171, 173).

Wives of the queen who were of the royal lineage received districts in which they ruled, as did brothers and sisters of queens (and of kings before them). These royal chiefs, like others, gave their daughters as wives to the queen, who in turn favored royal wives with chiefship and/or with bearing the heir. Royal district chiefs were the main source of confidential advisers. The emphasis on lineage endogamy, combined with direct political rule by its sisters (as well as brothers), highlighted the importance of brother-sister relations of production. In a sense the Lovedu were a nation tied together by a patrilineal core of brothers and sisters who established affinal links with other groups but who maintained their corporateness by endogamy. It is in this context that the prohibition of Lovedu queens from marrying can be understood. Wifely relations involved subordination to a husband, a relationship incompatible with ritual supremacy vis-à-vis one's lineage brothers and sisters.

Yet the estate of the royal group is not clear. In one sense the queen is said to be the owner of all of Lovedu through her control of the rain, without which the land would be barren. In another sense, she had the right to allocate unused land to newcomers after the manner of district chiefs. To the extent that the queen and her lineage can be said to control a means of production, they possessed a corporate estate, and that is the Lovedu conception. They did clearly hold the right to grant land. Yet any case for royal ownership of productive means confronts the same contradiction encountered with respect to chiefly relations with their people: so-called rulers had no apparent hold on the livelihood of their followers. They did not expropriate much in the way of produce or labor, nor were they in any way stewards of productive resources.

The formal political structure of Lovedu gives the appearance of hierarchy, but all information pertaining to royal lineage or district chiefs' control over productive means shows local lineage autonomy in owning productive means and in organizing production. Consonant with this latter is the stress in self-help in conflict resolution.

Although direct evidence is lacking, the most likely hypothesis is that the position of the royal lineage rested initially on its control of trade, which gave them a preponderance of cattle and perhaps of marriage hoes. The Kriges do mention that the Lovedu, though they possessed fewer cattle in the past, possessed them more unequally (J. D. Krige 1939b: 395). With the transition to queenly rule at the end of the eighteenth century, an additional source of cattle for the royal lineage may have been generated by the queen's renown as a rainmaker. Rulers of Venda, Sotho, and Nguni chiefdoms were said to bring cattle as gifts when they begged for rain. Lovedu history stresses the frequency of such visits, but how many cattle were involved is not known (Krige and Krige 1943: 10; Kruger 1936: 101).

MODE OF PRODUCTION AND GENDER

FORCES OF PRODUCTION

For both men's and women's tasks, productive organization centered around the neighborhood. Task groups for most agricultural events—hoeing, weeding, and reaping—were made up of both men and women of the locale. Herding, livestock tending, building, and tanning large skins involved groups of men, but little is known of their organizations. Less is known about men's smelting and woodwork. Carrying and brewing beer was often a cooperative activity, mainly of women (Krige and Krige 1943: 52–55; E. Krige 1964: 189). How women organized cooking, gathering, and carrying wood and water is not known either.

RELATIONS OF PRODUCTION

Corporate groups of brothers and sisters owned land and livestock, though the relations of brothers and sisters to the estate differed because sisters were simultaneously wives in another household as well as mothers to its sons and daughters. In the Lovedu case, sisterhood was a woman's chief relation to the means of production and indeed shaped her wifely relationship (rather than vice-versa). Similarly brother was stressed over husband. The economic corporateness of a mother-child house within a larger household and the relationship of mother and father to its children reflected clearly the centrality of sibling relations of production.

Sisters and Brothers

The labor of men in clearing land established male ownership. Sons were the direct heirs of garden land, generally that allocated by his father to his wife. Brothers often allocated gardens to married sisters for their use.

The center of the brother-sister relationship lay in bridewealth cattle. The sister's marriage was a necessary condition for carrying on her own corporate patrilineage: the house founded by her brother's marriage with the cattle brought in by the sister's marriage. This house was the sister's economically, politically, and ritually, as well as the brother's. She divided its property on her brother's death; she reallocated its wives in leviratic marriage to the extent they wanted to be so allocated; she was the person sought to adjudicate conflicts in which her brother was involved; she was the highest ritual head of the house vis-à-vis the ancestors. To the extent that the wife married with the sister's cattle was his chief wife, the sister was then co-authority of the entire household; and to the extent that her brother headed the local lineage, so too did the sister. All of these rights of sisterhood increased with age. As brother and sister aged, their house and its members and property grew.

A sister became a wife, working for and bearing children of her husband's family. In a sense this was her contribution to her own lineage. In return, that house was obligated to send a daughter to do for its sister what the sister did for her husband and his mother: cooking, stamping, and performing agricultural work for them. This generally involved marriage of a brother's daughter with the sister's son, but if no son were available the sister might take on the role of female husband and marry the daughter herself. At one level this system entailed a delayed reciprocity of service, with junior women of a lineage working for its senior women simultaneously as father's sister and mother-in-law. At another level, brother and sister became affines and established a perpetual relationship of affinity between their patrilineal descendants.

At the center of this affinity remained the shared house of brother and sister, with two stages of reciprocity:

1. Sister becomes a wife, allowing her brother to build a house within which both are property managers and decision makers.

2. Brother provides a daughter to his sister to work for her as she works for her husband. The cattle given by the sister allows her brother's son to marry and found a house for him and *his* sister, thereby continuing the patrilineal corporation of brothers and sisters.

When a household head died, the eldest son of the chief wife, who was a man's matrilateral cross-cousin, succeeded to the position of household head. He assumed responsibility for meeting debts and receiving goods owed the deceased; he also inherited the father's personal goods and livestock. Grain, fields, and personal property not allocated to specific houses could be administered by the heir or divided among the houses or children within the houses. Within each house, the eldest son became heir to the property of that house.

Because age and seniority were important and did not always coincide with the appropriate gender, it was not always clear who would inherit. The cattle-linked sister, together with a man's eldest and other sisters, made these decisions and divided up their brother's property. If there were no living sisters of the deceased, his eldest daughter, in consultation with her father's brother, performed the task. A sister's decision was backed up by the belief that after her death, her spirit could bring illness to her brother's children were she dissatisfied with them (E. Krige 1964: 177; Krige and Krige 1943: 402).

E. Krige cites three cases of actual division of a dead man's property. In the first, all cattle were divided among the sons. The deceased had no goats. In the second only goats were involved. Twenty of the thirty-six went to two daughters, one son received eight, and the remainder were distributed among the other sons, a son's widow and a sister's son. In the third, all cattle went to the senior son of the chief wife to be used for the marriage of his brothers (1964: 172, 174–75, 180–82). Only sons inherited cattle, but daughters did inherit goats.

A sister could also be called in to adjudicate property disputes between her brother and his children that might arise if the children's mother died. In this event, their father administered the property of the deceased wife's house. Its children could appeal to their father's sister if they felt unfairly treated by their father.

Sisters could also carry on the lineage by marrying a wife for a dead or nonexistent brother (E. Krige 1964: 165). Like many of their neighbors, the Lovedu practiced woman marriage to a woman. Women could make these marriages either in their own name or in that of a kinsman. Wives married to women bore children either by a man selected by her female husband or by men of her choice (on woman marriage see E. Krige 1974; Herskovits 1937; O'Brien 1977).

The sister was the ultimate arbiter of disputes in a brother's household, mediated with the ancestors on his behalf, and had rights to the services of his daughter. Enforcing her authority was the belief that her displeasure could bring serious illness to her brother's children. She might even have some influence in her brother's choice of a wife

(Krige and Krige 1943: 75). Finally, she could rule her brother's settlement or district after his death. Many women were settlement
heads. Especially when old or widowed, a woman moved into and
ruled in a deceased brother's settlement. But women could do this
even while married to a man of another village (E. Krige 1964: 182).

Cattle-linked sisters were the most important institutionalized figures in adjudicating disputes in which their brothers were involved.

> . . . legal arrangements appear to be made and controlled by men, but that is
> because we identify law with the *khoro*, the place of the men. In *hu khumelwa*
> [reconciliation—especially important in family, adultery, property, and blood
> cases] women are at least as important as men, and in family disputes no one
> occupies so pivotal a position as the cattle-linked sister, the legal "builder" of
> most houses in the country, she who "cuts" cases arising within the house and
> regulates the inheritance of goods and of widows. These "judicial"-like activi-
> ties cover vast provinces of the total culture, and they are fully recognized in
> *khoro* proceedings in which neither in arriving at a decision nor in safeguard-
> ing its execution can the men ignore the wishes, authority, or influence of the
> sister. In complicated cases, they often postpone their decision again and
> again until she appears, and they rely upon her to suggest a solution and to
> guarantee its being put into effect. [Krige and Krige 1943: 197–98]

Ancestral spirits were important in regard to health and agricultural success. They could harm those who neglected them or bring
illness on those they loved most in order to receive recognition from
them. Appeals were made and thanks given them for health, fertility,
and good crops. Smaller appeals to appease an ancestor could be performed by men or women.

Major rites were held yearly at the harvest thanksgiving and when a
diviner prescribed them for a particular purpose. The group involved
here consisted of three to five generations sharing a shrine to a common male ancestor. The participants were generally neighbors. In
these rites the chief priest for mediating with the ancestors was the
eldest sister of the lineage head or the head of the household initiating
the ritual. All members of the lineage, male and female, participated.
Women who were heads of households acted as priests. Harvest ceremonies at a lineage level were integrated into a national pattern in that
they were performed first at the queen's household, then at that of the

district head, and finally by lineage segments (Krige and Krige 1943: 234–38; E. Krige 1964: 158–59).

Wives

As wives, women's access to garden lands and livestock for their use depended mainly on their husbands, who allocated productive means and their products to each wife for the use of her house (mother and her children) and for inheritance by her own children. Wives worked under the direction of their husband's mother, and in the early years of wifehood, cooked and stamped grain at her hearth and cultivated for her. It was the mother-in-law who gave a wife permission to attend work and social events. With age and the arrival of new wives, a wife gained her own hearth and increasing independence of her mother-in-law. Wives were subordinate members of their marital household. Husbands and sisters, but not wives, entertained visitors. Although wives sometimes attacked their husbands when angry, wife beating was frequent and socially acceptable (Krige and Krige 1943: 71–73). All children a wife bore were her husband's. A husband could pledge a baby daughter in marriage. In this he had to consult his sister, but not the wife (E. Krige 1964: 160–61).

Sisters and Wives

On the other hand, sisterhood is the predominant relationship of women to the means of production. Sisters were not far from home. The organization of production, together with the sister's political and ritual responsibilities to her house, made these relationships frequently exercised. Moreover sisterhood was reinforced in a woman's older years by service and marriage of her brother's daughter into her marital house and under her authority. In her younger years as a wife, the ties to her father and his sister merged sisterhood with wifehood.

This may explain the power wives had over their husband's marriage through their claims as mothers and sisters to a daughter's bridewealth cattle and the marriages made with them. Mothers, because of the priority of their ties to their brothers, had rights to the services of any wife married with a daughter's bridewealth. Thus if her husband took them to marry a co-wife, that co-wife would stand in a subordinate, daughter-in-law relationship to the first wife. This gave a wife considerable de facto power over her husband's marriages even though, as a wife, she had no de jure authority.

As sister-mother a woman's rights to the bridewealth from a daughter's marriage went even further. If there were no son to use the cattle, she might take a wife for herself or give the cattle to her own brother who "establishes a 'house' where the son of his niece will find a wife" (Krige and Krige 1943: 72). The rights of a woman as cattle-linked sister were so strong that had she no son, she could demand her brother's daughter to provide the services of a daughter-in-law without marriage, or she could marry the daughter herself, even though she were simultaneously wife to a husband. Indeed wives often used live-stock to acquire their own wives, becoming husbands and sisters as well as wives and sisters.

In practice sister relations of production underwrote women's rights to own and dispose of property, to hold positions of authority, and to determine their own social and sexual lives, even while they were wives. Being a wife did not prevent a woman from gaining the neces-sary wealth to become a husband or household head. This she could do using her daughter's bridewealth or by being a successful medical practitioner. Cattle and goats (in addition to the more usual beer) were often paid for doctoring and divining. Both men and women practiced, but the women's specialty (*lelopo* doctoring), was more remunerative than bone throwing. Women were involved in both types of divina-tion. Women doctors were often quite rich in livestock, which were theirs to dispose of as they wished (E. Krige 1964: 175).

The organization of agricultural production, involving as it did both sexes in a neighborhood bilateral kindred, reinforced sisterly rela-tions of production. Each wife had her own field, and most tasks in-volved work groups, often with a beer feast supplied by the owner of the field. In one sense, the grain belonged to the husband's family be-cause it was grown of their land. Wives could not take the harvest with them in divorce. Yet the Lovedu differed from other groups in not pro-hibiting women access to the grain pits or to the cattle enclosure (seat of the patrilineage) in which they were located (Krige and Krige 1943: 19, 45; E. Krige 1964: 174–76). Moreover wives gave their own beer feasts to work parties and, as mothers and sisters, engaged in the affinal exchanges involving gifts of beer, grain, and goats.

Political authority was exercised in two arenas: the courts (*khoro*) and family or lineage channels of adjudication. In the former, men were the central actors, while the latter centered on women. Despite the fact that the *khoro* was under male authority, women appeared on their own behalf as defendants and plaintiffs as often as did men. Additionally the relative importance of age over sex is seen in a divorce case where the defendant was an old woman and the plaintiff a twenty-five-year-old man. The latter had presumptuously handed bride-wealth cattle to the bride's former husband instead of to the mother of the bride, who was the defendant. When the mother took her daughter, the young man demanded the return of his bridewealth. In the *khoro* the mother said, "I scorn to discuss the matter with you, a mere child. You know nothing about cases. Bring your father. I do not understand your complaint." The *khoro* agreed (Krige and Krige 1943: 198). In general, women sat around the fringes, often commenting tellingly on the proceedings, and a man's sister was often relied on for a decision by the *khoro*. Thus the two avenues of adjudication were linked.

Women held chiefly positions, including some of the more important ones; but only some 14 percent of the chiefs were women in the 1930s; however, the percentage of women rulers is much higher if one includes cases where sons ruled in consultation with their mothers (Krige and Krige 1943: 180). Women also acted as district mothers and councillors to the queen.

Political office was linked to relations of production. Women of the royal lineage who were wives to the queen were often made chiefs. Indeed until the 1960s, the queens sent lineage sisters to rule in the districts and kept lineage brothers in the capital as advisers and to preside over the *khoro*. In general, when women were chiefs they brought their brother to administer the court. Political chiefship was conceived of as containing both brotherly and sisterly aspects (E. Krige 1974: 16–17). And when men were chiefs, their sisters shared authority with them. A sister's son had a claim to inherit the chiefship, as did a chief's own son (J. Krige 1939b: 411; Krige and Krige 1943: 181).

As with decision making, mediation with the supernatural involved both sexes. Rainmaking was the province of the queen and her close relatives (of both sexes). District chiefs and apparently (the information is not clear) male initiation schools were linked with rainmaking and renewal rites (Krige and Krige 1954; 1943: 126–30; E. Krige 1931: 212–20). In agricultural ritual, particularly that of the harvest, however, lineage ceremonies predominated, as did women in sisterly roles as officiators. Finally, both sexes had age set organizations, but clear information on them is lacking.

Sister relations of production seemed to underwrite the norms by which adult women could conduct their social and sexual lives. But with respect to sexuality, girls were more potential wives than sisters and were restricted more than their brothers. Beer feasts and dances were attended equally by both sexes, but young wives were kept too busy working for much socializing. Deference seems not to have been an expected behavior (Krige and Krige 1943: 402–03).

Apparently both men and women had equal opportunities for extramarital affairs and took advantage of them equally. Although it was socially acceptable for both partners to have extramarital relations, husbands could fine their wives' lovers but not the reverse. Despite the de jure inequalities of the spouse relationship, the sisterly autonomy underlay the de facto situation. It was considered contemptible for a husband to watch his wife too closely, and extramarital affairs were not grounds for divorce. Both husband and wife could obtain medicines to make their spouse fall ill should he or she engage in extramarital sex (Krige and Krige 1943: 123, 137, 157–59; 1954: 79).

In contrast, premarital sexual behavior, especially of girls, was restricted. Pregnancy disgraced them and spoiled their chances of being married to a young man. The boy (actually his father) was fined double adultery compensation. Boys, however, were not prohibited from sex relations with married women. These restrictions seem to stem from relations of production centering around marriage and wifehood in a girl's youth: Before a girl can be a sister, she must be a wife. That is, the house in which she is a sister cannot be built by her brother until she marries and brings him bridewealth cattle. Thus a girl's sexuality and reproductive powers were not hers to control; they were owed by her father to his sister. More pressure was applied to girls than boys with respect to marriage; indeed this was the only circumstance in which suicide was mentioned (Krige and Krige 1943: 77). The same obtains with respect to sexuality. This difference seems to stem from the sibling relationship in the parental generation. A brother was obligated to provide a daughter for his sister's house, but the sister was not equally obligated to request one for her son. Moreover, even if her son chose his own bride, the sister could claim the girl for herself, thereby maintaining the relationship. For a daughter to choose her own spouse would jeopardize the ties between the two houses. In this way too, wifehood was a restrictive and subordinate relationship for a woman.

SUMMARY AND CONCLUSIONS

Lovedu corporate patrilineages centered around linked pairs of brothers and sisters, who jointly owned and administered a corporate estate in gardens, livestock and children. These estates were perpetuated by sisters working and bearing children as wives for another lineage and by brothers using the bridewealth to become fathers and perpetuators of their own lineage. With respect to both men and women, the sibling and parent relations to the means of production predominated over the marital relations and shaped adult political, economic, and sexual roles of both sexes, as well as the relationship of husband and wife. However, young women prior to marriage were primarily wives-to-be. In relation to their brothers, theirs was an inferior position specifically with regard to sexuality.

The forces of agricultural production stressed the bilateral local kindred, the central productive group in the society. It rested upon enduring relations of marriage and exchange of goods and services among the local patrilineages. In one sense the forces of production, together with the merging of kin and affines by cross-cousin marriage, were in contradiction with lineage control over its agricultural means of production and the crop. But in another sense this bilateral kindred generated the productive means—livestock, marriage hoes, and women's fertility—that constituted the other pole of lineage estates.

Chapter 6
MPONDO

The Mpondo live in the Transkei.[1] In name only, this is today an independent state; in reality it is a Bantustan wholly controlled, politically and economically, by South Africa. As is the case everywhere for black South Africans, land in the Transkei is inadequate for subsistence production, and many inhabitants are landless. The Transkei's major export is human labor power. Throughout 1960 the Mpondo rose in revolt against the imposition of the increasingly repressive policies of the Nationalist party government. The revolt was put down brutally, and government reprisals and partial occupation of Mpondoland continued long afterward (Mbeki 1964; Carter, Karis, and Stultz 1967).

Because the Mpondo lived close enough to the European settlement at the Cape of South Africa to be affected by European expansion and close enough to the Zulu, who threatened the Europeans as well as the Mpondo, a fair amount of published information exists on Mpondo history from the nineteenth century on. It is conventional for the most part, ignoring women as well as social organization and focusing on wars, cattle raids, chiefs, and alliances, but it does suggest that the Mpondo patrikin corporate mode of production was undergoing significant changes. They were not revolutionary in that Mpondo did not develop a new mode of production. But they seem to have involved a shift in or an increased development of productive forces and relations associated with acquiring and maintaining livestock. The relations of production developing from livestock acquisition and maintenance in the nineteenth-century South African context differed from those developed in agriculture. Both were corporate lineage based but in contradictory ways.

Following the decimation of their cattle by Zulu raids, Mpondo spent the latter two-thirds of the nineteenth century making up their losses by raiding their neighbors. The forces of production for acquiring and holding cattle joined large numbers of men together as lineage brothers and also as clients of a chief. Larger political units—paramount chiefs uniting all or half of the Mpondo (at different times)—stemmed from these forces of production, as well as from corporate lineage productive relations, but they also undermined the latter, specifically the relations of corporate brothers. Chiefs owned cattle taken in raids, and they came to own most of Mpondo cattle. These they loaned or gave to individual men as gifts. Clientage to a chief, an individual relationship, was an important productive relationship that could grow with success in cattle raiding. Yet there is no evidence that lineage corporations were in any way directly weakened. It took the imposition of an apartheid capitalist state to do that.

It is not clear what Mpondo relations of production were with respect to cattle prior to Zulu expansion. It is unlikely that clientage was a new development in the nineteenth century (Marks and Gray 1975: 427). The point remains, though, that as the Mpondo replenished their livestock, these cattle came to be largely owned by chiefs who distributed use rights to clients. Clientship inserted itself into brotherhood as a productive relationship.[2]

Women's place in the Mpondo political economy was decidedly subordinate to men's. Sisterhood existed but did not count for much with respect to political and economic power and authority. I will try to show that for most of the nineteenth century, the productive forces of cattle raiding and the productive relations of clientship, a totally male sphere, dominated those of lineage corporateness. Yet sisterhood was much alive with respect to women's control of their sexual and social behavior. The fact that lineage wives constituted task groups for agriculture and for wood and water carrying reinforced their claiming sisterly prerogatives in wifely roles.

HISTORICAL CONTEXT

The Mpondo speak the Xhosa dialect of Nguni. By 1686, survivors of the Stavenisse shipwreck met them in the general area to which they are confined today, the Transkei of South Africa. I will focus on Mpondo organization prior to 1894, when European rule was imposed, and after approximately, 1830, when the Zulu raids on the Mpondo ceased.

An understanding of the pre-nineteenth century context is helpful in locating the Mpondo in the nineteenth century. The Mpondo may have been formed in the sixteenth century by the southern vanguard of the dispersal of Mbo-Dlamini lineages from the Lebombo Mountains behind Delagoa Bay. It is possible that they are the Vambe who traded in ivory with the Portuguese by 1559. Their organization was said to be that of small-scale chiefdoms (Wilson and Thompson 1969: 79, 91–93; Marks and Gray 1975: 429–33). During the sixteenth and seventeenth centuries, ivory was the main export from Delagoa Bay, and much of it came from the south. Conflict over trade routes may have been involved in the rise of military kingdoms among northern Nguni (Marks and Gray 1975: 432–33). Hunter suggests that wealth from the ivory trade in the nineteenth century may have underwritten heightened power to Mpondo chiefs relative to their people (1936: xi).

Until near the end of the eighteenth century, there was a basic similarity of language, culture, and social organization among Nguni speakers (Lestrade 1934; Omer-Cooper 1969; Wilson and Thompson 1969; Murdock 1949; Schapera 1937, 1956; Marks and Gray 1975). Small-scale chiefdoms, with the senior member of the senior clan acting as chief, were the framework within which political life proceeded. The size and composition of these chiefdoms fluctuated with the flow of quarrels, character of the chief, and available stock. Chiefs may have been wealthy but appear not to have had much in the way of coercive means to hold their followers. Chiefdoms often divided on the death of the chief, between the eldest son of the great wife and the eldest son of the right-hand wife. Southern Nguni chiefs may have ruled only three to five settlements. The settlement pattern was one of scattered villages of twenty to forty houses inhabited by a group of patrilineally related males and their families (*imizi*, plural; *umzi*, singular). Subsistence was derived from livestock and horticulture. The Mpondo seem to have retained much of this Nguni pattern regarding economic and political organization into the twentieth century.

The nineteenth century saw the expansion of white settlements northward from the Cape and, in Natal, the transformation and rise of the Zulu. Each of these brought massive dislocation, fragmentation, and transformations of societies throughout southern and central

Africa; those stemming from Zulu expansion were called *Mfecane* (Omer-Cooper 1969). The Mpondo were affected by these events but were buffered from the initial waves of Zulu expansion from the north and European expansion from the south. Early in the nineteenth century, they were raided but not dislodged or transformed by the Zulu. Shaka, the Zulu leader, was reluctant to push too far south because he hoped to maintain friendly relations with Europeans settling at the Cape. Thus the bulk of Zulu expansion was among the northern Nguni, though the Mpondo suffered very heavy cattle losses (see Reverend J. Boyce letters in Steedman 1835, vol. 2: 274–315, for a contemporary account). South of the Mpondo, the Xhosa bore the brunt of white expansion from the Cape (Wilson and Thompson 1969: 233–46; Kay 1833: passim; Soga 1930; Marks and Gray 1975: 454–58).

The Mpondo and other southern Nguni societies retained a fairly decentralized political organization centered around a hierarchy of territorially based, largely clan recruited chiefs. Southern Nguni did not adopt the military regiments and centralization of more northern Nguni (Wilson and Thompson 1969: 124). Of the former only the Mpondo have not been dislodged from their past territory by Zulu or Europeans. Although they were very much involved in the wars and raids of the *Mfecane* and paid tribute to Shaka, they did not seem to lose their political and economic autonomy, nor did the Mpondo organization suffer as much as those of other southern Nguni. The Bhaca were a creation of the *Mfecane*; and at least the northern Thembu were pushed into close proximity to the Mpondo, broken up, and partially incorporated by the latter toward the middle of the nineteenth century (Omer-Cooper 1969: 156, 161–63). The Xhosa lost much of their independence and land to the whites early in the nineteenth century (Wilson and Thompson 1969: 243; Marks and Gray 1975: 454–58).

Zulu expansion practically depopulated Natal, pushing many refugees south toward Mpondoland. Some were incorporated as refugees by the Mpondo, but overcrowding led to friction over land, and scarcity of cattle led to raids. Mpondo fought against the northern Thembu who had been displaced by the first wave of Zulu expansion, dispersing some and incorporating others. They defeated the Qwabe, a group that broke away from the Zulu (Omer-Cooper 1969: 160–63; Hunter 1936: 404).

Although the nature and scope of Mpondo warfare varied somewhat over the nineteenth century, raiding for livestock and, to a lesser degree, for territory were constant features of Mpondo life and an activity that involved all men. In the early years of the century, the Mpondo lost the bulk of their cattle to the Zulu raids, so that by 1828 they were almost completely dependent on their agriculture for subsistence. During this period the Mpondo paid tribute to Shaka but retained their fighting strength and functional autonomy (Omer-Cooper 1969: 156, 159; Walter 1969: 261).

Wars between the Mpondo and their neighbors, the Bhaca, Thembu, Mpondomise, and Xesibe, were frequent. The goal was primarily livestock and, on occasion, territory. The Reverend J. Boyce, a missionary in Mpondoland between 1830 and 1832, noted that the Mpondo were poor in cattle and that Faku, the paramount, "earnestly covets the plunder of the country between the Umtata and Bashee rivers, where there are no chiefs of much ability to make any opposition" (Steedman 1835, vol. 2: 280). Theal (1915: 64) mentioned a thousand head of cattle captured in a single war. Who was an enemy and who was an ally depended upon the circumstances. This applied to Europeans as well as to Africans. When the Boers began their expansion into Natal about 1840, the Mpondo allied with the Bhaca and later the British, against them. Mpondo and Bhaca also forged an alliance against the Qwabe. Mpondo allied with the British against Xhosa and Thembu. Faku, the Mpondo paramount chief for much of the nineteenth century (ruling from 1824 to 1867), wrote Theal, "was always ready to fall upon the Xhosas and Thembus when the Cape colony was at war with them, and stock his kraals with oxen and cows at their expense" (Ibid.).

Although there were temporary alliances and large-scale wars, records of these seem to fall in the first half of the century. After the death of Faku, small-scale hostilities seem more frequent. I suspect these existed prior to 1867 but were overshadowed by major campaigns. Raids and alliances in the latter half of the century were made primarily by districts. Several Mpondo districts might raid a section of another people or might ally with several districts of another group to attack a third. Interdistrict fighting among the Mpondo over cattle and succession also occurred with some frequency (Hunter 1936: 412).

The Mpondo continued this pattern of raids and warfare after 1877 when colonial rule was forced on other Transkeian societies. Theal noted "large-scale" raiding by Mpondo against Bhaca and Xesibe in the 1880s (1915: 209–53). He also cited a large number of specific raids and one large campaign involving a Mpondo army estimated at fifteen thousand against the Xesibe in 1886. Some of the fighting in this decade was a result of crowding, caused in part by the expansion of Europeans. The eastern Mpondo used witchcraft accusations and raids to drive Bhaca, Mpondomise, Xesibe, and others who had settled earlier in Mpondo territory into the British colony of East Griqualand. Between 1890 and 1893 Eastern Mpondoland took part in an extended struggle between rival claimants for the position of paramount chief (Ibid.: 231, 236, 250–51).

In the turbulent nineteenth century, then, warfare for livestock and grazing land was a large part of Mpondo life. The Mpondo never took up northern Nguni military systems or their strong centralization. The district, under its chief, remained the basic political and military unit. There were no age sets; all able-bodied men fought. The strength of the Mpondo army depended upon the nature of the threat, as well as upon the strength of the paramount chief. Although the paramount theoretically declared war, he often sanctioned or acquiesced to independent cattle raiding organized by district chiefs. Wars frequently took place close to home and lasted up to a week or ten days.

SUBSISTENCE AND MEANS OF PRODUCTION

Like other Nguni societies, Mpondo subsistence in the nineteenth century was based on grain agriculture (maize and millet) and raising cattle and goats. Hunting was a relatively unimportant subsistence activity as early as 1830 according to contemporary accounts (Steedman 1835, vol. 1: 258; Kay 1833: 122). Gathering wild vegetable foods was of some significance, particularly in the diets of women (Wilson and Thompson 1969: 111).

The relative importance of agriculture and livestock varied during the nineteenth century. Between 1820 and 1830 when the Mpondo suffered severely from Zulu raids, they were almost completely dependent on their agriculture. They went from being poor in cattle in the earlier part of the nineteenth century to being primarily dependent on livestock for most of the latter part. In the 1930s milk and meat were still staple foods. Cattle and goat were eaten at a variety of ritual and social occasions, and sometimes slaughtering was done just for meat. Hunter calculated that about 8,278 cattle alone were eaten in one year in a district of 40,352 people (1936: 69): "All informants are emphatic that before the advent of Europeans, grain played a much smaller part in the diet of the Mpondo than it does today. Meat and milk were staple foods and the area cultivated per family was much smaller than it is now" (Ibid.: 113). The trend, then, over the second half of the nineteenth century, seems to have been an increasing importance of livestock as a major subsistence base and a relative decline in agriculture.

The main productive means were livestock, grazing land, gardens, gathering land and hand tools, weapons, and utensils (such as hoes, spears, and cooking pots). Wild vegetable foods and firewood were collected from uncultivated land. Livestock were also grazed there. Gardens were cultivated on the slopes and along the streams dissecting the ridge land of the Mpondo. Bottom land was the most fertile and could be worked for about ten years; poorer slope land could be farmed for two to three years, after which it was left to regenerate for future use. Forest land was preferred to grassland for gardens because its burning enriched the soil more. However, forests have been on the wane since perhaps the seventeenth century (Wilson and Thompson 1969: 110).

Women, particularly old women, wove kitchen utensils (plates, grain baskets, mats, brooms, and beer strainers). Not all women, even in the past, knew how to weave, and there was a great variety of skill among those who did. Each *umzi* usually had a weaver. The situation was similar with respect to men's crafts—sewing beer baskets, weaving meat trays, carving wood milk buckets and spoons, tanning hides, and sewing cloth. Pottery making and iron smelting were specialized crafts; the former was passed from mother to daughter and the latter from father to son. In either case, nonkin could be taught. Potters exchanged their wares for grain, but smiths were paid grain, spears, or livestock. Iron deposits existed in Mpondoland, but iron was not plentiful, even in the latter nineteenth century. While iron hoes existed, most cultivation was done with wooden hoes or with digging sticks, the iron being reserved for spears and ornaments.

MODE OF PRODUCTION

IN HISTORY

How to characterize the nineteenth-century Mpondo mode of production is not an open and shut case. From ahistorical ethnographic descriptions there appear to be two modes of production: (1) the warriors and cattle raiders (forces of production), clients of chiefs (relations of production) who obtained and maintained the herds (productive means and food supply); and (2) the *umzi* or corporate kin group whose estate in cattle, grain, and gardens (productive means) was held by its brothers and sisters (productive relations) and whose wives and brothers (productive relations) produced beer and vegetable food as a female work group (productive forces) and produced its animal foods as a male work group (productive forces). But chiefship and lineage were not really discrete in that both stemmed from relations of genealogical seniority being relations of stewardship over productive means. That is, senior kin were also resource managers. On the other hand, they were not identical either, in that chiefs' clients were not necessarily kin.[3]

Although the published historical information bearing on the Mpondo mode of production is not as full as one would wish, it does suggest that chiefship and lineage are historically aspects of a single mode of production. It also suggests that nineteenth-century conditions provided chiefs with more productive means to control than they had controlled in the early part of the century. For Mpondo, as perhaps for other Nguni, chiefs faced outward; they were historically much involved with trade relations. External relations, particularly trade in means of production—iron weapons and tools—seems to have been an integral part of a general Nguni mode of production.

Chiefs, trade (particularly in ivory, iron and cattle), and an association between them have long been significant aspects of Nguni social organization, perhaps since its genesis. The same seems true for corporate lineages. Thus in fifteenth- and sixteenth-century Portuguese accounts and in later Dutch accounts, Nguni chiefdoms were noted as territorially organized as well as lineage based; they included people of a variety of clans and origins. In addition, chiefs are recorded as having continually sought, with varying success, to monopolize trade with respect to their own people and with respect to other chiefs (Marks and Gray 1975: 425–39).

Chiefly control of trade was likely chiefly control over two critical means of production. Ivory and sometimes cattle were exchanged for iron, which was scarce among southern Nguni for most of their history. When cattle were in short supply, they were raided, and when abundant they were sometimes traded to Europeans for metal, as among eighteenth-century Xhosa. In Nguni life both cattle and iron weapons were means of production; ivory was only a means to iron. Particularly in the milieu of the nineteenth century, iron weapons were necessary means of production for keeping and acquiring livestock, which in turn were means of producing milk and meat. Thus to the extent that chiefs controlled iron and cattle, it is not difficult to see how they could have increased their acquisition of clients and thus enhanced their power at the expense of or relative to that of lineage corporations. This contradiction seems to have been an integral part of Nguni social organization since its inception. Hence chiefs and lineages historically seem to have been parts of a single Nguni mode of production.

The next question deals with possible nineteenth-century developments of that contradictory relationship. Did chiefly control over productive means replace lineage corporations with chiefly clients? There is no evidence that lineages were being lysed by clientage or that lineages lost their corporate estate to chiefs. But there is evidence that chiefly control over livestock increased, that it joined lineages to chiefdoms through clientage relations of production, and that it organized forces of production on a larger than lineage scale. That circumstances could have arisen under which chiefs expanded at the expense of corporate lineages is not in dispute. The point is that they did not. Rather the reverse occurred—chiefs increased their power relative to but not at the expense of corporate lineages—and Mpondo lived successfully with this contradiction for most of the nineteenth century.

The evidence is circumstantial. Nineteenth-century Mpondo chiefs had a monopoly on ivory and also traded with the San to obtain it. Hunter (1936) claims that chiefly power was enhanced by this monopoly and by the ivory trade. We have seen that iron was scarce and valuable through the latter part of the century. Mpondo chiefs did organize raids, did own and distribute cattle taken in raids, and were the richest people in livestock. Overall their organization of raiding was successful in building up Mpondo herds. However, to complete the argument that chiefs provided lineages with some of their means of production, we need to show that ivory exchanged for iron (and with whom) and that chiefs distributed iron. Regarding chiefly control over and distribution of cattle as *umzi* means of production, the evidence is fairly consistent.

IN SPACE

Territorial and kin relations were the relations of production that underwrote Mpondo political economy. Topped by a paramount chief, there was a hierarchy of headmen and chiefs, often related to each other, that ruled territorial divisions. The Mpondo settlement pattern was one of scattered *umzi* spaced anywhere from fifty yards to over a mile apart. An *umzi* included about twenty agnatically related married men and their families. Mpondoland is a country of ridges dissected by streams. A group of *umzi* in a neighborhood, generally those of a ridge, were under the authority of a petty headman. Several of these were grouped together into a district under the authority of the paramount. Depending on the size of the district, there may have been a number of levels in the hierarchy between headmen and district chiefs. Following Hunter, those in charge of large districts and the paramount will be designated *chiefs*. *Headmen* will be those in charge of subdivisions of large districts, and *petty headmen* those in charge of a group of *umzi*. The terminology is more rigid than the situation was. There was a good bit of fission, declarations of independence by district, and transfer of loyalty by groups within a district from one chief to another. And after Faku's death in 1867, Mpondo divided into an eastern and a western paramountcy, headed by the heirs of Faku's right hand and great houses.

It is difficult to ascertain the size of a Mpondo district. During Faku's rule, Steedman mentioned the existence of six "principal subordinate chiefs" (1835, vol. 1: 249). Hammond-Tooke (1965) lists eight chiefdoms for the Mpondo, but of these only five were independent of the paramount of Eastern Mpondoland. Presumably the remaining two were subordinate to him. Yet there were more than two such districts in precolonial days. It should be noted that Hammond-Tooke does not consider chiefs subordinate to the paramount to be independent political units. Although I think his classification is overly rigid, his estimate of eight powerful chiefs allows some guess at the size of political units. The Mpondo occupied a territory of about thirty-nine hundred square miles in the 1930s (Hunter 1936: 15). Based on a population of two hundred thousand in 1875 (Wilson and Thompson 1969: 255), the average political unit would have contained some twenty-five thousand people in an area of five hundred square miles. If we assume seven chiefs, as Steedman indicates, the average district was larger and more populous.

In war, all men served in the army of their district chief. When called, a district chief was expected to bring his army to fight for the paramount. In addition, districts near that of the paramount brought their armies to his place each year for magical treatment designed to strengthen them. Those who were distant enough or powerful enough possessed their own medicines and treated their own fighters.

The households or *umzi* of the paramount, of which there were several, were the foci for the organization of the Mpondo army. Each district was attached to one of these. There were four such divisions in the paramountcy of Eastern Mpondoland and four in Western Mpondoland. Actually the *umzi* in each half, and hence the divisions, were quite close together so that the army was fairly concentrated. Each division was under the leadership of a kinsman or councillor of the paramount. Despite its territorial allegiance, the army was able to act under a single leadership (Ibid.: 379, 400–06).

Actual centralization, as opposed to formal structure, depended on external threats and relative strength of the paramount and particular district chiefs. Under Faku, centralization seems to have been much greater than it was after his death. But even under Faku's rule, subordinate chiefs fought among themselves (Steedman 1835, vol. 1, 255).

A paramount had no special sanctions at his disposal and had to rely on loyalty. Omer-Cooper, writing of Faku, states that "his rule was generally mild. He rarely employed the death penalty except for witchcraft" (1969: 159). Political organization was at a district level, and the paramount was just first among equals.

Thus the powerful district chief merged into the independent ally and the tribe was no closely knit unit, but an affiliation of districts recognizing one paramount. The size and solidarity of the tribe varied with the extent of outside dangers and the personality of the paramount. During the period of Shaka's war many chiefs who had formerly been independent recognized the Mpondo paramount, Faku, as their paramount. [Hunter 1936: 379]

Indeed after the Zulu threat abated, many of these chiefs fought for independence. District chiefs gained their independence sometimes by armed rebellion and sometimes with the backing of the paramount, to extend Mpondo rule.

The formal territorial structure of the Mpondo was related to lineage. All Mpondo were members of an *umzi* (plural: *imizi*), a co-resident corporate patrilineage. *Imizi* fissioned, giving rise to agnatically related patrilineages, which tended to cluster in a neighborhood. All Mpondo were members of a patrilineal clan. Agnates shared the same clan; hence clans tended to be concentrated in a locality or district. Headmen and sometimes chiefs tended to be chosen from the senior line of the predominant clan in the area. On the other hand, the senior clan of the Mpondo (Nyawuza) was the clan of the paramount chief.

As senior representative of the senior Mpondo clan, the paramount tried to appoint brothers and sons as district chiefs so far as possible. Strong chiefs who were not relatives were not forced out, but weaker chiefs were replaced by Nyawuza kinsmen. Just as the paramount boosted his own relatives, so too did district chiefs with regard to headmen under them and headmen with regard to petty headmen. Within each district and to a large extent between districts, kinship tied each level of the hierarchy to its superior. In addition, there were ties of marriage among Mpondo, Bhaca, Thembu, and Xhosa chiefs. Generally chiefs chose the daughter of another chief as their principal wife; the senior son of this wife succeeded to the chiefship.

The *umzi*, a residential group of male agnates and their families, was the corporate kin group of Mpondo society. These may have included the families of up to twenty married men in the nineteenth century, although they sharply decreased in size under colonial conditions (Ibid.: 15, 59). Livestock, stored grain, and garden lands constituted the principal estate of an *umzi* and were allocated among the houses of individual wives with respect to daily use and inheritance. Although livestock were owned by individual men, they were under the overall authority of the senior male, the "owner" of the *umzi*. Succession was by the eldest son of the owner's eldest son by his "great wife." (The owner's eldest son was presumed to have already begun his own *umzi*.) It was said that all a man's property was his father's as long as the latter lived. Agnates were expected to consult each other, and especially the owner, in making decisions about killing or distributing their animals. Elder brothers were responsible for using inherited livestock to care for the needs of their younger brothers, sisters, and mother. But brothers were not responsible for providing bridewealth for each other's sons; this was a responsibility of the father or elder brother. The livestock of an *umzi* were kept in a single *kraal* and were herded together as a unit by the youths and boys of the *umzi* under their elders' management.

Milk, meat, and vegetables were prepared from the stores of each wife for the *umzi* as a whole. With respect to wives, *umzi* members, male and female, shared clear collective authority. All brothers had authority over all wives (and their children) "because she has been [married] with the cattle of the *umzi*," and her "husband's brother . . . (is her husband)" (Hunter 1936: 30). Wives called their husbands' sisters *female husbands* and owed them much the same obligations owed male affines. Thus male and female members of an *umzi* commanded the labor of wives and were entitled to be served by wives. Sisters were entitled to claim wives' possessions and to ask wives to weave for them. A wife's youngest son inherited all her possessions— gardens, tools, and any livestock—which were earned or given her by her father or brother. Yet as mothers of grown sons, they had a place of their own and a blood tie to *umzi* means of production.

The relations of *umzi* members to wives was contradictory. Wives were a collective force in the production of beer and vegetable food and in its allocation throughout the *umzi*; they performed this work under the collective control of *umzi* members; and they produced the next generation of *umzi* members. But wives did not "own" either grain or children. On the other hand, they did allocate the *umzi*'s means of production to their own children; and as mothers they had a claim on the *umzi*'s property through their sons. This contradictory relationship of an *umzi* to its wives was also a contradictory relationship among *umzi* members themselves. Thus an *umzi* estate in cattle was congruent with *umzi* forces for their production in herding and defense. But cattle had two ends. As milk and meat they were produced by the collective male forces of production and were allocated throughout the *umzi*. But as bridewealth, the means of marriage, they belonged to individual men and were used for themselves or their own sons. Thus the *umzi* contradiction is between *umzi* care and maintenance of the herd and individual allocation of cattle. The assertion of collective authority over *umzi* wives is in some sense an *umzi* assertion that this contradiction is resolved. But actually it is simply displaced onto the contradictory relationship between wives and *umzi*.

A chief "owned" his district and was father to his people in ways analogous to the owner of an *umzi*. He had stewardship of uncultivated lands and might allocate them to newcomers upon payment of cattle and their acceptance of his authority. While chiefs had no claims on *umzi* livestock and land or the right to evict residents, in practice they exercised some control over *umzi* means of production. First, chiefs and headmen held claims to grazing land in the form of cattle posts. While herds grazed for most of the year on the ridges of an *umzi*'s neighborhood, cattle were moved for part of the year to better grazing at these cattle posts. Some posts were for the use of all under a chief's jurisdiction, but others were reserved for chiefly use. Given the scarcity of grazing land as nineteenth-century European expansion reduced the land available to Africans, this may have become a significant inequality in control of productive means. Second, chiefs often used witchcraft accusations as means of dispossessing those who posed a threat to their power, particularly wealthy commoners (Steedman 1835, vol. 1: 257). Those convicted were punished by banishment or death and their property was confiscated. Third, chiefs claimed a share of cattle captured in war. Although indirect, the information indicates that chiefs controlled the bulk of Mpondo livestock, much of which came from raids. Mpondo claimed that chiefs always wanted war, while their subjects were frequently opposed to it, indicating that a chief's share was substantial. Hunter implies that chiefs had claim to captured livestock: "When an independent raiding party attacked an enemy tribe, the chief of the raiders, if they were successful, was always given at least one beast" (1936: 385). And Schapera (1956: 100) and Lestrade (1934: 435), writing generally, noted that Nguni chiefs claimed all cattle taken in war. They gave some to successful warriors and other men but kept many themselves. Fourth, chiefs had a monopoly on all elephant tusks and certain hides, regardless of how they were obtained. With respect to hunting associated with the yearly ceremonies to strengthen the army, chiefs organized the hunters and claimed all game obtained. Fifth, an undetermined amount of livestock found its way to the chiefs as a result of fines levied in judicial proceedings and as gifts. Chiefs were the wealthiest people in Mpondoland. Yet the difference was quantitative. Chiefs and wives performed the same labors as nonchiefs, but chiefs had more wives—from ten to twenty—and thus more grain and beer. They also tended to have several *imizi*, the best garden lands, and more meat.

The significance of chiefly advantages in control of productive means lay in its use to control the labor of people: to develop clientship relations of production, or *indunas* ("one who comes to serve").

Such a relationship was not restricted to chiefs. Any wealthy man could obtain such voluntary clients. An *induna* was a person who came to a chief or wealthy man to ask for a gift or a loan of stock and was prepared to offer his services in return. Indeed anyone coming to a chief's place was liable to be called upon to run an errand or perform another service. As the richest person in his country, a chief was expected to be generous. Distribution of wealth attracted followers, and the service of clients brought wealth. Much of a chief's authority derived from his loans and favors to his subjects. Hunter says of one chief that "a very large proportion of his people in his country had cattle from him on loan" and implies this was in no way extraordinary (Ibid.: 388). Often chiefs did not have to do their own work; they had enough clients to do it for them. Some clients stayed only as long as it took them to get what they wanted; others attached themselves to the chief's household for years or served him even though they had their own household.

Clientage was an important productive relationship and part of the lives of many Mpondo men. "Cattle raiding afforded an opportunity for enterprising men to get rich quickly, but the principal way in which a poor man acquired wealth was to serve a chief or a wealthy man, and receive in return the loan or gift of cattle" (Ibid.: 135). Such loans and gifts underwrote an *umzi*, and hence clientship underwrote lineage productive relationships.

Wealth in livestock was a central aspect of chiefship, and anyone who was wealthy was in some respects chiefly. "Generosity is a primary virtue and the mark of a chief . . . beggars interlard their solicitation with 'You are our chief, give to us' or 'Give to us and you will be our chief'" (Ibid.: 387–88). Chiefs had the advantage over nonchiefs in their legal ability to expropriate the property of the latter. But nonchiefs had the same incentives as chiefs to distribute their livestock to establish a following (as well as to avoid seizure by a chief). Those who were successful in gaining clients might be made headmen. Chiefship, then, was somewhat fluid. Undue extortion from a following or lack of success in gaining livestock for distribution likely decreased a chief's following. Alternatively followers might transfer their allegiance to a competitor for the position.

Beyond their wealth in productive means, chiefs had limited control over coercive or cooptive means. The army was the adult male populace, organized locally and massed for war or chiefly ceremonies to strengthen them. Chiefs stood as intermediaries between their people and rain, appealing to their own ancestors or to a rainmaker for rain.

In much the same way as an *umzi*, a chiefdom was rooted in contradictory relationships. First, livestock were captured by large scale collective productive forces in warfare but were claimed by individual chiefs and allocated among individual clients. Stemming from this, chiefly control over productive means created clients and fed clientage relations of production in that voluntary service (together with *umzi* membership) was an important relationship for obtaining the means to livelihood. Yet those means to livelihood, particularly livestock, could be used only to create and sustain *imizi*, or lineage productive relations, which in turn undercut clientage. From this perspective, then, *induna* and *umzi* are not separate modes of production but rather two sides of a contradictory relationship in a single mode of production. The two sides of this contradiction were not equal in the latter nineteenth century. The chiefly side dominated *umzi* access to the means of production and thus shaped the framework within which lineage life proceeded. There is another critical difference in the two sides of this contradiction: The forces and relations of production on the *induna*-chief-warfare side were all male and those on the *umzi* side included both sexes.

MODE OF PRODUCTION AND GENDER

In the nineteenth century the forces and means of production associated with acquiring and keeping livestock were the collectivity of armed adult men of a district. Their productive relations were at once those of chief and client for warfare and allocation of cattle on the one hand, and brothers of an *umzi* for herding, stock tending and consuming on the other. While these were the core relationships of Mpondo political economy, that core presumed productive forces and relations giving rise to chiefs and brothers in the first place. The genesis of chiefs and clients is not central here. Suffice to repeat the earlier suggestion that external trade relations and metal goods may have been important forces in generating chiefship.

The productive forces and relations generating corporate agnatic groups are central to the concern with gender roles and relationships. Women and men in their capacities as producers are forces of production. Their productive relations are those of sisters (*idikazi*,singular, *amadikazi*, plural), wives, and mothers on the one hand and brothers, fathers, and clients on the other. It was the labor of women in producing vegetable food that created part of an *umzi* estate in productive means as well as creating the people of the *umzi* itself. But that labor was performed in the relationship of wives to the *umzi*. Likewise, the labor of men in stock tending, raiding, and serving chiefs created another part of an *umzi*'s estate in productive means. This labor was performed in the relationship of brothers, or of fathers and sons on the lineage side, and as clients and followers on the chiefdom side. As a corporation, an *umzi* was created by its brothers (and clients) and its wives. Wives were producers but not owners or members; brothers were both producers and owners. As wives produced children, they became mothers and entered a new relationship to the *umzi*. This relationship stemmed from a mother's supplying her sons with their means of production and hence creating a relationship to the marital *umzi* independent of the one established through her husband. The relations of husband and wife presume relations of brother and sister in a corporate kin mode of production. Sisters and their marriages are necessary conditions of brothers' marriages. Lineages need sisters as well as brothers as members. Mpondo sisters are owner-members, but they are also nonproducers. These then are the principal productive forces and relationships generating the variety of female and male roles and relationships. The point to be recalled is that there is no "essential male" or "essential female" lurking underneath brother or sister, husband or wife; they are the essentials.

FORCES OF PRODUCTION

I will consider the way Mpondo organize the tasks involved in livestock keeping, agriculture, collecting firewood, and preparing food and in hunting for meat as well as for ivory and skins.[4] The organization of craft production appears to have been mainly by individual effort. While the tools and implements involved in production were used by individuals, the organization of subsistence work itself was most commonly in groups of either men or women. In brief, the creation of vegetable food and beer (agricultural tasks, collecting and cooking) involved mainly women's groups, and hunting and most stock-related tasks involved groups of men or boys.

Women were responsible for and performed most of the agricultural work, and they placed high value on their gardens and gardening. Although men were responsible for cutting trees and digging grain pits, they sometimes assisted women in piling brush, planting, weeding, reaping, and threshing. Women carried the grain in from the fields. Agricultural work could be performed with several different types of organization. Each married woman had her own field or fields, the produce from which belonged to her and her children. A husband and wife occasionally worked a field together. Generally the wives of an *umzi* worked together planting, weeding, and reaping the fields of each in turn. If *imizi* were small, several combined for harvesting and sometimes weeding. When one *umzi* was involved, there were no gifts for service, as there were in the case of several *imizi* combining. Men might participate in this work but did not do so with any frequency. In reaping, for example, Hunter estimated one (generally old) man for every ten women. Besides group reciprocal labor, there were also frequent work parties (*amalima*, plural; *ilima*, singular) for planting, clearing land, weeding, shelling maize, and occasionally reaping. These were organized by wives in consultation with their husbands. The wife whose field was to be worked killed a goat for meat or brewed beer to reward the workers. A weeding *ilima* might draw as many as two hundred people. *Amalima* were considered parties and were used for all agricultural tasks. In these, men and women participated in about equal numbers. Very often for a single task, cooperative labor within the *umzi* was combined with an *ilima*.

Both men and women worked for chiefs. Both the paramount and district chiefs called on men as well as women for agricultural labor service and for hut and *kraal* building. The paramount chief had *imizi* in several districts and called upon the people of these districts to cultivate the fields of the *umzi* in their district. At least under white rule, these rights were small scale and much like an *ilima*; chiefs had to provide meat or beer to reward the workers. In the case of either a rich commoner or a chief, workers would expect a head of cattle to be slaughtered, but then two or three days' work were expected. The work was organized, as at other *amalima*, by the wife whose field was being worked.

Cooking and collecting wood and water were heavily cooperative. Some time after about a year of marriage or after the birth of her first child, a wife began cooking in her own hut. Before that time, she cooked in the hut of her mother-in-law. Household tasks were time-consuming. Until she had a daughter old enough to do so, a woman had to draw water at least twice a day, from perhaps half a mile away, and cut and carry firewood three to four times a week from perhaps five miles away, in addition to cooking. Grinding grain took about an hour on a daily basis. Water and wood gathering were generally done in groups, though each woman did her own work. Collecting firewood was hard work, and sometimes *amalima* were held for this purpose. When preparing for a feast, when a woman was near birth, or as a friendly gesture, one woman might make an *ilima* for another. Women also brewed beer. This too was a cooperative venture, with the women of a neighborhood working together. Young women and girls were principally involved here. This work was done in a party-like atmosphere, with food for the workers being provided by the *umzi* for whom beer was being brewed. Each worker was given a pot to take home with her. Daily cooking was also cooperative; it was organized by wives and was a collective force of production. Meals were taken in groups within the *umzi*. Several dishes were prepared: one for the owner of the *umzi*, one for men and youths, another for women, and one for children.

Herding and milking goats and cattle were the responsibilities of boys and youths. Girls before puberty and nonmenstruating older daughters performed these tasks if there were no boys available. Overall responsibility and management of livestock, however, was in the hands of adult men. Each *umzi* took its stock to pasture separately, but once there the herds of a neighborhood or a ridge were joined together. Some coastal districts moved their cattle to inland cattle posts in the summer, while inland districts moved theirs to the coast or to river valleys in the winter. It is not known whether men or boys herded at the distant posts. Given the importance of cattle raiding in the nineteenth-century milieu, it is surprising to find boys doing the herding. Yet pre-colonial travelers in the Transkei confirm this (Kay 1833: 118–19; Kidd 1904: 329), though they did not mention Mpondo specifically. The importance of warfare as a productive task in obtaining livestock and pasture has already been discussed. Men placed a high value on warfare and on fighting abilities. The organization of war involved men of a chiefdom or district fighting under their chief. Occasionally larger armies combined under a paramount chief. Thus while stock tending involved boys and men of an *umzi* or neighborhood, stock maintenance and acquisition involved cooperation among men of a chiefdom.

Hunting contributed some food and skins for clothing and ivory for trade. Information about its organization, particularly with reference to the ivory trade, is sparse, but its organization seems parallel to that of livestock. Hunts were organized among men of an *umzi* or ridge. Larger hunts were organized by the paramount chief in the context of ceremonies to strengthen the army.

RELATIONS OF PRODUCTION

Men were related to the means of production as clients and chiefs mainly with respect to livestock, and as sons and brothers of a lineage corporation or *umzi*, mainly with respect to garden land and live-stock. To discuss men's relations of production is to discuss the relationship of lineage and chiefship. Productive relations centered on livestock were the foundation of the Mpondo chiefdom. Men, whether husband, brother, or client, were simultaneously owners and producers of livestock. From these relations as producer and owner stemmed men's participation in the decision-making relations of the chiefdom. Only men were headmen, councillors, and chiefs. The Mpondo occasionally held a national or district meeting on important matters such as war, endemic faction fighting, or the unauthorized killing of a sorcerer. Such meetings were open to all men. Any man and only men could participate in the courts of chief and headmen. The national ritual of a first fruits ceremony to mass the army for magical strengthening by the chief dramatized the relations of the chiefdom and the centrality of its adult men. This three-day ceremony involved only men, as warriors. At its conclusion, the warriors brought some of the medicines back to their *umzi*, where men and women of their family were treated. This ritual was repeated after the wars.

As owners and producers of livestock for their families, fathers had authority over the labor and marriage choices of unmarried children. They paid and received compensation in cases where they were involved. Wherever possible, a father supplied his son's bridewealth. His daughters' lovers owed him gifts for permission for premarital partial sex relations. They also claimed similar payments from the lovers of divorced daughters.

Regardless of whether they acted as sisters, wives, or mothers, women did not exercise authority over marriages of their children, did not in any way act as guardians (though their influence as wives and mothers was quite significant), and did not participate in chiefdom or *umzi* decision-making forums or in the major avenues of settling disputes. Yet they did act as witnesses in court, did bring cases on their own behalf, and did stand accused in their own right. Hunter (1936) describes a married woman acting as plaintiff in an assault case and a woman fined for giving false evidence. Women convicted of witchcraft were punished.

An *umzi* rested on more than cattle. Women were productive forces and their relations to the means of production as sisters, wives, and mothers were not the simple opposite of men's. Responsibility for productive labor in agriculture rested with wives rather than sisters, though the latter participated in this when at home. It was principally task groups of wives who gardened, who collected wood, water, and vegetables, and who cooked and brewed. Thus wifely relations stand at the center of the discussion. The relationship of husband and wife required also the relationship of brother and sister. As far as possible, a man tried to pair a brother and sister of the same house so that the former received his sister's bridewealth cattle for his own marriage. The right to dispose of these cattle, though governed by certain rules, was held by fathers and brothers of the *umzi*. A father could take bridewealth of a daughter and use it to marry another wife for himself. A father (or brother) who received bridewealth cattle from a girl's marriage was linked to her by the obligation to provide her with livestock for her initiation rite, a wedding outfit, domestic utensils, and other gifts, especially clothing, for herself and women of her husband's *umzi*.

Wives took to their husband's *umzi* the utensils necessary to their work. A wife and her movable means of production were a unit. Her father or brother was responsible for supplying her throughout her life with the wooden or metal tools and utensils she needed for her work. Woodworking and metalworking were men's crafts. Similarly a woman's brother or father was responsible for supplying her with skin clothing, the making of which was also a men's craft. Husbands were not responsible for supplying wives with any tools, utensils or clothing. In addition, fathers gave a heifer to their daughter on marriage to supply her with milk. However, sisters (*idikazi*) of an *umzi* could and often did expropriate these possessions (save the cattle) from the wives. Moreover, they could demand that wives make or obtain such an item from the wife's own *umzi*.

Cultivation by wives created an *umzi*'s estate in garden land. Garden land came to a woman largely through her husband. Land that had been cultivated had an owner, the husband of the woman who worked it or a man of the husband's *umzi*. This land was inherited from the mother by her youngest son, presumably for use by his wife. It was the act of bringing the land into cultivation that created its *umzi* ownership. That ownership continued as long as anyone of that *umzi* lived in the district. Land over which no such claim existed belonged to the chief in the sense that chiefs had overrights to all land in their district and the right to allocate unclaimed land to settlers for gardens. Uncultivated land, be it fallow or unclaimed, was open to all for collecting firewood and wild vegetables. Land that had not been gardened, and hence possessed by an *umzi*, could be claimed by anyone who lived in the district. Since women were producers in their capacities as wives, they began to cultivate after they married and at the husband's *umzi*. The land they brought under cultivation passed to the husband's *umzi*. Hence over the generations, wives of a lineage brought new garden lands from the chief's domain into ownership of the husband's lineage. Over time, the wives of a lineage served to expand the lineage's claim to productive land relative to that of a chief. Brothers and sisters did not have the same relations to garden land of the *umzi*. While sisters living permanently in their own lineage worked fields belonging to their *umzi*, they did not inherit land; this was restricted to men of the male line. Sisters' share in the estate lay in a lifetime supply of tools and clothing.

While Hunter noted that garden land was not scarce in the 1930s, there is ample evidence of friction over grazing land in the nineteenth century. Since livestock grazed on uncultivated land, and on garden land after the harvest, the two uses of land are closely related. It is possible that there was a basis of conflict between resident lineages' claims on land for both gardens and grazing, and chiefs' desires under latter nineteenth-century conditions to use some of that land to attract new clients and followers.

In addition to bringing tools and garden land to the *umzi*, its wives also created grain, vegetable food, and beer. In some sense the grain belonged to the husband, but in another it belonged to the *umzi* and its wives. On the one hand grain, the product of wives' collective labor, was stored in individual grain pits dug by husbands in the cattle *kraal* or courtyard, from which wives were prohibited.[5] The produce of a wife's fields belonged to her house, but once it was stored its de facto allocation lay with the husband and men of his *umzi*. Moreover wives needed their husband's consent to brew beer or allocate any of the produce beyond their house. On the other hand, much food was harvested daily and not stored. Much of what was stored remained for a large part of the year in a wife's individual storehouse. Thus wives had access to most of what they produced. The wife or wives who cooked for the entire *umzi* decided what and how much to cook. Therefore a woman's garden produce was not confined to her own house. Wives as a collectivity of cooks necessarily made decisions about the *umzi*'s allocation of food. In grinding grain for brewing beer, wives of an *umzi* invited neighboring women to assist them. They fed these women and gave them beer to take home. In addition, wives distributed food and beer at the *amalima*, or work parties, they held for garden tasks and wood gathering. Although husbands had overrights to wives' produce, husbands' de facto management was curtailed by the organization of these tasks.

To summarize, bringing their utensils and tools from their own lineage, wives of an *umzi* working as a collectivity were a productive force of garden land (a means of production) and of vegetable food and beer. Collectively their labor transformed chief's land into garden lands belonging to the *umzi*. Wives' collective labor also produced grain, which belonged to individual husbands. However grain was an intermediate product. Its final forms, beer and cooked food, were also produced by the collective labor of wives. Wives labored collectively to create *umzi* means of production yet did not own them, and their claims to the product were at best shared. Expropriating the products of the collective labor of *umzi* wives created the *umzi* as a kin corporation by creating a productive estate. However, this was not the total *umzi* estate.

Within the *umzi*, brothers and sisters shared a claim on the labor and product of its wives. An *idikazi* was called "female-husband" by the *umzi*'s wives and was entitled to be served by them much as were her brothers. Sisters laid claim to wives' possessions as brothers claimed the produce of their gardens. Sisters could expect economic and moral support from their father or from the brother who received their bridewealth cattle. There they found a home, temporary or permanent, upon leaving a husband. A permanent *idikazi* almost certainly gardened, but sisters, unlike brothers, were not responsible for any production.

Although some of a wife's productive means and possessions passed to sisters of the husband's *umzi*, the rest, particularly gardens, passed not to its brothers or to the woman's husband but to her own youngest son. A husband's possessions, especially livestock, passed to his sons through his wives. Men allocated their herd among their wives for use by their house and for providing bridewealth for its sons. Thus both husband and wife contriuted the means of production to a son's household, but that contribution passed through the mother. Thus, as a mother, a wife's relationship to the productive means of her husband's *umzi* becomes similar to that of her husband through a mother's relationship to her son. It is in this proprietary sense that wives became members of their husband's *umzi*.

The contrast between wife and sister relations to the means of production generated contrasting social roles with very different behavior expectations, but in neither role did women exercise power or authority over others beyond the *umzi*. In considering why this was the case, it is necessary to explore and explain the differences between wifely and sisterly behavior, as members and nonmembers of the *umzi*. A wife has a whole constellation of restrictions centering around contact with her husband's agnates, particularly senior male ones. She must walk around the back of all huts and may not enter the men's side of any hut or the cattle *kraal*. She may not drink milk of cattle from her marital *umzi* for up to a year after marriage. In addition, wives must observe various forms of deferential behavior to members of her husband's lineage. "Women agree that *ukuceza* [prohibition on entering or walking past the men's side of huts] is one of the trials of life. It adds enormously to the work of the bride" (Hunter 1936: 36–37). Wives must also avoid the river in which their husband's clan sacrifices; they may not use the water or gather rushes there. These restrictions mark the wife relationship as one of a not-quite-trusted outsider. A sister faced none of these restrictions. At all ceremonies pertaining to the ancestors, men and women of the *umzi*, but not its wives, took part. Wives did join in the feast however. As a stranger herself, a wife, unlike an *idikazi*, did not greet or entertain visitors to the *umzi*. She needed also to show respect to her husband's sisters, treating them as honored guests and supplying them with goods. When a wife disregarded one of these restrictions, all the wives were punished collectively. They were sent home to bring a gift to the head of the *umzi*, who then made a ritual killing to restore good relations. This procedure was rare. Most often it was initiated by visiting sisters when they needed something to take back to their marital *umzi*. Wives, but not sisters, were frequently accused of witchcraft, often by a husband's sisters, co-wives, or mother-in-law. A woman's own kin defended her against these accusations. Such charges seemed to reflect conflict between the sisters of an *umzi* and its wives. Since husbands often supported their wives, witchcraft accusations may have also worked to split an *umzi* where friction among men of the lineage existed but where the ideology was one of fraternal solidarity. By blaming an outsider, the ideal of lineage solidarity could be maintained.

Over the years, especially as a wife became a mother and her children grew up, the number of avoidances decreased. The mother of grown sons, wife of an *umzi* head, was primarily a mother and member of her husband's lineage and hence free of wifely restrictions. She could assist in distributing meat at ceremonies to the ancestors. Sisters past childbearing could officiate at these ceremonies, and so too might the mother of an *umzi* head if she were old and knew the names of her husband's ancestors. "She is no longer of another clan" (Ibid: 257). After death "a woman becomes an *ithongo* [ancestral spirit] to her children who belong to her husband's clan, but she is never completely assimilated" (Ibid.: 43).

There is also a contrast between sisters and wives with respect to authority. Wives live and work under the collective authority of members of their husband's *umzi*: his brothers, his sisters and his mother. Husbands claimed exclusive sexual rights over their wives and could demand compensation from a wife's lover. Husband's brothers, as well as a husband, could beat a wife for improper behavior. In daily productive tasks, a wife worked under the authority of her mother-in-law, and it was she who gave a wife permission to visit and to attend beer and meat feasts. Until they were married about four years, or had two children, neither sex attended these feasts, the principal forms of socializing activity involving adults of both sexes. Wives of an *umzi* needed permission to attend meat or beer feasts. In this regard chiefs' wives tended to be more restricted than others. Wives were expected to attend festivities only for the day; older mothers, *amadikazi*, and men could sleep there or go from party to party and not return home for a week. Wives attended feasts less frequently than *amadikazi* and men. Especially younger wives were too busy with work to travel around.

Submissive behavior, restrictions, and hard work applied only to a wife living in her husband's *umzi*. When a woman was in her father's or brother's *umzi*, she was free to attend social events without asking and need not observe any avoidances. She had the right to take things from her brother's wives and to expect them to wait on her. She generally participated in women's work, though she was not so obligated. For these reasons, many women preferred to live the life of an *idikazi*—either abandoning their husbands permanently or taking long, frequent visits to their own kin. Hunter cites a "short" visit of three months, though elsewhere she speaks of visits of two weeks or more about three times a year (Ibid.: 40, 128). Included in this category of *idikazi* are married women on visits, as well as divorcees, widows, and women who have never married but have had a child. Those who have husbands differ from others in that they should not have extramarital affairs. If caught, their husbands may claim compensation. Many women ran away from their husbands. Some had many affairs; others had a stable relationship with one man. To be an *idikazi* was an easier position, requiring less work and granting a woman much more freedom. They were well supplied with gifts from their lovers. "Any woman is flattered if you greet her as an *idikazi*. 'That is the name we like best' " (Ibid.: 107).

The rate of divorce, judging by the number of *amadikazi*, seems to have been high. Either party could initiate it. Although the return of bridewealth was required where the wife was seen to be at fault, this was not much of an impediment. Bridewealth was given over many years and deductions were made for children and services, so there was often little to return. If a wife left her husband because of poor treatment or under suspicion of witchcraft, the bridewealth was not returned. Likewise if a widow left her dead husband's *umzi*, the bridewealth, with deductions made for children and services, had to be returned before she could remarry. If the widow were a chief's daughter, the bridewealth was never returned, but she could remarry. A widow could also remain in her husband's *umzi* and live with a man not of that *umzi*. In that case the man with whom she lived lacked a husband's rights; instead he was an *induna* to her.

The existence of *idikazi* as an alternative (even a short-term one) to wifehood had some impact on the treatment of wives by husbands. Mistreated wives could appeal to their own kin. To run home was no disgrace, and a woman could expect her family to take her side. "Fetching a wife who has run away is a dreaded task" (Ibid.: 42). Husbands had to be submissive and could be forced to pay compensation to a wife's father or brother.

These two productive relationships come together, however, with respect to the sexual activity of women and girls. Regardless of whether they were sisters or wives, men (as fathers, brothers, and husbands) claimed authority over women's sexual activity in a nonreciprocal way. Women as a gender—as wives, sisters, and mothers—did not accept this authority, but they did not confront men either. They simply evaded it, collectively, along gender lines.

How sex is related to relations of production is not immediately obvious. It is necessary to distinguish between premarital sex and extramarital sex. Premarital sexual relations and pregnancy were prohibited for girls. Women as well as men shared these norms and helped to enforce them. When an unmarried girl exceeded the limits of proper premarital sex relations, she and her age-mates of the neighborhood were held collectively responsible and were punished as a group by being allowed no festivities. In some clans the women of the girl's family descended on the boy's *umzi* and threatened to beat him and fight the *umzi*. They seized a head of cattle from them and kept the meat. The boy (presumably his father) was liable to a heavy fine in cattle. The girl was disgraced. Mothers had a stake in their daughters' virginity to the extent that they received an extra head of cattle from the bridewealth in the event that a daughter was a virgin.

Extramarital sex for women was prohibited by men's norms but not by those of women. Women evaded these rules as men sought to enforce them. With respect to such conflicts, men and their courts condoned extramarital sex for men but maintained a husband's exclusive sexual rights over his wife, regardless of where she was living. Chiefs' wives were more carefully guarded than others, and there were cases of chiefs killing a wife for actual or suspected adultery. Most women, however, did have lovers. Some husbands objected, others did not, but adultery was no grounds for divorce. If a man sent his wife home for adultery, he forfeited his bridewealth. It was permissible for a man to kill his wife's lover if he caught them in the act, but it was more common for the lover to pay the husband a fine. Some husbands used medicine to harm or kill their wife's lover. Hunter cited one case where a man committed suicide over his wife's adultery. Women did not regard extramarital sex as wrong; they only feared getting caught. Women of an *umzi* stood together against the men in this regard. A co-wife, husband's sister, or a husband's mother might act as a woman's go-between. If they were caught, the men fined all the wives of the *umzi* by making them eat part of the cattle received after it had been made unpalatable. Though not severe, this was the only punishment Hunter could discover for women.

Men, as fathers, brothers, or husbands, claimed the right to control women's sexuality, but the control over girls, perhaps because this norm was shared by women, was more effective. Both sexes had considerable de facto freedom in choosing a spouse, but it was not equal. Theoretically a boy's father could veto his son's choice. In practice sons were never forced into marriage against their will, but daughters sometimes were. Even though it was not socially approved, some fathers did beat their daughters. There was a high rate of elopement, and many girls ran away from husbands they disliked. There were cases from precolonial days of girls committing suicide rather than marry against their will. An *idikazi* without a husband was free to have lovers, but their lovers were supposed to give the same gifts to the woman's father that were required of lovers of unmarried girls. For each pregnancy an *idikazi*'s lover was expected to pay five head of cattle to claim the child. But many *amadikazi* were effective in refusing to let their fathers claim this, so they could keep their children.

The normal round of women's work joined wives and sisters of neighboring *umzi* together. In addition ceremonies joined women and girls of a neighborhood. A crucial part of a girl's initiation ceremony was the dancing performed by married women of the girl's neighborhood at frequent intervals throughout the initiate's three-month seclusion. Prior to the 1820s, boys were circumcised at an initiation ceremony, but this ceremony was viewed as depleting Mpondo military strength and was eliminated by Faku in the face of Shaka's raids. It was never resumed.

Sisters and wives of several *umzi* were also able to enforce at least something of a shared standard of husbandly behavior. Hunter cited a case of a husband unjustly beating his wife for a suspected extramarital affair so that she ran away. In this case, the women of his own and neighboring *umzi*, in addition to the wife's kin, acted against the man. The latter refused to return the woman, and the former refused to do any work for him.

It seems, then, that fathers' and brothers' contrasting standards for their own sexual activity and that of their wives and daughters was part of a process of controlling marriage, livestock transfers, and children of the *umzi*. Their double standard was an assertion of male control of marriage and children based on their control of livestock. I see women's assertion of a single sexual standard by collective evasion as an agreement that fathers, brothers, and husbands do and should indeed control marriage and children. Mpondo women were not challenging the social order. Indeed they actively upheld it with respect to the sexual behavior of daughters before marriage. But they were disputing an implicit equation of sex and marriage-reproduction with respect to women's adult sexual activities. (Perhaps it is in this light that Mpondo women were prohibited eggs, which were said to make them "lascivious.")

SUMMARY AND CONCLUSIONS

It was with respect to married women's extramarital sexual activity that the contradictory relations of Mpondo society and a corporate kinship mode of production were most sharply manifest. As long as there were *umzi*, there were sisters. Sisters were owner-members of an *umzi* and asserted equal rights to travel, to socialize, to be supported by fathers and brothers, and to represent the *umzi* in a few social contexts. Yet brothers and fathers claimed control over sisters-daughters' sexual activities as part of their control over marriage and livestock. They supported sisters' social prerogatives, even against husbands, but they challenged their sexual prerogatives. In this sense fathers, brothers, and husbands all claimed compensation or gifts from daughters', sisters' or wives' lovers. The contradiction between sisters on the one hand and brothers, fathers, husbands on the other was weighted in favor of the latter.

That women actually exercised their sisterly role to the extent that they did seems to stem from the forces of production—from the ways in which women's work was organized. The collective organization of an *umzi*'s wives, as well as collective task performance by women of a neighborhood, was also an organization of women who were sisters in other *umzi*. Their collective work allowed wives to exercise the options of *idikazi* together with marriage as well as an alternative to it. And it was with respect to sexual activity that sisters, wives, and mothers joined along their work lines, within an *umzi* or neighborhood, to assist sisterly rights. Mpondo *imizi*, then, at once subordinated women as wives and made them group members as sisters.

It is worth noting that wives of chiefs were more restricted than other wives. In a sense their sisterhood was downplayed. Wives were punished for extramarital affairs but apparently not especially effectively. This was less the case for wives of chiefs. On the other hand, chiefly sisters and daughters were somewhat more sister than other wives in that their husband's *umzi* could not demand a bridewealth return should they leave. In Mpondo society these were minor distinctions.

NOTES

1. Unless noted otherwise all information is from Hunter 1936.

2. Meillassoux (1972) emphasizes the relations of junior and senior within a lineage. While chiefs were senior kin, they were also more; and clientship differs from lineage juniority in that very few clients became chiefs or could hope to do so. I use the term *clientship* to refer to a situation of personal dependence separable from lineage membership. Thus I see clientage as growing within a lineage productive mode but also in contradiction to it. Its source is that stewardship of productive means was vested in a member of that lineage. It became clientship under conditions when a steward used those productive means to develop forces and relations of production that transcended the lineage (Sacks 1974: 212).

3. One can postulate all sorts of Ptolemaic just-so stories about "hierarchies of determination" and about how chieftainship and lineage "modes" were articulated. But if one sees "mode of production" as a summation of those political and economic forces, means, and relationships that are the organizational framework within which people make their lives, it defeats its usefulness as an analytical tool to let the number of "modes" in one's analysis run amok as surface appearances dictate.

4. I can find no information on gathering vegetable food beyond the fact that women do it, sometimes as part of a wood-gathering trip.

5. Sisters were not prohibited this area, but I do not know whether they were allowed access to the grain pits.

Chapter 7

MODE OF PRODUCTION II: SEX AND CLASS

So far I have discussed nonclass modes of production at two levels: that of evolution, or metahistory, and that of particular comparative history. The categories of communal and kin corporate modes of production were evolutionary in that each was intended to include a large number of societies at particular points in their histories. Further, I assumed that communal modes of production appeared before kin corporations and that modes of production characteristic of class societies appeared still later. But, as was noted in Chapter 3, an evolutionary discussion cannot speak to questions of change—the processes by which communal modes were transformed into kin corporations. These questions can be answered only by comparative historical inquiries into particular transformations. Just as these two modes of production are abstractions from particular studies, mainly of stasis, statements about transformations need to be abstracted from particular studies of change in mode of production. The information on such transformations, particularly for the preclass world, is sparse. However, when we enter the world of states, the possibilities for comparative history are richer. The following chapters will begin to explore these areas for African states, again at an evolutionary level and at the level of particular historical cases.

This discussion will have a different emphasis from that of preclass modes of production. In ethnographies, preclass African societies seem to be organized along either communal or kin corporate lines. However, in ethnographies and histories of African states I have not found the kinds of categories available—ancient, slave, feudal, Asiatic or capitalist modes of production—to be helpful in illuminating either static description or historical process in Africa. I have therefore approached the world of African class societies much as I have that of preclass societies by making women's productive relations the center of attention. Although this focus has not generated particular modes of production as it did with nonclass societies, it has suggested an evolutionary dynamic for the process of class formation, with particular respect to women's and men's relations to the means of production. In other words, focusing on women's places has generated a hypothesis about how the process of a ruling class's taking control over productive means has transformed women's and men's relations to these means in very different ways. This and the following chapters then speak to the relationship of class to sex.

SEX AND CLASS IN EVOLUTIONARY PROCESS

Putting women at the center of an analysis has illuminated their contrasting relationships of sister and wife. Looking at kinship as relations to the means of production opened up new ways of seeing kin corporations and of understanding women's relations to their means of production. This in turn has stimulated a new way of seeing the rise of class society as a process of struggle between a ruling class and kin corporations for control of productive means. In an evolutionary sense, the former has won. Historically the process was most uneven: kin corporations resisted, often successfully; at other times and places the result of the struggle was their maintenance in distorted or subverted form; and in still other cases they have been largely destroyed. This view differs from more conventional evolutionary ones not only with respect to its focus on women but also with respect to which class occupies the center of analysis. Thus conventional evolutionary anthropologists (Cohen 1974; White 1959; Sahlins and Service 1960) tend to enumerate progressive trends such as productivity of human labor power, variety and quantity of goods available, and proliferation of occupational and life-style choices. But instead of being counted as societal gains, these criteria should be looked at as gains for ruling classes and a small proportion of nonruling but affluent people. Such criteria, or analytical centers, obscure evolutionary losses for the majority of humanity. Workers, for example, do not own the results of their great productivity, and most of the world's population is denied even an adequate diet and has little meaningful choice of occupation or life-style. In nonclass societies, necessities were generally available and fairly equitably distributed. Although occupational or life-style choices were indeed limited, the lack of specialization forced adults to command a wide range of mental and manual occupations. From this perspective, then, the rise of ruling classes and state formations initiated a long and uneven process of destroying kin corporations.

For women, particularly women of the underclasses, class struggle has taken a particular form, which centers around sisterhood. As ruling classes have usurped control over productive means, destroying the economic basis for sisterly relations of production, they have also enforced wifely relations of production in their sociolegal treatment of women. Women's struggle has been to retain or recreate sister relations in the context of intraclass relations of production. The myriad ways this struggle has been and is played out is, of course, a historical question and needs to be investigated and analyzed historically. Clearly sisterhood in class societies does not involve women of the nonpropertied classes in a corporation of owners of productive means; that is more appropriate to women of the ruling class. But it may involve underclass women in some forms of struggle to control productive means, and it almost certainly involves them as wives and mothers—relations of production stressed in ruling class sociolegal systems—in creating productive relations with other wives and mothers, which add to their own and their class's collective wherewithal to resist both the class and sex dimensions of dependency in wife and mother productive relations. Indeed this may be much of what underlies so-called matrifocality in a variety of cultural contexts in today's world of class societies (Tanner 1974; Caulfield 1974; Young and Wilmott 1962; Stack 1974; Sacks 1979). In one sense I am suggesting that long before industrial capitalism (which created conditions making proletarians need each other at the point of production), wives and mothers of the underclasses linked men and women of their class together in class-based matrifocal kin networks that represented class-based productive forces for women's work and established class-based relations of sisterhood and brotherhood.

While ruling classes often denied sisterhood in ideology and legal systems, in many African systems sisterhood was not destroyed as a productive relationship of ruling-class women; hence it was retained to varying degrees—though not without contradictions—in ideology and legal systems. However, its meaning was transformed to emphasize a gender dimension of class productive relations. Sister became a relationship of privilege over both women and men of the underclasses. Yet sister, even within the ruling class, was in some ways contradictory to the fact of class rule with male property ownership.

If the history of women and of the family in the world of class societies is one of class struggle, underclass women and underclass families are not winning. Class modes of production, most notably industrial capitalism, have seen ruling classes claim more control over more means of production than ever before. In capitalist ideology and legal systems, wifehood and motherhood have been affirmed as women's essence, while sisterhood has been denied, even for women of the ruling class. Yet capitalist expansion and intensification have driven underclass women into proletarian productive relations and work organization. We might expect to find them involved in two-pronged efforts to recreate and reconceptualize sisterly places in union and feminist ways in paid labor (Rowbotham 1972; Sacks 1976b; Baxandall, Gordon, and Reverby 1976) and in formations of kin networks and welfare rights organizing in unpaid labor (Glassman 1970; Tillmon 1976).

SEX AND CLASS IN AFRICAN HISTORY

I must stress at the outset that what I am doing from here on is presenting a hypothesis illustrated with pieces of African history, but I cannot show that history really happened in the way I think it did. Let me explain. The following illustrations of class societies discuss specific histories of class formation. In the discussions of the kingdoms of Buganda and Dahomey, there is clear historical evidence of ruling classes' taking control over productive means, particularly agricultural land, away from kin corporations. In the case of the city of Onitsha, there is historical evidence of no ruling-class gains in control over productive means and the persistence of strong kin corporations. We thus have historical data for comparative processes of class formation and can see how ruling classes gained strength and power by taking them away from kin corporations. But on women's relations to the means of production, we have only ethnographic, not historical, material. For example, we have late nineteenth and twentieth century descriptions of Baganda and Dahomean women's relations to the means of production—after ruling classes of these states had broken kin corporate control over productive means—but there is no information on women's relations to productive means prior to the rise of these ruling classes. So although I can say that peasant women's productive relations in Dahomey and Buganda were wife and not sister, I can only guess that women in these societies were also sisters in the times when kin corporations controlled productive means. Such a guess lacks independent evidence and thus is not especially convincing or clarifying. I have therefore added a discussion of the Nigerian city of Onitsha, an almost (or not quite) class society with stable kin corporate group control over productive resources and a very clear delineation of sisterly prerogatives. This case provides comparative but not historical support for thinking that the weaker the ruling class's hold on productive means and the stronger that of kin corporations, the stronger will be sisterly relations of production for women (assuming similar productive forces). I am suggesting an evolutionary process of women's relations to productive means and hence to women's places.[1]

NOTE

1. Most of the rest of the book deals with what ruling classes did to sisterly relations. We need to know what women did for sisterly prerogatives, that is, how they organized to retain or recapture them, and what new shapes women have given them in the world of class societies. These questions are clearly beyond the scope of this work. They are being addressed particularly by feminist social history. In the conclusion I will suggest some linkages between this discussion of precapitalist sisters and wives and some recent social history of women in Europe and Africa.

Chapter 8
BUGANDA

By the middle of the nineteenth century, the kingdom of Buganda, with somewhere between one million and four million inhabitants (Kiwanuka 1972: 151), on the northern shore of Victoria Nyanza in Uganda, was the most powerful and centralized of the interlacustrine states. Its history from the seventeenth through the nineteenth centuries reveals a two-sided process of state formation: expansion conquest and heightened ruling-class control over productive means at the expense of corporate kinship group control. During the seventeenth and eighteenth centuries, the area under Buganda rule grew enormously. This expansion was coupled with and facilitated the transformation of political organization from one based largely on a federation of ranked, territorially based patriclans to a centralized bureaucratic organization. It resulted in the progressive destruction of independent power in the hands of clan leaders. Buganda's increasing participation in the nineteenth-century ivory and slave trade further increased the wealth and power of its already consolidated ruling class. From about 1800 on, Buganda's wars became oriented toward predation more than annexation and toward control over trade routes.

Given the rise of a ruling class and the demise of clan-based power, the ideal situation would be to show how the destruction of patrilineal kin corporations entailed the destruction of sisterhood and the rise of wifehood as women's sole relation to the means of production. Unfortunately the published historical materials do not speak to the transformations in productive forces and relations in general, and with respect to women they are totally silent. But there is an adequate body of information pertaining to the nineteenth-century mode of production and gender. Therefore only the discussion of how corporate kinship groups were transformed into kin relations compatible with class society can be treated historically. The relationship of gender and mode of production has to be discussed in the context of the Buganda state as it existed in the nineteenth century.

At that time, peasant men's primary productive relations were as clients of ruling officials. Peasant women's relation to productive means was that of wife. The ruling class, on the other hand, as owners of productive means, maintained something of a kin corporate organization and kin corporate productive relations. While productive means (including slave labor) were attached to offices, those offices were largely the hereditary property of specific lineages. Sisterhood persisted in the ruling class, but in a weak form. Part of the weakness stemmed from the way in which forces of production undercut sisterly relations of production among the rulers as they did among peasants.

POLITICAL ECONOMY IN HISTORY

Buganda's expansion from a small client of the powerful Bunyoro kingdom began in the seventeenth century and appears to have been linked to salt and iron. Lacking iron deposits, Buganda relied heavily on Bunyoro for metal tools and weapons prior to conquering eastern Kyaggwe and Buddu in the eighteenth century. Buganda also lacked natural salt, which Bunyoro possessed as well. But there was also conflict over control of Katwe and the salt lakes southwest of Buganda (Tosh 1970: 104–07). Kiwanuka (1972: 144) suggests that control over Kyaggwe and Buddu, together with the excellent ironsmiths of those areas, added significantly to Buganda's supply of weapons and hence to its greatly increased military power.

As Buganda expanded its territory over the course of the seventeenth century, the balance of control over productive means and political power shifted from chiefs who headed corporate clans to a class of appointed officials who owed their positions to the institutional power of the kingship. In the seventeenth century, the *kabaka*, or king, Kateregga allocated lands taken from Bunyoro to his war leaders and created posts for other loyal followers. This change departed from the usual practice of exacting tribute from conquered peoples while leaving their organization untouched. Although these offices became hereditary, the families controlling them needed royal approval of their choice of official, and these could be deposed. Kiwanuka de-

scribes one way in which clan-based rule was transformed into hereditary class rule:

[Kaggo] was chief of Kyaddondo because Kyaddondo is the claimed great
ancestor of the Nvuma clan to which the first Kaggo belonged, settled in, and
used to rule over that area known today as the county of Kyaddondo. This
group of people of the clan claim to have come to Buganda during the time of
the Kintu migration and settled in or around Kawempe, near modern
Kampala. When the original leader died his name was given to the whole area
and hence the first central county was known as Kyaddondo. Members of the
Nvuma clan, therefore, remained the territorial administrators of Kyaddondo until they presumably fell out of favour and were replaced by the members of the Colobus Monkey clan. [Ibid.: 113]

The productive relations were hereditary clientage relations. This
class of king's men increased in size relative to that of clan leaders as
Kateregga's successors increased their numbers as Buganda incorporated more territory. By the early eighteenth century, independent
clan chiefs were outnumbered and declining in influence (Alpers and
Ehret 1975; Kiwanuka 1972).

Perhaps before the nineteenth century, under the reigns of Kya-
baggu and his successor, Semakokiro, Buganda became increasingly
involved in the Arab trade networks to the south, going through Tan-
zania to the coast. Ivory was the principal export, with manufactured
goods, particularly cotton cloth, coming into Buganda. Ivory was
made a royal monopoly. By the end of the eighteenth century,
Semakokiro employed elephant hunters and carriers to pursue trade at
the southern end of Victoria Nyanza. In the nineteenth century, Buganda came into conflict with Bunyoro over control of the trade routes
to the coast (Unomah and Webster 1976; Alpers and Ehret 1975;
Tosh 1970).

Toward the end of the eighteenth century, Semakokiro initiated a
policy of killing or putting into custody the king's brothers and most of
his sons to prevent rebellions and succession conflicts, a practice that
diminished the size of a royal family. Southwold (1968: 141) points
out that the effect of this policy was to strengthen the class of appointed rulers, making the kingship a pivot or unifying institution
among them. In this process relations of production were transformed
from direct patriclan control over productive means to control by a
network of chiefly families of a few of these clans who held hereditary

rights to goods and plunder by virtue of their ties to each other through the king.

The point is important. Clans and their component lineages were decorporatized rather than destroyed. Kinship became a basis for establishing vertical, dyadic clientage relations, the central relation of men to productive means. Clans were deprived of their independent base of power by expropriation of clan land and installation of appointed officials, together with cooptation, or harnessing clanship to class organization. By the mid-nineteenth century, clan lands were basically small burial grounds with relatively few peasant residents. Particular clans were granted hereditary rights to appointive positions in return for clientage to the king. In this way potentially divisive clan interests were transformed into class-centered patronage networks. Baganda did not seek to rise in a clan hierarchy. There was none. Yet ties of clanship were quite important in gaining entry into state positions, and these were the ones that promised access to wealth and the services of others (Fallers 1964: 92; Mair 1934: 164; Roscoe 1966: 134, 180, 196; Kiwanuka 1972: chaps. 4–7). Thus a few clans had hereditary rights to provide the king with a specific wife or with services and thereby serve as overlords of royal estates (Roscoe 1966: 152). The clientage chains extended to local level political economy. Richards, in dealing with an area of fifty-four square miles in the district of Busiro, listed seventeen villages ruled by lineage heads; of these, eight lineage heads also served as overlords of the king's estates (1966: 106). The priests for the national temples to the two important war gods came from two clans. These temples were sustained by the king's and chiefs' gifts (Roscoe 1966: 154, 303). Although particular lineages within clans had power, this power rested on their class rather than their clan position because it was as a class that they owned the means of production.

The nineteenth century saw an acceleration of predatory warfare (related partly to conflicts over trade routes) and a concomitant expansion in the predation-derived wealth controlled by the ruling class (Kiwanuka 1972: 137–38). Above all, Buganda was a warfare state. Kagwa noted, though with some exaggeration, "The people did not learn to sell (or produce for sale), for they obtained all their requirements by force of arms of gift of the Kabaka" (quoted in Wrigley 1964: 18). Kamanya's reign in the early nineteenth century was known as one of "restless warfare" (Kagwa 1934: 43). His successor,

Suna, carried on sixteen major military expeditions in a twenty-six-year reign. Kagwa (Ibid.: 93) speaks of wars being waged regularly every six months. Under Mutesa (c. 1860–1884), there were sixty-six wars in twenty-eight years. Buganda was able to field a huge army. Stanley estimated the army sent in 1875 against the Buvuma Islanders contained 125,000 Baganda soldiers, 25,000 non-Baganda soldiers, and 100,000 camp followers. The navy used 230 large war canoes, which could carry 16,000 to 20,000 men. An army usually carried at least a month's supply of food, though it generally lived off the countryside, even in Buganda (Kiwanuka 1972: 144).

The spoils of war were mainly women, children, who became slaves within Buganda or were sold to coastal traders, and cattle. According to Kagwa's figures, the king received between one-fourth and one-third of the total booty (1934: 91–92). Additional large shares were given to chiefs who commanded their own men. These reserved their share, or part of it, before presenting the spoils to the king. Even though half the spoils may have been distributed among the warriors, the vast majority were left empty-handed. War was a major means of enriching the ruling class with cattle and slaves. The herds of the king and major chiefs ran into the thousands. These were divided up and pastured in different parts of Buganda by Bahima herdsmen taken prisoners in war (Roscoe 1966: 415, 422; Mair 1934: 122). Although war represented a hope of wealth and advancement for peasants, it was a reality for very few.

By the nineteenth century, Buganda ideology conceived the nation as organized along male patronage rather than kinship lines. The political hierarchy was said to consist of an elaborate structure of territorial overlordships. Everyone save the king had an overlord, and all save peasants had subordinates. One owed an overlord goods, services, and loyalty. This ideology denied the existence of classes in its stress on dyadic, vertical relationships between ranked individuals. Horatio Alger-like, it proclaimed the possibility of individual mobility through competent, loyal service to one's superiors. At one level such an ideological denial of kin corporateness and stress on individual political relations accurately reflected the demise of corporate patriclans. But at another level it denied Buganda's class organization and the transformed role of kinship into classs relations of production in uniting the ruling class as well as in dividing the underclasses. Despite open competition for high offices, a few clans remained disproportionately influential over the centuries. Prolonged political influence rose from the fact that a clan or family that had long been close to the corridors of power had a large number of its members in important positions, all of whom would look after the fortunes of their struggling fellow members (Kiwanuka 1972: 122).

NINETEENTH-CENTURY MODE OF PRODUCTION

In its most general outlines, Buganda's class structure consisted of two producing classes divided along gender lines. Free peasant men as clients, together with male war captives as slaves, produced the bark cloth for clothing, smelted, made beer, tended livestock, constructed buildings and roads, carried, and traded. Most of their labor and produce went to the ruling class. In addition these men constituted the army and the lower ranks of retainers and servants for the rulers. Free peasant women and slave women produced and prepared the kingdom's staple vegetable foods, plantains and root crops, as wives. Free women were mainly wives of peasants, and slave women were mainly wives of rulers or servants of their wives.

Although there was a large slave population, made up mainly of women and small boys captured in war, their circumstances seem to have been similar to those of peasants, and their status was not hereditary. Children of slave women by their masters were free Baganda. Most slaves were in the households of important officials and worked as servants or wives. Peasant women too became domestic servants and wives in chiefly households. Domestic slavery preceded the slave trade, which involved Buganda only after mid-nineteenth century. After Mutesa ended Suna's prohibition on slave trading, chiefs sold war captives of both sexes to Arab traders (Kiwanuka 1972: 167; Mair 1934: 32).

The formal hierarchy of chiefs, officials, subchiefs, and retainers was exceedingly elaborate. Its power rested with the number of people, goods, and services a ruler controlled and the scope of that control. Officially the king owned Buganda and had absolute power. He appointed officials and was ultimate adjudicator of conflict, as well as military decision maker. He was in theory an absolutist king. There were four other officials, however, who, like the king, had their own estates (overlordship of one or more villages), collected their own taxes, and commanded their own services. Two of these were women:

the king's mother (*Namasole*) and the queen sister (*Lubuga*). The
other two, the *Katikiro* and *Kimbugwe*, were men. For their own subjects, the *Namasole* and *Lubuga* were the final decision makers and
arbiters. *Lubuga*'s palace was about twice the size of that of an important wife of the king. The others had more elaborate palaces. Also
among the most powerful rulers were the chiefs of the ten great districts of Buganda and the chiefs of their major subdivisions. These
were ranked, but all were wealthy, maintaining large palaces in their
districts as well as households of several hundred people in the capital,
where they spent much of their time. Both were provisioned with food
and beer by peasants. They commanded labor from those under their
jurisdiction and received a portion of the king's tax. In addition, they
had estates of their own, administered by their own appointed retainers, most of whom were chosen from among the fellow clansmen
who flocked to a chief's court. The king also appointed personal retainers as overlords of his estates. These provisioned the king's household with a particular product—beer, firewood, or barkcloth. Royal
estates and their officials became much more numerous and important
after about 1860 when Mutesa developed the practice of granting
them to military officers (Fallers 1964: 94).

The king, *Katikiro, Kimbugwe, Namasole, Lubuga*, chiefs, and a
few royal retainers received the bulk of all tax goods and, except for
the retainers, had additional sources of revenues: market fees, war
plunder, court fees, fines, tribute, a portion of the king's tax, and a
monopoly of ivory sale. Smaller subchiefs, on the other hand, were
themselves taxed in cattle, goats, and hoes. Officials thus were divided, roughly speaking, into taxpayers and tax receivers (Roscoe
1966: 234, 244–46, 269, 447; Kagwa 1934: 95; Fallers 1964: 110).
The ruling class, consisting of the receivers, enjoyed a standard of
living far above that of peasants. There was no mass redistribution of
goods back to the producers. Most were redistributed among chiefs
with some trickling to peasants in the form of hospitality and stock
loans.

The Baganda rulers relied on their control of armed force to maintain their rule. The king and district chiefs had their own armed body-
guards even before Mutesa was said to have created a standing army.[1]
The king also had his own secret police and executioners. The courts
of the king, his mother and sister, and the district chiefs could and often
did administer the death penalty, frequently for minor offenses

(Roscoe 1966: 201, 208; Wrigley 1964: 21). Finally the ruling class was organized in a military chain of command; they alone had the forms to organize peasants for fighting—for the interests of the rulers (Ibid.: 19).

Despite the ideology of royal absolutism, it is clear from looking at family and clan ties that a fairly small number of families predominated in the ruling class over the generations (Cox 1950; Fallers 1964; Kagwa 1934). The genealogy of Sir Apolo Kagwa, *Katikiro* from 1889 to 1926, shows the disproportionate representation of sons of important chiefs in the governing hierarchy (Fallers 1964: 172–74). Moreover the important wives of the king came from a relatively small number of families. For example, of Suna II's 148 ranking wives, 16 were from the Mbogo clan. Six were daughters of one man and 7 were daughters of another (Kagwa 1934: 44–49). The few clans from which most district chiefs came were those from which important royal wives came. These predominated and benefited as the clans of most queen mothers, a major ruler in her own right (Kagwa 1934; chapter 7; Cox 1950: 159; Southwold 1968: 150; Fallers 1964: 106; Kiwanuka 1972: 122–23). Fallers's conclusion seems accurate: "Appointive offices which were increasing in numbers and importance, were to some unmeasurable extent monopolized by a kind of incipient gentry, which held a measure of control over recruitment" (1964: 176).[2]

MODE OF PRODUCTION, GENDER, AND CLASS

Garden land and livestock (cattle, goats, and chickens) were the major means of production. Metal tools and pottery seem to have been made by male specialists and sold to peasants. The Baganda diet was basically vegetable; plantains, the staple food, were supplemented by root crops. Meat was occasionally obtained through hunting, by slaughtering cattle (among rulers) or goats (among peasants), or perhaps by purchase in a market.[3] Meat was a regular item in the diet of chiefs but rarely on the menu of peasants. Fish was eaten by rulers and shore-dwelling peasants but was not a regular item of inland peasant diet (Roscoe 1966: 420, 438–39).

Women did the horticulture, cooking, basket and mat weaving, wood and water gathering, vegetable salt making, and thatch cutting. By and large they worked individually, mainly as food providers for their marital households. Only in planting and winnowing simsim, a minor crop, did women of several households combine on an informal basis. Gardening was extremely productive. "It was said, with some, but not very much exaggeration, that one old woman could feed ten men" (Wrigley 1964: 18). However, this estimate ignores the cooking and wood and water carrying, which were time-consuming parts of feeding.

Men's contributions to subsistence—hunting, fishing, stock tending, and beer brewing—were secondary regarding both dietary contributions and the portion of men's time they consumed. Unlike women's work, the men of a village most often worked as a task group. Peasants had few animals, perhaps a cow, and a few goats or sheep. Herding was done mainly by boys of a village who herded their families' stock together. Fishing was often a full-time collective specialization of men in lakeshore villages. Hunting of small game was done by anywhere from three to a dozen men in the form of a collective net hunt. Beer brewing sometimes involved cooperation of men from several households (Kagwa 1934: 94; Mair 1934: 115, 122–24; Roscoe 1966: 5, 391, 394, 415, 422, 449). Men were the main craft workers, making barkcloth, dressing skins, and building houses. Barkcloth, important for clothing and for taxes, was manufactured either by men of two households working together (Roscoe 1966: 405) or by the men of a village working together as a team (Nsimbi 1956: 27). Houses were rebuilt about every three years. Here all men of the village worked collectively (Ibid.).

Craft specialists included blacksmiths, woodworkers, ivory workers, and potters. They too were men and worked cooperatively (Ibid.). The wives of these craftsmen were agriculturalists. Some craftsmen were employed by the king or chiefs and supplied them with free wares, but they also sold to peasants. Other craftsmen apparently sold only to peasants. Most men were not full-time craft specialists, however.

Midwifery was a woman's craft. It was organized on a clan basis, with each clan or subdivision having its own practitioners who were paid for their services (Roscoe 1966: 57).

If peasant women's principal labor was in feeding their families, peasant men were largely occupied in service to the ruling class, as builders and soldiers and producers of barkcloth, a major tax item. Peasants paid one barkcloth for every five trees planted. It was common for a peasant to have about two hundred trees, hence a tax of forty barkcloths per household. It took about two days to manufacture a cloth or eighty labor days to pay this tax (Wrigley 1964: 17; Mair 1934: 133). Building and roadwork were still more time-consuming. Building houses, halls, temples, and enclosures for the king and chiefs probably took at least as much time as warfare. Kings frequently moved their palaces, temporarily for directing warfare, consulting oracles, or putting down rebellions. Peasants did all this building. The so-called permanent capitals of the king were often moved also: Mutesa, for example, moved ten times during his reign (Fallers 1964: 84). Houses in Buganda could last up to four years, but they often burned before that. With 450 important buildings, plus hundreds of smaller structures in the royal enclosure alone, several buildings were under construction or repair at any given time. There was a large, constant supply of labor of at least a thousand men. It took about two hundred workers two months to build one of the large houses. Building was rotated evenly among the population; the labor time involved per call-up was between two and six months. Peasants on the job supplied their own food. Other construction was organized in the same way for chiefs and the temple for the dead king's jawbone, which lasted fourteen to sixteen months (Roscoe 1966: 303; Mair 1934: 132, 196). Roadwork may (Fallers 1964: 83–84) or may not (Roscoe 1966: 243) have been time-consuming, but it also involved all men. Miscellaneous tasks such as hunting lions and leopards, carrying beer, and supplying pottery and other items to the king's or chief's capital rounded out the labor required of a peasant man. Speke described sixteen hundred men involved in carrying firewood to the royal enclosure (1937: 338). "*Bakopi* [peasant] men probably contributed as much to the support of the non-productive superstructure as they did to their own households" (Fallers 1964: 83).

Just as peasant wives produced and prepared the staple vegetable foods, so too did wives of the ruling class—though not all such wives did so. Although almost all the information on ruling-class households pertains to that of the king, those of important chiefs were organized in a similar manner (Roscoe 1966: 8–10, 246). The population of the Buganda capital was estimated at tens of thousands in the latter half of the nineteenth century (Fallers 1964: 85). It contained the households of the king, his retainers, his important chiefs and their retainers, as well as visitors. These were all provisioned with vegetable food and beer by wives and female domestic servants. Stanley (1878, vol. 1: 393) described the capital as "a hill covered with tall conical huts, whose tops peep out above the foliage of plantains and bananas." Speke described essentially the same scene in 1861 (1937: 274, 294, 301). The royal food producing establishment was of considerable size. Gardens of the kings' wives were worked mainly by their servants if they were ranking wives (Roscoe 1966: 8–10; Kagwa 1934: 75). Kagwa's data allow an estimate of the size of the domestic labor force commanded by the king (Kagwa 1934: 37–55):

King	Named Wives	Other Wives	Maid Servants
Djundju	4	200	400
Semakokiro	13	1,500	7,000
Kamanya	37	1,000	9,963
Suna II	148	2,000	18,000
Mutesa	82	1,000	17,000

In summary, the ruling class did no productive labor. Instead it commanded goods and services from peasant men organized as production teams, as well as the persons and labor of nonruling-class women as wives (non-ranking) and servants. Wives drawn from ruling class families seem to have done no work themselves.

GENDER AND CLASS RELATIONS OF PRODUCTION

Rulers and peasants had diametrically opposed relations of production. The former owned the land and the bulk of the livestock, especially cattle. They determined peasants' land allotments, could evict peasants at will, and could seize their livestock (Mair 1934: 155–56). Peasants obtained access to land by entering into clientage relations in which they provided labor and tax to their patron. Peasant men and women had very different relations to the means of production. Only men's work fulfilled clientage obligations, only men were clients, and thus only men had direct access to land. Women obtained access to land and houses mainly as a wife through her husband and secondarily through any other man who might be her guardian. Women could not inherit land or houses. In the eyes of the Buganda state, women were wives, dependents of men, and men were clients. Because the state effectively controlled channels of decison making, dispute settlement, ritual life, and institutionalized social activities, it could enforce wifely dependency. Women were effectively excluded from direct involvement in political and economic processes.

An examination of how clanship and kinship reinforced clientship also reveals the way in which kinship simultaneously reinforced the differences between men's and women's relations of production. Land was plentiful, and men could easily acquire it by inheritance or clientage. Baganda moved frequently and preferred living in a village where they had clansmen. From whom and where a man got land depended upon his choice of a patron. Children were members of their father's clan. Clans were large, dispersed groups divided into branches and lineages, which themselves were dispersed. Children were brought up in the household of a clansperson rather than in their natal household. Boys developed closer relations as they grew older with a particular clansman, who might or might not be an official, or with an unrelated official. This person became his patron, often paying his bridewealth. The client acquired land from the patron or opened up new land in his patron's village (Mair 1934: 59–61; Southwold 1965: 98–99; Kiwanuka 1972: 118–19). For some peasants kinship linked them to political superiors in a way that undercut clan unity.

Kinship also operated among peasants to build up horizontal ties among the men of a lineage in the face of the vertical ties of kin-based clientage. Each married person had an heir who was a clansperson of the same sex and who acted as the social equivalent of the deceased on ritual occasions. In the case of a peasant, heirship was not particularly remunerative, as it was in the case of a chief. Prior to Mutesa's reign, succession passed to a man's brother, his brother's son, or to his paternal first cousin, emphasizing the interfamily links within the lineage over individual family lines. Baganda gave this as their reason for fraternal succession (Mair 1934: 211–20; Roscoe 1966: 121–26; Southwold 1968, 1965: 97–103). But these horizontal productive relations were among men of the lineage. Sisters and daughters could not inherit land or houses, and wives inherited nothing from their husbands. Moreover wives could not dispose of land, though peasant men could allocate use rights to some of their land to others and in return could expect gifts and service from their clients (Mair 1934: 96, 155–56).

Because they lacked productive estates, clans were not corporate groups. For peasant women, there was therefore no sisterhood. It was peasant men individually who obtained access to productive means not as brothers but by entering into clientage relations of production with a patron. Clans, or lineages within them, gained hereditary access to political office by the clientage and appointment of individual members by the king. Peasant women could not enter clientage relations of production.

The productive relations of ruling-class women differed from those of peasant women. While certain clans or lineages within them acquired access to political office (and productive means) by the clientage of an individual male in the lineage to the king, these offices were largely hereditary in practice. This meant that the lineages of ruling officials had productive estates and thus a basis for sisterhood. Yet ruling-class women shared with peasant women an exclusion from clientage relations; thus they could not inherit any property of chiefship, either as wife or sister.

The difference between a wife (woman) and a client (man) were drawn sharply in ideology and law. Women, regardless of class, were assigned a male guardian (generally a married brother, followed by her husband upon marriage) who controlled and was responsible for her behavior legally and informally (Roscoe 1966: 12, 55, 74, 232, 264; Mair 1934: 41, 220; Richards 1966: 93–94; Mukasa 1946: 139). The political life of the state, its bureaucracy, councils, and courts for the settlement of disputes were all-male spheres, composed of patrons and clients. The same was true concerning clan courts and officials. These were concerned mainly with matters of inheritance and intraclan affairs. They articulated with the state sphere in that the king, himself clanless, was head of all clans (Ibid.).

The institution of blood brotherhood, while not in the pattern of clientage or in the state control, was an important relationship among men. It may have rested on men's involvement in trading ventures. Men generally had one or several blood brothers of different clans with whom the strongest bonds of mutual assistance obtained; they were like clansmen, only more so. Brotherhood bonds transcended clan and national loyalties and were guarantees of hospitality and safe conduct away from home (Roscoe 1966: 19; Mair 1934: 70–73). Women were excluded from such ties because they were wards of men and not responsible for their actions.

The single exception to women as wives and wards was the king's mother and sister, both officials. In this respect Buganda seems to have shared in the widespread African pattern of shared rule among a brother, sister, and their mother (Lebeuf: 1971: 99–107). Southwold (1965: 91) claims that the powers of the queen sister and mother were "much inferior to that of the king, though the queen mother often had considerable influence over her son." It is difficult to tell to what extent their weakness is an artifact of general sexist blindness to mothers and sisters as power holders and to what extent the tripartite sharing of royal power was undermined in Buganda. Given the destruction of corporate kinship in Buganda, the latter may be accurate. Both women had estates and courts (male administered) and commanded labor and tax, but there is no indication of their authority in national political economy (Roscoe 1966: 348; Mair 1934: 178).

Wifehood, as women's basic relation to productive means, shaped women's social and sexual lives just as clientship shaped men's. Within the general pattern of wifely subordination to husbands, the restrictions on wives of rulers were somewhat heightened.

Women's sexuality and reproductive powers were central aspects of their productive relations and directly shaped their movements and behavior. Childless women were despised and often badly treated. During pregnancy sex relations were prohibited, and women were ideally semisecluded, particularly from male contact. Ruling-class wives were more isolated than peasant women. The king's wives, isolated in the house of the midwife, were referred to as "being a prisoner." Chiefs' wives were cared for by an old woman of the chief's clan (Roscoe 1966: 49–50, 53, 57). Many common foods were also prohibited. Failure to observe these prohibitions could sicken or kill the child or mother. Any defects in the baby were attributed to disregard of the rules of pregnancy or postpartum behavior by the mother. Women were also barred from sexual relations for the three-year nursing period. In ruling-class households this involved separation from the husband; however, a king's favorites could resume sex immediately by having a peasant woman nurse the child. This decision, however, was the king's, not the wife's (Mair 1934: 39–41, 55; Roscoe 1966: 49–55, 95, 101; Johnston 1904: 640). Menstruation also demanded a woman's sexual abstinence, and in ruling-class households, wives could have no contact with their husbands.

Sexuality in general and that of women in particular was separated from male and state forces of production. Women were not allowed any contact with male craft production, hunting, fishing, and care of cattle. Baganda believed that women's presence (but not that of young girls) or contact with the equipment would spoil these ventures. In addition, men engaged in or preparing for these pursuits—as well as for warfare—could not have sexual relations. No such restrictions applied to women's work (Mair 1934: 121; Roscoe 1966: chapter 11). Women were associated with sex and reproduction, men with collective production and national political economy. This dualization denied women's importance in production and deemphasized men's role in reproduction. Buganda ideology posed an antagonism between sexuality and male productive forces. This seems to be a sexual phrasing of a class contradiction. That is, peasant men worked largely for the ruling class, while peasant women worked largely for their own class. Tension surrounding female sexuality was also tension surrounding claims on labor and produce.

Another association of sexuality with private and household life pitted it against an asexual national political economy, which also distorted the class terms of conflict. Forms of socializing for men were centered on state-clientage channels. Peasant men spent much time eating and drinking at their chief's households; chiefs' guests were male. Men and women generally ate separately. Women were confined to the household without a guardian's permission to go visiting. Wives of the rulers lived in guarded, restricted-access compounds, and royal wives needed an escort to go visiting. Thus wives, especially of the ruling class, were physically restricted to the household, while peasant and ruling-class men were encouraged to center their social and economic lives with other clients in attendance on a patron.

Husbands and wives were no more equal than patron and client, household and state. The state enforced a double sexual standard for husbands and wives. Extramarital sex was approved for men, provided a husband kept his wife informed. It was not approved for wives. Courts fined women's lovers and meted out death and mutilation to women offenders. Husbands who killed their wives for extramarital affairs were within their rights. A wife's clan could claim compensation only by proving she was innocent. Superimposed on the sexual double standard was a class double standard. Peasant or slave men caught in sexual affairs with wives of ruling-class men were almost always killed, but a peasant man had no legal recourse against a ruling-class man who had an affair with his wife. We do not know what the risks were to a peasant woman for rejecting a chief. The only women allowed sexual affairs were princesses, sisters and daughters of the king. However, they could not marry, and any children born to them were killed. Death was the penalty for marriage and children (Roscoe 1966: 85, 101–02, 187, 232, 261, 263; Mair 1934: 97; Johnston 1904: 689). Regardless of class, wives were subordinate to the authority of husbands. They were expected to be submissive, to take beatings, and not to discuss these or their marital fights with others. A husband had the right to put his wife in the stocks for disobedience and to kill her (as he did a slave) without suffering any consequences. A woman's revenge for mistreatment was to kill herself and her husband by burning down the hut during the night (Roscoe 1966: 20, 23; Mair 1934: 97).

Sisterhood existed only in a somewhat perverse form with respect to state enforcement. Thus clan membership distinguished free men and women from slaves, who were basically kinless people. However, sisters were perennial clan juniors under the protection and authority of a brother or husband. For a married woman, her clan represented a weak check on the authority of her husband; however, the way in which the state enforced the clan ties of a married sister were of no help to the woman. If a woman were killed for adultery by her husband and subsequently found to have been innocent, her clan could demand a fine from the husband. Likewise, if a woman died in childbirth, her clan could fine the husband. In the Buganda legal system, women were wards and thus could not be wronged in their own right; only their clan or their husband could be wronged and thus seek compensation. This notion was not confined to the courts. A woman needed to have her brother (and clan) return her bridewealth for her to divorce her husband, but brothers generally acted to preserve the marriage. A husband's relation with his wife's brother was to cultivate an ally in returning a wayward wife. In marriage as well, brothers had veto power over sisters' choices (Mair 1934: 92–98; Roscoe 1966: 87–88; Johnston 1904: 687).

As marriage became less important than clientage, particularly among nonruling-class men, in generating political and economic ties, sisterhood was further undercut. In this context premarital sexual activity and pregnancy, while frowned upon for girls (and for which their partners were punished), was of little consequence for her future marriage chances (Roscoe 1966: 79, 263). Clan or lineage social relations among peasants did not hinge on control over their daughters' sexuality, as it did for example, among Lovedu.[4] The single exception to this leniency was that girls who had premarital pregnancies could not be married to chiefs. Such marriages allied a girl's family to a political and economic patron (unlike other marriages), and hence her behavior implicated them.

While the Buganda state and the subordinate clan channels clearly defined women primarily as wives and secondarily as daughters, there were two areas in which a shadow of sisterhood persisted: among the ruling class and among peasants in informal contexts. The former was stronger.

Among the ruling class, the queen mother and the king's sister wielded political and economic authority. Other sisters of the ruling and prior kings had no power but were allowed to take lovers and move about freely, and they were economically provided for from royal estates. No royal sisters were allowed to rear children or marry. In the royal family, children took the clan of their mother, the wife of the king. Royal wives, particularly ranking ones, were chosen largely from a few ruling families who comprised a ruling circle over the centuries of the kingdom.

> . . . clans struggled to give women to the kings so that their daughters might give birth to the next successor. Even when a royal wife did not give birth to the next successor, she might become one of the favourite wives, in which case her family and clan would have royal gifts showered upon them. Wives also did their best to promote the fortune of their families. They would, for example, bring with them their brothers, sisters or other relatives and introduce them to the king. [Kiwanuka 1972: 122–23]

Kingship was the organizing principle that regulated intraclass relations among ruling families. Women of these families were principally wives and daughters, links among men, but they were also sisters in that their class as a whole possessed a corporate estate to which they had certain rights, the most obvious of which was to be maintained by the goods and services of that estate. Thus, the ranking wives of the king, together with their daughters, were assigned servants and the produce from particular estates (Roscoe 1966: 189).[5] In addition, the king's sisters shared the sexual freedoms of ruling-class men, but these were clearly incompatible with wifehood. Royal and chiefly wives were tightly controlled and severely punished for extramarital affairs.

The only context in which nonruling women seemed to exert authority was in nonstate channels. A group of old women in the village often adjudicated marital disputes, though they lacked formal sanctions and were not recognized by the legal system. Private beer feasts and socializing, unlike that associated with patrons, often involved women as well as men (Nsimbi 1956: 30). Unfortunately it is difficult to tell whether any of this is associated with women's relations to their clans or lineages. Overall it does appear that the Buganda state all but obliterated both corporate kin groups and sisterhood in all save the ruling class. In the case of women, the agricultural forces of production reinforced wifely relations of production to give women a sole and essential role: that of wifely ward.

NOTES

1. Kiwanuka (1972: 145–46) presents a convincing case that Mutesa's army corps armed with rifles was more a display to impress foreigners than an effective fighting force.

2. Fallers, along with others, denies that Buganda was a class society on the grounds that there were conflicts among rulers stemming from patronage ties and that clan loyalties cut across class lines (1964: 177). There is no evidence that clan loyalties cut across class lines. Moreover, there are no class societies that have managed to eliminate intra-class conflict. Clan loyalty meant simply that chiefs favored clansmen in choosing retainers and clients. Rulers needed retainers and clients, and clansmen were a likely source. Clans served class rather than being in conflict with it. The shared economic and political interests of the ruling class prescribed the limits of and channels for intraclass competition. They required the civil and military labor of peasants for their maintenance and distributed the fruits of this labor in such a manner as to insure the continuing flow of labor and goods. Their high standard of living and their prerogatives were dependent in part upon success in this area and in part on their superior organization of armed force.

3. The question of markets in nineteenth century Buganda is unclear. Mair (1934: 130–31) claimed that markets were introduced by Mutesa shortly prior to European colonialism. She and Kiwanuka (1972: 151) speak of the regional trade in foods and craft items in which Baganda participated and in which blood brotherhood played an important part. In the nineteenth century, Buganda contained a large concentration of resident Arab traders (Unomah and Webster 1976; Tosh 1970; Alpers 1968; Bennett 1968). While Mair claims that women did not trade in the markets, there is no information on market organization, on who supplied them, and on the links between men who went on trading expeditions and market sellers.

4. But premarital leniency contrasted sharply with strict control in Buganda over wives' sexual activities. Here too Baganda contrasted with Lovedu, reinforcing the analysis of wifely relations of production in Buganda and sisterly relations of production in Lovedu.

5. After Semakokiro, sons were killed or exiled for the most part.

Chapter 9

SISTERS AND RULERS
IN WEST AFRICA

In Buganda class relations of production buttressed productive forces that separated underclass women from each other in their work and joined underclass men together as clients of rulers in their work. Productive forces reinforced wifely relations of production, leaving no basis for sisterly relations or the prerogatives sustained by them. Women's work was very different in West Africa. Through much of the area, trading was women's central work, requiring some form of collective organization in travel, setting prices, and buying. While long-distance trade has a long history in West Africa, women's trade was usually within a fairly circumscribed area and tended to center on buying and selling of daily needs. Most goods were locally produced, but market women also retailed goods brought from afar. Women's marketing integrated a regional subsistence economy by making available a wider variety of goods than was produced in any one area. In one sense cultivation, fishing, and craft work were production for exchange, but in a more fundamental sense, the ultimate goal of such production in West Africa was household consumption. And women's trading activities too had household provisioning as their end.

Within this broad pattern of collective organization for women's trading, there were many differences in productive relations across precolonial West Africa. Women were central to internal marketing systems in class and nonclass societies alike; they traded in places where they did and did not also farm; they traded in places where they did and did not inherit land.[1] In all of these places, the purchase and sale of goods was an integral aspect of household maintenance.

Women traders and their associations did not have the same range of responsibilities everywhere, nor did they articulate with channels of power and authority in the same way. Differences within West Africa in the power and autonomy of women and women's groups seem to stem from different relations of production, specifically the relative power of class and corporate kin groups over the means of production. Where corporate kin group control over productive means was strong, as it was in the city of Onitsha on the Niger River, sisterly relations of production were reinforced by the productive forces associated with trading. Here associations of wives and of sisters held a wide range of social responsibility, power, and authority, and they protected sisterly personal autonomy even in wifely relations. Heightened ruling-class control over productive means led to subversion and shrinking of sisterly relations in Dahomey. Dahomean productive relations were in contradiction to the productive forces of women's trading. As long as women were responsible for internal distribution, preparation, and sale of basic foods, they sustained some form of women's collectivity which was in some aspects contradictory to class relations of production. Powerful ruling classes sought to limit women's collective responsibilities to the conduct of market relations and mutual economic assistance and to substitute themselves or their agents as decision makers in most nonmarket spheres of women's lives, transforming women's associations from defenders of sisterly relations in their sexual, political, and economic aspects (as in Onitsha) into mutual aid and marketing associations (as in Dahomey).

I see the transformation of women's associations as related to and part of the process by which ruling classes gained control over the means of production at the expense of patrilineal kin corporations—patrilineal with respect to control over land. The latter lost land to private-, slave-, and client-worked estates of the ruling class or had their importance as producers undermined by the development of such estates.

It bears repeating that a proper demonstration of this hypothesis would entail one or several cases in which historical transformation in productive relations were documented together with the predicted transformations in women's associations. It is possible to document more or less successful attempts by ruling classes to undermine lineage control of productive means in several West African states. I have not, however, been able to uncover parallel historical depth on women's associations or on women's internal marketing participation.

However, these thoughts about class and sex were generated by the contrast between Igbo and Dahomean women and can be illustrated by a discussion of these contrasts. Comparing productive relations and women's organizations for particular points in the precolonial histories of Onitsha and Dahomey shows significant differences in the degree of ruling-class control over productive means and corresponding differences in the scope of authority wielded by women's groups. Synchronic contrast between Onitsha and Dahomey suggests that strong women's groups coexisted with weak or protoruling classes. While I will document a history of ruling class attempts in Dahomey (not always successful) to usurp lineage control over their productive means, a parallel usurping process with respect to women's organizations needs to be demonstrated to argue the reverse: that strong ruling classes weaken what had been stronger women's groups. Basically I am comparing peoples with similar productive forces but different productive relations to generate a hypothesis about evolutionary processes.

The first section deals with the city of Onitsha, an Igbo community on the Niger River. Onitsha was not really a class society in that corporate lineages held firm control over productive means. The description of nineteenth-century Onitsha provides a very clear case of productive forces reinforcing productive relations to underwrite a full elaboration of sisterhood and brotherhood at a greater level of stratification, or wealth inequality, than is usually thought to be associated with sexual equality. The second section focuses on Dahomey, a state with strong ruling-class control over productive means. Here women's associations, stemming from women's marketing activities, were able to maintain some of the elements of sisterly relations, particularly women's abilities to avoid the subordination of wifehood. Even more significantly, but tentatively, women's market-based associations organized from below suggest germs of a recreated sisterhood under conditions of severely weakened corporate groups.

Thus the evolutionary progression of this chapter is to see ruling classes destroying corporate kin groups and hence sisterly relations as they become strong by seizing more control over productive means. For women of the underclasses, who are the center of this analysis, this meant reduction to wifely subordination. But in precolonial West Africa heightened ruling-class control of productive means also heightened women's importance as internal marketers and hence heightened the importance of their productive collectivities. Under these circumstances, there was a second strand to an evolutionary progression in women's efforts to regenerate sisterly relations in new forms. Instead of stemming from corporations of brothers and sisters, sisterhood in class relations of production came from nonkin work organizations. These in turn partly sustained the economic and personal autonomy of wives vis-à-vis their husbands.

The histories of Onitsha and Dahomey, or at least of their ruling groups, have a common source in the ancient Yoruba and Edo kingdoms of present-day western Nigeria (Akinjogbin 1967; Nzimiro 1972; Forde and Jones 1950). Akinjogbin has described the shared social order of the Yoruba and the Aja, the ethnic group from which the Dahomey rulers developed, and the continued influence Oyo maintained over Dahomey. Onitsha was founded in the sixteenth century by refugees from Benin (Henderson 1972: 76–82).

ONITSHA

The Igbo town of Onitsha was located at a crossroads of the Anambra and the Niger rivers, where the uplands ecological zones on both sides of the Niger joined the riverain region (Henderson 1972: 65–75; Ukwu 1969: 117–18). Its population in 1860, shortly after the beginning of European penetration, was sixteen thousand (Meek 1937: 14). The Niger River provided the main trade route. Riverain trade networks involved in exchanges of salt and fish for uplands vegetable products and upriver products have a long history. The European demand for slaves brought slave trading and raiding up the Niger in the sixteenth century. While Igbo people were the principal victims, they were also engaged in the trade (Ibid.: 5–8; Jones 1963). In general, European goods were traded upriver, while slaves, ivory, and livestock from Igala and palm oil and woven cloth from the uplands were traded downriver. It was in this milieu of an expanding slave trade along the river that Onitsha developed as a unified town. From its early days, it was raided for captives and was engaged in the riverain slave trade (Henderson 1972: 91–93).

The sandbar in the Niger opposite Onitsha was a meeting point for traders from Igala, the major kingdom upriver, and Aboh, downriver at the entrance to the delta. Both kingdoms maintained commercial and kinship links to towns along the rivers and through these with upland villages. Political control beyond the town was unstable, however, and the complex web of riverain trade and kinship alliances often broke down, erupting in warfare. The area around Onitsha was particularly turbulent as the city states of Igala or Aboh sought control at various periods. In the nineteenth century with the development of the Aro network to the east as a third areal power, it became even more so. Prior to European penetration, Onitsha was not a center of political or economic power in the riverain milieu and did not seek such control over a hinterland. Indeed its expansion took place away from the river, into the higher ground (Henderson 1972: 65–75, 91–93, 499–502; Meek 1937: 13).

It is not known what, if any, effect the nineteenth-century transition in European demand from slaves to palm oil had on the internal organization of Onitsha. Slaves continued to be sold in the river market as late as 1881 (Mockler-Ferryman 1892: 20–23). In 1857 the first missionaries, trading stations, and river steamers were established at Onitsha (Nzimiro 1972: 9–10; Anene 1966: 39, 41). The traders initially paid subsidies to kings and chiefs for the privilege of settlement; however, before long traders, backed up by the British navy, established their hegemony, sacking and razing the town to enforce their terms of trade (Meek 1937: 13–15; Henderson 1972: 91–93; Ukwu 1969: 139–41).

MODE OF PRODUCTION IN HISTORY

Prior to the sixteenth century, the site and area around Onitsha was occupied by riverain Igbo and by uplands Igbo, both organized in corporate descent groups. The institution of kingship was developed sometime in the sixteenth century by migrants from west of the Niger and from Benin and later by refugees from wars between Benin and Igala. They settled in several descent groups at Onitsha, expropriated land from the original occupants, and established an ideology of kingship modeled on Benin's as a unifying principle. The migrants became the royal lines or those with claim to kingship, and over time came almost to predominate numerically over commoners, or lineages lacking such claim (Forde and Jones 1950: 45–51; Basden 1966: 121–22; Meek 1937: 11–13; Henderson 1972: 76–95; Nzimiro 1972: 7–9, 41–42).

Henderson's analysis suggests that throughout its history, Onitsha remained fundamentally a confederation of corporate descent groups of diverse origin, each of which was internally stratified and all of which were integrated by the institution of kingship and chiefship (Henderson 1972: 76, 182–92, 511–25). Ideologically Onitsha people saw themselves as "both stratified and segmentary" (Ibid.: 105). Patrilineages as corporate bodies owned farmland, home sites, trees, and shrines. Lineages were not equal either in size or in land holdings. There were mechanisms for the transfer of land to take place, apparently without open conflict. Thus a man of a large lineage, with many single sons, daughters, husbands, slaves, and agemates to help him farm, might seek additional land from his maternal kin or his wife's kin. Small lineages, those with few members, might be pressured to lease out portions of their land in this manner. Within a lineage, too, land was distributed unequally, based on each male member's command over labor power; however, all lineage members had rights to the land. "The essential definition of the status of a freeman is given by his relationship with a particular land" (Ibid.: 182–83). The lineage priest was responsible for allocating plots each year and for acting as general steward of the group's property. Lineage members collectively cultivated a plot for him.

Somewhat separate from the corporate descent group was the town's political authority. Authority rested with a class of senior chiefs, ostensibly officials chosen by the king for their wealth, influence, and success in warfare. Although they were not viewed as lineage representatives, they were based in the component lineage villages of Onitsha. They played a prominent role in warfare and slave trading and are described as the elite of the town (Ibid.: 315–20, 516–17; Nzimiro 1972: 44–46, 135–36).

Information about Onitsha's organization of warfare and trade, particularly the slave trade, is almost nonexistent. It does seem that external warfare and trade were the foundation of chiefly wealth and authority (Nzimiro 1972: 7), while land and production rested firmly in lineage control. Chiefs appear to have had much in common with Melanesian big men, and indeed Meek makes the comparison explicit (1937: 111, 184n). Their basis of wealth and influence seems to have been in organizing external relations in warfare and trade rather than in control over the means of production. Intercommunity trade in general, and the slave trade in particular, were not monopolized or organized on more than a personal level. Trade up and down the river was heavily dependent on kin ties and trade partners for hospitality and safe conduct. Influential people were sought out as partners, and chiefs were guarantors of outsiders' safety (Ukwu 1969: 131–32; Henderson 1972: 334). The slave trade in Onitsha was not conducted in the market but in the houses of chiefs, other influential men, and influential women traders. Chiefly ties of safe conduct gave them, their wives, and their lineage daughters a prominent role in the trade. "It is said that chiefs traditionally particpated directly in the inter-community slave trade of Onitsha, a trade whose extent may have caused the road eastward from Onitsha to be called by some peoples the 'road of slaves' " (Ibid.).

The information available suggests that Onitsha was more proto-state than state or class society, particularly with regard to lineage control over land. But it also suggests that the institution of kingship in the context of the slave trade, combined with Onitsha's location at a trade crossroads, may have underwritten a more elaborate organization among chiefly power holders than existed among nonriverain Igbo. That is, Benin influence elaborated along the Niger fit with the elaboration of the slave trade.

SISTERS OVER WIVES

By the latter nineteenth century, the city of Onitsha was made up of a number of localized and internally ranked corporate patrilineages whose estates in productive property—gardens, farmland, trees—together with shrines and house sites comprised the major wealth of the city (Ibid.: 183). For men the major productive forces were the organized brothers of a lineage who worked the land together. The ideal was to divide lineage farmland into seven strips and to farm one strip each year, with each man cultivating his own portion. The senior lineage priest and other priests had somewhat more land. All brothers cooperated in clearing the senior priest's land and in building a lineage yam barn in which each man had a section (Ibid.: 188–89). Farming was men's principal work, and the men of a lineage constituted a productive team for much of their work. Women's central work was trading, with the wife and resident daughters of one or a group of localized lineages trading together. Trading involved women's organized activity at the city level as well. Women also grew a significant amount of food in gardens near their houses. Trade here was a productive activity (as opposed an exchange activity) because it stems from lineage or individual production and flows back to household consumption in a direct way. Women sold the crops they and their husbands grew, and bought goods, produced locally and beyond, for their direct consumption. Look at in this way, women's trading organization was a production team for the central part of a process by which women transformed what they and others in town grew into what they and the rest of the town consumed.

Onitsha ideology about men's and women's work was that they were sharply separated. Ideally houseland and farmland were kept spatially separate because the yam spirit, resident of farms, disliked women's presence. Houseland, the province of women and children, contained intensively cultivated (by women) gardens of banana, taro, and vegetables. In reality the dichotomy was not quite so rigid. Men cultivated tree crops on houseland, and women sometimes worked on farmland and claimed part of the cotton grown there (Ibid.: 159–60). In Onitsha, then, the productive forces were such that men and women each constituted a separate single-sex productive team.

Okonjo (1976) has characterized precolonial Igbo political organization generally as a dual-sex political system in which power was shared between separate and parallel hierarchies of men and women within the lineage and the city, together with its component villages. In Onitsha, as among Igbo elsewhere (Green 1964), the basis for such organization rested in both sexes' relations to corporately owned means of production, as brothers and sisters (or adult daughters). Thus an Onitsha patrilineage was made up of its brothers and sisters, each ranked by seniority, sharing political and economic decision making with respect to the lineage estate and exerting authority over wives married into the lineage. The political organization of the city involved parallel hierarchies representing senior men and women of each lineage or the senior lineages of each of the component villages of Onitsha. Wifehood also was a productive relationship to the husband's corporate lineage. Wives of a patrilineage were collectively subordinate to its brothers and sisters. Wives' relations to each other regarding economic authority and political decision making were set by their relationship to their husband—specifically by their order of marriage—and by their husband's seniority among his lineage brothers.

These relations of production, which joined brothers and sisters of a lineage together in parallel interdependent hierarchies of decision making, were central to lineage and city political economy. The proverb, "On the day of the sibling, one's lover departs," refers to the primacy of the brother-sister tie in Onitsha. Brothers were expected to look out for their sister's welfare and to assist them in trading ventures. Often they helped their sisters repay their bridewealth, leave their husbands, and return home. Villages frequently had a core of resident daughters trading from their marital lineages. At least in colonial times, if not earlier, daughters were the main organizers of village trade (Henderson 1972: 234–35). Sisters were obligated to feed and care for their brothers and to pay homage to the senior brother. Sisters were the only ones who could purify a brother's house. Senior sisters were important in settling disputes between lineage segments, as well as in sharing authority over brothers' wives and punishing those offending either a brother or sister. Head daughters were important as ritual figures in much the same way senior sons were as lineage priests. Head daughters were responsible for cleansing children, cleansing new wives and incorporating them into the husband's village, purifying the houses of all lineage wives, and washing the dead of the lineage. "Remarkably, both male and female members share control of the spiritual authority that underlies their interdependence, which is irrevocable and all-embracing. The basic role structure is linked to the statuses of 'senior sons' and 'senior daughters' " (Ibid.: 156). Lineage daughters were organized in a parallel and separate hierarchy to lineage sons. The head daughter was parallel to the senior lineage priest and was his senior sister. Daughters mediated conflicts between priests and others of the lineage. Just as the senior priest was given homage gifts by lineage brothers, so too was the senior daughter given such gifts from lineage sisters (Ibid.: 40–41, 153–56, 206).[2] Henderson (Ibid.: 432) gives an example of the strength of the daughter's organization. At a funeral ceremony, one group of daughters demanded that their segment's head daughter be given ritual seniority equal to that of the lineage's senior head daughter. When they were refused, they boycotted the funeral and established an autonomous lineage segment. Lineage sisters also frequently retained direct control over a portion of the lineage estate. When a woman married, the gifts given to her by her family sometimes included farmland or rights to economic trees (Ibid.: 205).

A wife's subordinate relationship to her husband and his lineage was ideologically in sharp contrast to sisterly equality in her own. All members of the husband's lineage, including its brothers and sisters, called the woman *wife*. The term *husband* connoted mastery when used in a nonkinship context, while that of *wife* implied obedience and service. Wives were expected to work for their husbands' mothers and could be punished by the mother-in-law as well as by the husband's brothers and sisters (Ibid.: 215–16). But this subordination was in some ways undercut by wives' organization as simultaneously a productive collectivity and a lineage and local political collectivity.

The forces of production centering on trading reinforced a woman's sisterly relations and undercut those of wife, ameliorating the contrast in role expectations in an egalitarian direction. This can be seen in the women's organizations in Onitsha, as well as in a woman's motherhood relationship to her husband's lineage. Co-wives were expected to move together in getting firewood and water, as well as in trading. The women of a village also were formed into a group under the authority of a lineage daughter. Although they were under a woman of the husband's lineage, wives were ranked, with the senior wife of the lineage convening the group. Wives' groups were concerned with village markets, cooking for village ceremonies and fining husbands for mistreatment of wives. Their main activity was funerary dancing, the chief occasion for individual public display by women (Ibid.: 217–18). The organization "Women of Onitsha" included all past and currently married women of the town and was headed by the *Omu* (mother) and her council. As such it appears to have included both wives and daughters.[3] This organization was responsible for cleansing the city of evil, making various protective and curative ceremonies on behalf of the town's welfare, and arranging market affairs. Their place of convocation was the great waterside market and lowland square. Market squares in general were deemed women's places in Onitsha. It was sisterly rather than wifely relations of production that determined a woman's place in the Women of Onitsha, though here too the contrast was mitigated. Thus the *Omu* was head daughter of her lineage segment of the royal clan, and the councillors were also head daughters of their own lineages. All traders gave her market tribute. The *Omu* and her council were the women's parallel to the king and male chiefs (Ibid.: 375–76, 309–14). The wealthiest and most senior families of the city seem to have been intermarried so that senior men and women of powerful lineages also held the highest town offices. This appears most clearly in Henderson's discussion of the slave trade, apparently a significant source of wealth. This trade was pursued largely outside the marketplaces in the houses of chiefs, wealthy men, and major women traders. The latter were often wives and sisters of chiefs, and chiefs were in a good position to underwrite sisters' and wives' success in slave trading since they were more able to offer the protection and security the trade demanded (Ibid.: 313). A large part of the Onitsha population were slaves and were employed in farming, fishing, and warfare (Nzimiro 1972: 25). We know that chiefs had more land than the average person (Hendrson 1972: 485), but there is no direct evidence that they had more slaves.

Motherhood also mediated the sister-wife contrast, but within the context of a husband's lineage. When women requested help from their own gods, it was for children and wealth "in that order" (Ibid.: 231). Bearing children for a husband's lineage was politically and economically, as well as emotionally, important for a woman, even though it was seen to be in contradiction to trading; "when a woman gets wealth, children run away," was a favorite proverb (Ibid.). Motherhood established a new and less subordinate relationship to her husband's lineage. Upon bearing children, especially a boy, a wife was referred to as "mother of [child's name]." This marked changes in the relationships to her husband's lineage, which "do not eliminate, but tend to overshadow, her designation [that is, her productive relationship] as a wife" (Ibid.: 219). Symbolically, it was expressed in a link with the ancestors of the husband's lineage—an eligibility to be buried on her son's residential land and to be brought into that lineage's ancestor system. As a mother-in-law, a woman shared some aspects of sisterly authority with respect to overseeing sons' wives and having them work for her so that she might trade or visit. Children were seen as necessary defenders of a woman's place in her husband's lineage (Ibid.: 232–34).

There was also friction between sisterhood and wifehood. Women were expected to trade, but trading was seen to be in conflict with household duties. Moreover the independence from a husband combined with the collective organization with other women, which was required for trading, was in contradiction with the ideal of wifely deference to a husband. Henderson suggests that the society's contradiction (or perhaps that of its men) was manifested in the belief that traders tended to be sexually unfaithful, a practice that the society believed could harm or kill the children and husbands. This same contradiction was manifest in Onitsha men's beliefs that market women became witches at night and inhabited the waterside market and lowland square (women's turf) where they victimized any man who approached. "Symbolically, the marketplace is defined as outside the sphere of assertion by males" (Ibid.: 311). These beliefs seem to reflect ideological resolutions of the conflicting ideals inherent in women's two relations of production. However, this ideology was belied by women's behavior with respect to their sexuality, behavior highlighting the predominance of sisterly behavior. Green (1964: 193, 198–204), Van Allen (1972: 171), and Henderson (1972: 525) all reported incidents of Igbo women's organizations successfully resisting husbands' attempts to prevent them from having lovers, in the face of a double sexual standard for husbands and wives.

More than did men, women required the structural support of corporate patrilineages for their economic independence and broader social autonomy. On the basis of such ascriptive support, Onitsha women had erected a system of councillors and queen [*Omu*] that mirrored the men's system and wielded signigicant power; it is said that at one time the queen led a boycott by all the women of the community against cooking for their husbands, which brought the men to accept their demands. With descent group support undermined, however, the trading roles of women would have been seriously affected. [Ibid.]

DAHOMEY

The history of Dahomey is, among other things, the creation of a ruling class that transformed control over the means of production from the system existing throughout the area, of descent group ownership with control vested in local lineage heads, to a system where the Dahomean king became the owner of all lands and reallocated them, each generation to a new generation of officials (generally the heirs of the previous incumbents). The critical aspect of this transformation lay in the long-term shift of land from control by free peasants organized in lineages to control as something like hereditary prebends by a ruling class dependent on slave labor (prisoners of war or kinless people). The demographic consequences of this revolution for the peasantry were clear from rather early in Dahomey's history: peasants disappeared, unfree labor became increasingly important for production as well as for exchange in the slave trade, and demographic transformations were visible manifestations of changes in the relations of production. This part of Dahomean history does not occupy center stage, but what data exist suggest that this was the process.

RISE OF THE STATE

Fortunately there is a historical study of the Dahomean beginnings in the latter seventeenth century and of the process by which the ruling class expanded in the eighteenth and nineteenth centuries to the detriment of a peasantry organized in territorially based kin groups. This information and interpretation is consistent with much of the ethnographic description provided by Herskovits (1938). Two major reexaminations of Dahomean history (Akinjogbin 1967; Argyle 1966) agree on the beginnings—the social innovations or revolution carried out by the founders of the kingdom.[4]

Akinjogbin speaks of an overthrow of the social order, which he characterizes as an "*ebi* commonwealth," or family-kin group commonwealth. This was a social order shared by Yoruba and Aja alike and represented most powerfully by Oyo, senior kingdom and overlord of the region. It was an order based on internally stratified descent groups associated with a village or town, overarching and kin-based chiefships or kingships uniting a number of such towns into a kingdom or confederacy (Akinjogbin 1967: 13–18). Argyle, too, emphasizes the importance of lineage ownership of land and the role of lineage head-king as owner (1966: 7–8, 55–56, 95–96). Akinjogbin suggests that the Dahomean transformation of the social order was a response to the conditions of social insecurity created by the presence of Europeans and their demands for slaves (1967: 18–38).

Both agree that several key transformations had their roots in the period between 1625 and 1680. The most important of these lay in the new idea of citizenship and the state (Ibid.: 25; Argyle 1966: 8–13, 55–56). The Dahomean royal group claimed as its own the land of those whom they conquered. As owner it claimed the right to inherit the land worked by the inhabitants. In practice the descendants of the previous owners retained possession and were reconfirmed by the new owners. But often their leaders, who had been heads of descent groups and owners by virtue of their position in the kin group, were killed or replaced by the conquerors. The replacements stood in a new relationship to both those on the land and to the Dahomean rulers. They were not owners but rather something akin to prebendal officials, theoretically in the service of the Dahomean king and in no way beholden to the peasants they ruled. This new relationship theoretically obtained even in the cases where leaders who submitted peacefully to Dahomean rule were left to rule as before. Other prerogatives claimed by the early Dahomean kings and attributed to Wegbaja (prior to about 1680) include ending the rights of kin groups to punish offenders and ending the right of local chiefs to collect tolls (Argyle 1966: 8–11). The promise of these transformations was to strengthen the new rulers at the expense of the peasantry by uniting rulers to each other along class lines, through the institution of Dahomean kingship, and away from the peasants by weakening kinship and territorial bonds and prerogatives.

Thus both studies see the rise of the Dahomean rulers as a blow to the power and autonomy that kin groups held in the old order of Yoruba and Aja society. In this respect, Herskovits's interpretation of Dahomean organization in the latter nineteenth century appears to be the end product of a process begun two hundred years earlier. Herskovits describes a situation in which a ruling class of absentee landowners controlled large estates responsible for a large percentage of the kingdom's food production and in which the peasantry is much reduced in size.

Akinjogbin's study is particularly helpful in elucidating the interplay between external forces and the internal dynamic that led to a transformed mode of production. He emphasizes the Dahomean system as at once a response to the seventeenth-century erosion of earlier patterns of organization in the face of the slave trade and an attempt to end the trade, or at least its penetration to what became Dahomey. He traces the process by which the Dahomean rulers became enmeshed in and dependent on the trade for much of their wealth and hence their power to preserve organization against subjects and neighbors alike. However, they could not control the terms and conditions of the European trade, nor could they control Oyo, the most powerful presence in the region. This external weakness of the Dahomean rulers led it to policies that had profound impacts on their relations with citizen peasants.

From mid-seventeenth century until the last quarter of the eighteenth, Dahomey expanded in territorial power. From about 1730, shortly after it turned Whydah into its own slave trading port, until the end of the slave trade, the Dahomean ruling class looked to this trade for its wealth. Although there were significant ups and downs, the European demand for slaves from Dahomey remained high for most of the eighteenth century under Tegbesu's reign (1740–1774) and declined under his successor, Kpengla (1774–1789). Tegbesu's policies involved resolution of conflict with Oyo and other Aja states in such a way as to secure Dahomean access to the slave trade and to secure a supply of slaves for it. Oyo, as the most powerful and senior state in the area, protected other Aja cities and states against Dahomean expansion, claiming all, including Dahomey, were subordinate to Oyo. Its military devastation of Abomey lent weight to the claim. By accepting Oyo overlordship (which included Oyo's rights to intervene in Dahomean affairs) and agreeing to pay considerable tribute, Tegbesu obtained Oyo's acquiescence to Dahomean control of the coastal trade at Whydah at the expense of other Aja peoples, and hence obtained a secure ruling-class access to the wealth brought by the trade (Akinjogbin 1967: 123–25). Tegbesu restricted the number of people who were to have direct access to the wealth of the trade by making—and more or less effectively so—the slave trade a royal monoply delegated to particular officials.

Two intertwined problems arise at this point. (1) What were the sources of slaves destined for sale to the Europeans? (2) What was the preslave trade source of unfree labor in Dahomey, and how was it affected by the trade?[5]

On the eve of Dahomey's entry into the slave trade, Dahomean rulers used unfree labor. According to Snelgrave, Agaja (1708–1740) had large numbers of captives working his lands, whom he refused to sell to European traders (Dalzel 1967: 24, 34–35). Under his successor, warfare was undertaken for slaves to sell, but Tegbesu's armies were weak and not notably successful.

There were more important sources for slaves to sell abroad in the middle eighteenth century. Akinjogbin gives purchase from Oyo great importance in Tegbesu's time (1967: 132), but he also speaks to internal predation: potential competitors to the throne and large numbers of political enemies were sold to Europeans (Ibid.: 116). Dalzel (1967: 70–71) tells us that when a person was convicted of a crime, he, his family, and all of his retainers were killed or sold into slavery:

When the delinquent happens to be a man of consequence, with numerous dependents and connexions, who are deprived of their lives or liberty on this account, the state must suffer a considerable loss: yet this is a calamity which often happens; and together with the carnage of war, must have contributed greatly to depopulating this unhappy country.

Akinjogbin suggests that significant numbers of ordinary free Dahomeans were also sold (1967: 134). Dalzel agrees: "The innocent inhabitants of whole villages were sold for slaves" (1967: 97). Indeed the slaves sold from Whydah were Fon, Allada, Whydah, and Yoruba. Other writers deny that anyone born in Dahomey could be sold (Argyle 1966: 143; Herskovits 1938, vol. 1: 101). Yet Argyle seems to rest on Snelgrave's experience, which was before Tegbesu's time and before the period of ruling-class dependence on the trade.

Ordinary Dahomeans seem to have faced great variation in their life chances. Though the actual conduct of external trade was effectively restricted, its existence underwrote prosperity for large numbers. Whydah thrived. The conduct of the slave trade required the services of a myriad of Dahomeans to serve the European factories, ships, and indeed all involved in the trade. Royal control of the conditions of trade required that Europeans employ many Dahomeans and pay them substantial and standardized wages in cowries and in goods. Thus washerwomen, canoe men, water carriers, messengers, porters, and others prospered along with the slave trade and the Dahomean rulers. On the other hand, labor service was enforced for peasants around Abomey, and taxes in both cowries and produce were imposed on those farther away (Dalzel 1967: xii; Akinjogbin 1967: 129). Agricultural production was not encouraged and declined.

Behind the prosperous facade of the slave trade in Tegbesu's time lay a depopulation of the peasantry on the Abomey plateau. There may have been an additional decline in war captives employed in food production. Norris describes plantations that provisioned the kings' household as being cultivated by women (Dalzel 1967: 121). This could have come about from both a shift in captives away from production and to sale, or Tegbesu's deemphasis of the military (in the context of Oyo's watchful eye) could simply have meant fewer captives.

Tegbesu's exertions also produced unfavorable reactions which increased the insecurity of his achievements. His repressive measures drove away many people from Dahomey. These exiles were able to live in other territories under the general peace imposed by Oyo. This meant that Dahomey no longer had any special advantages to offer anyone seeking security or adventure as it had during Agaja's reign. It was therefore no longer attractive to new immigrants who might have made good the losses through emigration. By 1750 the population of Dahomey was noticeably diminished, a further contributory cause of military weakness. [Akinjogbin 1967: 132]

By the last quarter of the century, then, Dahomey was at the peak of its apparent power, but it was also facing grave internal difficulties. The peasantry and their agriculture underwrote ruling-class wealth from the slave trade. But squeezing the peasants also made for a crisis in peasant agricultural production manifested in—and exacerbated by—a severe famine in 1780 followed by an epidemic that killed many Dahomeans (Ibid.: 161).

To revive agriculture required something of a new mode of production. The peasantry was decimated and apparently remained so through the nineteenth century, although its size fluctuated (Burton 1864; Forbes 1966, vol. 1: 12, 21). At this point, after 1775, the first wars explicitly "to supply labour for royal plantations" were undertaken (Newbury 1961: 27). Actually Newbury suggests a dual economic motive: to obtain laborers and to supply the population of the Abomey plateau with captured food, particularly in times of drought (Ibid.).

Kpengla reemphasized warfare and taking captives, but his reign saw a decline in European demand for slaves. It seems likely that much of this warfare was an effort to provision his kingdom (and class) with food and laborers. Thus the rise of direct ruling-class control over land and unfree labor was not really a product of successful subjugation of the peasantry; it was almost the reverse. Having squeezed the peasantry into flight—to Whydah or neighboring states where their chances looked better—or selling or impoverishing them, the rulers found themselves lacking producers when the slave trade waned. It is in this context—their need to populate Dahomey with producers— that the rise of royal plantations seems most comprehensible. These plantations were important for provisioning food in the nineteenth century prior to the palm oil trade (Argyle 1966: 142–43; LeHerisse 1911: 46, 52–53; Forbes 1966, vol. 1: 31, 68, 70, 113, 115; Herskovits 1938, vol. 1: 99–100). Forbes says that "industry and agriculture are not encouraged" (1966, vol. 1: 21), that the military was the road to success, and that all soldiers were fed. His description of "royal plantations' " being intensively cultivated (Ibid.: 30–31) suggests that it was specifically free peasant agriculture that was discouraged. Thus perhaps as early as the end of the eighteenth century, the Dahomean ruling class, through the royal house, expanded its control over land and labor power at the expense of a kin-based peasantry. In the mid-nineteenth century, during Gezo's reign, Forbes estimated that only about 10 percent of the population was free; the rest were slaves (1966: 14). Although this figure sounds too high, it does suggest that the peasantry had been truncated prior to the height of the palm oil trade.[6]

Palm oil became a significant item of trade with Europe by mid-nineteenth century, and after 1854 it largely replaced the slave trade as a source of ruling-class revenue (Ross 1965). There is evidence, too, that ruling-class officials developed sizable palm oil plantations along the coast in Whydah and inland (Argyle 1966: 103; Ross 1965; Forbes 1966, vol. 1: 31, 115; Coquery-Vidrovitch 1971). While the rise of palm oil may have entailed ruling-class expansion of its estates, such estates preceded this period. Nor is it clear that such estates, at least inland, expanded in size or importance during this period. Burton (1864, vol. 2: 230–53) speaks of a decline by the 1860s (Glele's reign), of abandoned agriculture, and of depopulation around Abomey. He contrasts this situation with happier days several decades prior.

Whether Dahomean rulers grew richer or poorer with the transition to palm oil production is not central. What is important is whether the transition entailed any significant transformation in the social organization or any changes in the mode of production, class composition, or relations in Dahomey. Coquery-Vidrovich (1971) argues that the old ruling class made the transition smoothly from slaves to palm oil by continuing to monopolize the channels of trade and by its control over land and labor power. Ross (1965) confirms this analysis, at least for the class relationships at Whydah.

CLASSES, SISTERS, AND WIVES

Discussion of women's work and organization comes principally from Herskovits (1938) and combines colonial observation with precolonial information. Dahomean history exhibited an expansion of ruling class control over productive means in some ways similar to that of the Buganda kingdom, yet it differed with respect to how lands were worked and with respect to how households were provisioned. Buganda lands were worked mainly by a free peasantry in clientship relations with political patrons, while in Dahomey estates or villages of unfree cultivators under ruling-class officials produced a large portion of that kingdom's food. The more significant difference with respect to free peasant women lay in the contrasting organization of work, or productive forces, in the two kingdoms. Unlike their Baganda counterparts, Dahomean women were traders and pursued this activity collectively as elsewhere in West Africa. But Dahomean trading contrasts with that of Onitsha in that neither wives nor sisters constituted a group for market activities in Dahomey.

Although the information on Dahomey's women is not rich, it does suggest the following picture. The forces of production associated with trade seem to have sustained remnants of sisterhood, particularly with respect to peasant marriage patterns and preferences. There is also some evidence that the state's ideology and law stressed wifely subordination of women. Most intriguing (but requiring more information) is the possibility that peasant women and men were generating a recreated sisterhood and brotherhood from below in the mutual aid organizations and relationships formed by both sexes for the performance of their labor and in their use of these organizations to sustain sisterly prerogatives within marriage. Although I cannot fully sustain this suggestion with the existing data, it appears that Dahomean peasant women struggled to generate new sisterly relations of production. These stemmed from their collective trade organization, were reinforced in sisterly mutual aid societies, and in turn partly countered the destruction of kin corporations by sustaining brotherhood and sisterhood relations in marriage.

A large but indeterminate part of the Dahomean populace did not engage in food production and depended on raw and cooked food purchased in the markets for their subsistence. In addition to full-time craft specialists, many people, women as well as men, were employed in the slave trade, in provisioning European forts, in carrying goods and people from the coast to Abomey and back, and in caring for the rest houses and their occupants along the way. Such people were "subsisted" in cowries with which they purchased their needs from market women (Forbes 1966, vol. 1: 51–52, 70). The organization of agriculture and craft production, as well as the slave trade, depended on an elaborate internal marketing system of raw and prepared food. Lineages had long been subordinated to slave-worked estates as suppliers of basic foodstuffs. By colonial times and very likely long before, market women's purchase of foodstuffs was cut loose from their village and from their relations with male affines as women traders traveled long distances to large estates to buy the crops they retailed in towns, villages, and crossroads (Herskovits 1938, vol. 1: 50–60; Forbes 1966, vol. 1: 58, 70). The corporate unity of producer-distributor villages was ruptured by the hegemony of estate production. Market women were oriented more toward trade relations with nonaffines and nonkin, toward wholesaling estate produce, and toward intensifying food preparation for sale to nonfood producers in towns and at trading crossroads.

Peasant men too were organized to work collectively in the *dokpwe*, a group consisting of the adult men of a village. This functioned in men's major tasks: cultivating fields, roofing houses, and building walls. In the past, it may have built roads as well, and it was critical for holding funerals for men. The head, or *dokpwega*, was a hereditary position and in Dahomean ideals was one of great power, able to command labor from king and peasant alike. In reality this was not at all so. The *dokpwega* was installed by the king and swore loyalty to him. The *dokpwe* was called upon by individual men to aid them in performing the tasks husbands were expected to do for their wives' parents. Every man was expected to do a major job every year or two for his wife's father and to repair his wife's mother's house. Persistent neglect of these duties might cause his in-laws to take their daughter back (Herskovits 1938, vol. 1: 63–73).

The organization and scope of activities of Dahomean patrilineages was sharply restricted. Extended families seem to have been the effective corporate groups while the larger and dispersed patrilineage, the sib, together with its head and council, seems to have had mainly ritual functions. It is noteworthy that the king installed even the male heads of sibs and extended family compounds, thus stressing male headship and incorporating it into the state sphere as with the *dokpwega*. However in both the dispersed sib and the extended family, there was a council of old men and old women. The latter were particularly powerful. Their responsibilities included mediating with the ancestors, officiating at funerals, and installing the sib and family heads from below (that is, on behalf of the sib's living and dead members). Thus sisterhood seems to have persisted, at least no more precariously than lineages themselves. Male headship was sanctified from above, but headship from below rested on acceptance by sisters and functioned as part of a group of senior brothers and sisters (Ibid.: 139–40, 156–58).

Marriage too pulled in opposite directions. Wives were never incorporated into the husband's lineage but retained membership in and some protection from their own. But this protection could be and often was forfeit in institutionalized ways. Marriages fell into three general types. In the first, *akwenusi*, the husband gave bridewealth, the wife's father arranged or approved of the marriage, and children were the husband's. The second, *xadudo*, involved no bridewealth but rather the woman's going to live with her husband generally against her family's wishes; children did not belong to the husband's group. In the third type, *vidotowe*, the wife, at the request of her lineage, chose a husband to live at her natal compound and kept most of the children, while the remainder belonged to the husband. Men's preferences seemed to be for the forms that gave them greatest control over their wives (and not the children). Thus they preferred *xadudo* because their wives could not run home to their own families and therefore had to be loyal and obedient to the husband. Women disliked this form because, without protection, *xadudo* wives were often mistreated, and when they grew old were often poor and neglected; moreover the husband had no obligation to the children. Women praised *akwenusi* marriage as giving a woman and her children both protection and the security born of two kin groups. Men seemed indifferent to this form, complaining about intervention from wives' families but also stressing their ownership of wives by virtue of the bridewealth paid (Ibid.: 301–38). Both sexes thought well of *vidotowe*. This marriage was generally undertaken by a woman in order to increase the size of a shrinking lineage segment. Woman marriage also was practiced and approved as a variant of *akwenusi*. *Vidotowe* wives did not found their own families but instead contributed toward building their lineage. Woman marriage on the other hand provided a way for a woman to translate earned wealth into family headship by marrying a woman and founding her own compound. This status was passed on to subsequent generations of daughters who succeeded to family headship and inheritance of property, becoming "free" women, or women with sisterly prerogatives (Herskovits 1937). Thus success in trade could underwrite alternatives to wifehood for a few women. I could find no information on motherhood as a productive relationship. Women's security as wives rested largely with protection from their own family or retention of some sort of sisterhood, but the content of the wife relationship itself is not clear. Wives had a significant degree of economic autonomy in that they owned all that they earned in trade, in gardening, and what was given to them by their own families (Herskovits 1938, vol. 1: 86). But without help from a husband or one's own family, this was apparently inadequate to support a woman and her children. There is no information about peasant women's extramarital sexual standards. However, Forbes (1966, vol. 1: 26) claimed that the state prohibited any extramarital sexual affairs and punished them by sale of both partners into slavery.

Sisters and wives within the ruling class were more sharply contrasted. Wives of the king and ruling-class officials lived in closed compounds, segregated from social contact. Wives' extramarital sex was punished by death in practice as well as theory. On the other hand, the king and male officials were able to take any woman they desired, whether she was married or not. When the king's wives marched through town to get water or to carry the food they prepared for the houses of various officials, all people on the road had to turn away (Ibid.; Herskovits, vol. 1: 338–39; vol. 2: 35, 46–48). Sisters, princesses or daughters of the royal sib, had all the sexual freedom of ruling-class men. They could also marry and have sexual affairs with men of their sib, their half-brothers. This was regarded as a mark of class privilege (Ibid., vol. 1: 339). The king used to marry off princesses to men of his choosing. Such husbands exerted little control over their wives' behavior, and children of the marriage did not inherit from their father. Royal sisters were also given several girls, whom they in turn married off to men of their own choosing. Children of these marriages were under the "paternal" control of the royal sisters (Ibid.: 325–33). The sister-wife contrast within the ruling class of Dahomey was not too different from that of Buganda. In a similar way, the double standard of sexual behavior was governed by rules of class privilege. Thus ruling-class men had access to any peasant or slave woman they desired. While there is no indication that ruling-class sisters seized men, to have many affairs was socially approved behavior for them.

Among the peasantry, men and women had different attitudes toward marriage to a ruling-class person because the consequences were very different from each sex. Men stood to gain, women to lose. Fathers liked to marry a daughter to a chief in order to enhance their prestige even though they could not protect the daughter as they could if she married a peasant. Women were "unanimous in their feeling that such a marriage was distinctly undesirable" because it curtailed their freedom and denied them protection (Ibid.: 339). On the other hand, men chosen as husbands to princesses were often elevated to office and were generally enriched, though they exerted no control over their wives. In cross-class marriages, the ruling class was able to enforce class privilege, manifest as subordinating nonruler husbands to ruling-class sisters and nonruler wives to ruling-class husbands, particularly by secluding them.

There is some evidence that Dahomean rulers were sensitive to the dangers of organization along class lines among the underclasses. Herskovits suggests that the rulers were hostile to all societies and associations that could act collectively and independently of the state because they feared their potential for subversion. Such groups existed on the peripheries but not in the core areas of the Dahomean kingdom, he suggested, because they were barred or eliminated (Ibid.: 243–44, 256). We have noted, too, the king's practice of investing both *dokpwegas* and heads of lineages in their positions. The tradition of how the *dokpwe* originated claims it preceded the institution of kingship and also suggests royal cooptation of a prestate local organization (Ibid.: 65–66).

So far I have stressed the precarious persistence of sisterly relations among peasants in marriage and sib ritual, as well as the transformation of sister to a relationship of class privilege among women of the royal sib. Herskovits's discussion of mutual aid, though it is very slim, suggests that a new sisterhood and brotherhood may have developed independently of corporate kin groups, stemming instead from productive organization. These organizations sustained some autonomy in women's wifely relations. There is thus the possibility that underclass Dahomean women and men recreated a modicum of sisterhood and brotherhood on a new basis after the old was undercut. Herskovits described the prevalence of mutual aid organizations, *gbe*, informal, small groups of men and women or of men only. They assisted each other in giving the gifts required at the funeral of a wife's parents and in other undertakings requiring financial assistance to affines and others. These groups had their own banners and functioned for public dancing as well. Women in the *gbe* were free women, that is, wealthy women who headed their own compounds either because they were daughters of ruling-class sisters or because their mothers established their own compound through woman marriage. These women were able to translate wealth into power by their contact and influence with officials and powerful men. Rich wives were allowed to join these societies only if their husbands were members.

Women had their own mutual aid societies, said to be richer than men's. They seemed to be associated with marketing and with defending women against men. Part of their public singing included songs of "allusion—of the type sung in the market places—which these organizations of women possess, and these are not too rarely directed against men." In Glele's reign, oral tradition speaks of husbands' attempts to stop their wives from attending the meetings because they were often away from home. It is said that through free women's influence, the king held a public hearing and decreed that women could join as many associations as they wished (Ibid.: 254–55). Herskovits's account suggests that mutual aid associations had been for men and for the wealthy or ruling class women who were sisters and not wives. This tradition, perhaps from the early nineteenth century, suggests that peasant women who were wives struggled to win a certain amount of the personal autonomy of sisters through developing their own organization. The information is too fragmentary, however, for any but the most tentative statement.

NOTES

1. I have confined my examination to places where inheritance of land was patrilineal and to males not because matrilineal inheritance or women inheriting land was unusual or unimportant but because I want to stress the existence of sisterness even where women were not heirs to land.

2. Henderson (Ibid.: 140) claims that lineage daughters were "defined as quasi-male" on the grounds that the *ofo* (ritual objects representing lineage authority) hated menstrual blood and women, but that daughters were exceptions in that they could hold *ofo*. It seems to me more likely that it was not the gender woman but rather the relationship wife-sexual that was antithetical to lineage *ofo*. Patrilineage ghosts were said to hate female sexuality; thus, when asking for their help, it was necessary to avoid sexual activity for several days (Ibid.: 145).

3. This would be the case if most marriages were made within the city. Direct infor-

mation is lacking for Onitsha. However, Green (1964: 180–232), in discussing a more dispersed village pattern among Igbo to the east in the village group of Agbaja, noted that most marriages there were within the village group and that the organization of women's work and productive relations formed the core of the local political economy of some eleven villages. Here women belonged to two separate organizations—of wives and of daughters in their marital and natal homes respectively. Their organized marketing activity as wives brought the women of the market (and intermarriage) area together, and their organization as daughters brought together the sisters of each lineage, who were dispersed as wives. Both organizations had wide-range ritual and adjudication roles in both village and areal affairs. "But it seems to be less generally grasped that the Ibo system of exogamy [village exogamy] works like a cement binding the villages together, or like a consolidating network which has to some extent, among other things, made trading between the village units possible. It has certainly made for the mitigation of inter-village fighting. And in all this the leading part has fallen to the women.... Women, as daughters of their native village, have also their far-flung inter-village organization which has no parallel in that of the men and which has thus a special interest and importance as an inter-village system of links" (Ibid.: 232). Green's discussion challenges conventional wisdom in anthropology on the alleged contrast between patrilineal-patrilocal and matrilineal-matrilocal organizations, where the latter are asserted to marry within a small area so that men can run lineage affairs, while the former can marry its women far away because women do not exercise political authority in their natal lineages. In Agbaja it seems to be women's activities and women's organizations that provide political and economic unity above the village level.

4. Argyle (1966) argues against the king's control over economic and political processes, suggesting instead that the Dahomean king sat precariously atop a group of officials who controlled the revenues of tribute—slaves and, in the nineteenth century, palm oil. He points out that the Dahomean innovations did not look quite so revolutionary when seen from below, that many of the new officials throughout the eighteenth and nineteenth centuries were old local and kin group leaders, that perennial rebellion and seccession existed, that officials withheld tribute from the center, and that these practices indicate royal weakness and perhaps a persistence of localism and kin-based loyalties—in short, a continuity with less centralized prekingdom patterns of Aja and Yoruba organization. First, while Argyle's analysis stresses the continuities of the kingdom's organization with prekingdom organization, it must be recognized that the old was transformed; it persisted with new meaning in a new political and economic context. In this sense, Argyle's point is consistent with anthropological notions of transition from kin to class organization (Kirchhoff 1959). Akinjogbin's analysis shows the institution of kingship as tying the ruling class together (not always harmoniously) through its function of allocating offices and their attached estates or their rights to collect taxes and carry trade. Second, Argyle's analysis, which focuses on the relationship between the king and local power holders, speaks less to the strength of the rulers vis-à-vis the underclasses than to the state of relationships within its ruling class. The issue of central concern here is the relations between rulers and underclasses over control of the land and its fruits. Here historians and contemporary observers agreed that rulers gained at the peasants' expense from the late eighteenth through the nineteenth centuries.

5. The same word is used for unfree laborers in Africa and those sold to Europeans. Several writers have noted how inaccurate this usage is for Dahomey and elsewhere, and some have suggested other terms (Davidson 1961; Argyle 1966). Yet *slavery* is still applied to describe unfree labor in West Africa (Meillassoux 1971). This usage has produced some confusion over what is meant. Yet Argyle makes the essential point that a slave in Dahomey (and elsewhere in West Africa) was "essentially a kinless person" (1966: 143), thus emphasizing the relationship between the weakening of kin ties and the strengthening of class ties on the one hand and the weakening of the peasant control over the means of production in relationship to ruling class control on the other. A remark by Norris in connection with Tegbesu's allocation of wives to his officials bears on this destruction of kin groups. Norris speaks of the king's allocating wives to officials as part of the general pattern by which all children "belong entirely to the king, are taken from their mothers at an early age and distributed in villages remote from the places of their nativity; where they remain subject to his future approbation of them. . . . The motive for this, that there may be no family connections or combinations; no associations, that might be injurious to the king's unlimited power. Hence each individual is detached, and unconnected; and having no relative for whom he is interested, is solicitous only for his own safety" (quoted in Dalzel 1967: 122–23). While Norris was surely overstating the case, he does indicate the hostility of the ruling class to kin group strength.

Dahomean kings emphasized the importance of warfare for obtaining captives. They also emphasized the noneconomic use of captives, particularly in sacrifice, and denied consistently that they made war mainly to capture slaves for sale to Europeans (Burton 1864; Dalzel 1967: 217–21). Newbury (1961: 26) claims that Gezo (1820–1858) was the first king to undertake yearly war for this purpose (Forbes 1966, vol. 1: 15). Thus warfare was important as a source of captives, but their disposition was not uniform.

6. Thus Meillassoux's suggestion that slaves were items of exchange and became producers only when palm oil replaced the slave trade as a means to ruling class wealth is too simple (1971: 59).

CONCLUSIONS

I have tried to do three things in this book. First, I tried to show how an intellectual heritage of social darwinist thinking has retarded understanding of what women's places are and why they are what they are. This heritage has asserted that a historically specific, industrial capitalist ideology about sexual spheres represents timeless biological and cultural truth. Biology has been used metaphorically to confound a construct of essential woman with a distorted version of nineteenth-century wife and mother capitalist relations of production. Second, I tried to show how a focus on sisters and wives as contrasting relations of production in preclass societies can at once free the study of women from spencerian blinders and allow use of mode of production in a nonsexist way to illuminate women's places in noncapitalist societies. Third, I also tried to recast how we see the rise of class society and the state as it affects women. Private property became one manifestation of a more fundamental process: the destruction or subversion of kin corporations. I stressed seeing class formation as a process, and an uneven one at that, a focus that allowed room for exploring differences in women's places in class societies. Thus, the kingdoms of Buganda and Dahomey went through somewhat similar processes of class formation but seem to have developed from very different productive forces and to have retained or built on these differences in their developments. Dahomean marketing organization seems to have provided peasant women with a base to retain some measure of sisterly prerogatives even as the corporations that presumably had originally sustained these were severely weakened.

I have dealt mainly with precapitalist organizations and have focused on nonclass societies more than I have on states. Most of the book detailed the ways an analytic approach to political economy generated from the viewpoint of European male proletarians—marxism—could illuminate the places of African women in precapitalist modes of production and could also help free such study from sexist assumptions of bourgeois ideology. Yet almost everyone in today's world lives under the effective rule of a state. More than that, almost everyone has been subjected to capitalism—not only as a mode of production but as rule by European state organization and imposition of its cultural traditions. I think it would be particularly appropriate to suggest some ways that this marxist understanding of African women's places can in turn help free our understandings about women in European history and women in capitalism from sexist blinders. I am not a historian, and I am not going to reinterpret European history or the history of capitalism in this conclusion. Instead I want to look at some of the pieces of women's history with which I am familiar from the perspective generated in this book and to suggest leads to be explored with future research.

ESSENTIALISM AND WOMEN'S PRODUCTIVE RELATIONS

If we assume that there is no more an essential woman in European than in African modes of production, I think we may be able to see, or at least to discover, multiple and changing productive relationships of European women. I think that we may also discover that patterns of those relationships that came to be particular to Europe contained different forms of African sister and wife relationships and may indeed have developed historically from a prefeudal mode of production similar to African kin corporations. Pursuing the genesis of European patterns from this perspective may also aid in reconceptualizing women's places in tribal and early feudal Europe.

From the vantage point of the present, European and African productive relationships present a basic contrast. In the African societies discussed in this work, land, the major means of production, was inherited by males in the male line; women did not inherit land. In Europe, though, women did inherit land from parents. A longstanding and widespread European pattern has been for daughters to receive their inheritance upon marriage in the form of a dowry. The European pattern of providing daughters with part of their natal family's means of production stands in sharp contrast to African patterns of a woman's retaining rights in, but not possession of, her corporate group's means of production. There are indications that this contrast may have come into being in feudal times when European organizations shifted from earlier, African-like patterns of bridewealth, inheritance, and lineally recruited kin corporations to systems of dowry, bilateral inheritance, and some types of conjugal corporate property.[1]

There is confusion about the position of women in prefeudal Europe and a consequent cloudiness in attempts to ascertain whether it rose or fell with the rise of feudalism. Thus Tacitus ascribed high status to Germanic women in prefeudal times. McNamara and Wemple (1974) dispute this evaluation, noting that bridewealth went to a woman's family and not to the woman herself and thus concluding that women's economic position was weak. But they also note that these same women seem to "have occupied an exceptionally important place in the rudimentary public life of the barbarian tribes" (Ibid.: 104). Muller (1977) agrees with Tacitus's evaluation of "barbarian" women's position and suggests that prefeudal kin corporations were positive forces for women. If prefeudal European groups had patrilineal kin corporations, the contradictory data on women's places could be manifestations of women's having contradictory sister and wife relations of production rather than having a single essential relation to the means of production. Tacitus and Muller, as well as McNamara and Wemple, would then be right, each having a different piece of the elephant—or different relation of production.

Both of these articles implicitly see women as having one essential relation to the means of production, and both have implicit notions of the kinds of productive relations necessary to protect women's autonomy and well-being. McNamara and Wemple are historians and share in the European historical perspective that sees conjugal property as normal and women's ownership as necessary to their independence. Muller is an anthropologist and shares that discipline's perspective that lineal kin corporations are normal and that some of their protection and benefits can underwrite women's independence.

This contrast extends to the way in which they answer the question of whether the position of women rose or fell with the rise of feudalism. They agree on what happened: that the rise of local powerholders with their client-followers undermined the estates and power of corporate kin groups. But they apply different notions of essential woman—

wives for McNamara and Wemple and something akin to adult powerholders for Muller—and come up with opposite answers. McNamara and Wemple see the transition from kin group to conjugal ownership as part of a positive process by which women came to inherit and transmit property. They show how property ownership and control underwrote women's high status and power in early medieval times. Muller focuses on the other side of the picture, the ways in which medieval clientship became a central political relationship, but one among males from which women were excluded. She stresses the decline in women as public powerholders with the transition from kin corporations to clientship.

Historians, given European postfeudal patterns, tend to see property as protection; anthropologists, given their study of nonclass organization, tend to see group membership as protection. It is possible that European historical evolution has been from prefeudal organizations in which kin corporations underwrote women's autonomy to feudal and postfeudal patterns where women's autonomy was sustained by property control. Islamic traditions speak clearly to these being two different relations that can sustain similar things. Theoretically daughters have rights to inherit shares of the family property, but if they accept their inheritance, they forfeit their right to membership in their natal family and protection by their brothers. It appears that daughters are given the option of retaining sisterly relations of production or property ownership relations as alternate bases of social standing and protection. Anthropological and historical analyses could be joined and strengthened by nonessentialist inquiry into historical processes by which women's relations to the means of production changed drastically as an integral part of a transformation from a corporate kin mode of production to one based on clientship and some forms of conjugal ownership.

If women were sisters and wives in prefeudal times, what did they become with the rise of feudalism? Does inheritance by daughters and the breakdown of kin groups mean that European women came to have one essential relation to the means of production? It does seem that sisterly relations ceased early on among the nobility as clientage chains developed, but it also appears that the prerogatives sustained earlier by kin corporations came to be sustained by direct possession of property by women *as wives*.[2] It was upon marriage that medieval women became property owners through their dowries. Thus it appears that the meaning of medieval wife as a productive relationship connoted many of the prerogatives sustained by African sister and, perhaps by European premedieval sister. Both McNamara and Wemple and Kelly-Gadol (1977) strongly suggest this line of argument. The former focus on the power, both economic and political exercised by wives in property owning families; the latter adds a discussion of the personal and sexual autonomy of wives in early medieval times. Both argue for a combination of women's control of property combined with an absence (or near absence) of more than local level political power in feudal society. That is, family manors were the basic form of property, and clientship chains of property owners were the totality of effective political control. Because women could inherit property, they could also be patrons and clients and thereby exert political control and in general control their own personal and sexual lives.

Kelly-Gadol describes the political economy of clientship in pre-Renaissance Europe, stressing the autonomy upon which it rested: "Of the two dominant sets of dependent social relations formed by feudalism . . . vassalage, the military relation of knight to lord, distinguished itself (in its early days) by being freely entered into. At a time when everyone was somebody's "man," the right to freely enter a relation of service characterized aristocratic bonds, whereas heritability marked the servile work relation of serf to lord" (Kelly-Gadol 1977: 141). For women of the nobility, early courtly love was an expression of their autonomy at a personal and sexual level. It stood in frank contradiction to the expectations of husband-wife relationships, which were not freely entered and which demanded sexual fidelity of women. Kelly-Gadol points out that feudal society had two contradictory expectations of women's relations to men—inside and outside marriage. She roots the latter in noble women's participation in relationships of patronage and clientage: "Courtly love, which flourished outside the institution of patriarchal marriage, owed its possibility as well as its model to the dominant political institution of feudal Europe that permitted actual vassal homage to be paid to women" (Ibid.: 148). Although Kelly-Gadol does not discuss what underlay patriarchal marriage, her analysis of courtly love does suggest that marriage in early feudal Europe conferred two diametrically opposed productive relationships on women: that of a wife given in marriage unfreely to a husband and subordinate to him, and that of a property owner able to enter into political and personal relationships freely. Instead of being at once sister and wife, noble women were at once vassal and wife.

WEAK STATES AND STRONG WOMEN, STRONG STATES AND WEAK WOMEN

Europe has had class societies for a long time. It is clear that the position of women did not decline and fall abruptly with the rise of class society nor has it been uniform since that time. I think that the variations (or such as we know of them) in European women's places can be illuminated by seeing women's relations to the means of production in relationship to changes in the strength of ruling-class control over productive means. Here too European and African processes may exhibit the same relationships but in very different ways.

Strong African states, at least those discussed in this book, seem to have developed in a milieu of strong corporate kin groups. This does not seem to have been the case in Europe where such groups were broken and transformed by feudal clientage and property relations. Most writers describe early feudal organization in terms more appropriate to a protoclass society than to a strong state organization. The key transformation seems to have been from the private and voluntary clientage of feudal political economy to the class and state control over land and people from Renaissance and late feudal times.

David Herlihy sees women's importance as administrators of feudal estates as well as heirs of property under early feudal conditions where husbands were often away at war. Early feudalism, he suggests, was characterized by a dichotomy between "inner" and "outer" political economies. The former was the domain of women and involved administering the manor and entering social relations pertinent to this; the latter was the domain of men and involved war, the acquisition of estates, and the establishment of social relations dealing with these affairs (Herlihy 1976: 7–11, 24–25). He stresses that "inner" and "outer" are not the same as "public" and "private"; they were both. He describes them in terms reminiscent of the discussion in chapter 2 of Iroquois and Delaware relations. That is, medieval "inner" and "outer" economies were separate but not hierarchically ranked spheres of responsibility for noble women and men. Both were public as well as private because the private fief was also the center of public polity.

The Renaissance and subsequent developments of strong feudal states brought about changes in women's productive relationships and in their places. Anderson (1974) sees the rise of absolutist states as manifesting a strengthened hold by the feudal ruling class over the land and the peasantry but at the expense of lesser members of the nobility itself. Part of this transformation involved changes in the ownership of productive means. Several writers have stressed the shift from a conditional and personal ownership of productive means characterizing feudal times to unconditional personal ownership, which grew up in late feudal times and came into its own as capitalist property (Anderson 1974; Thompson 1976; Kelly-Gadol 1977; Stuart 1976; Herlihy 1976). Feudal ownership was conditional upon clientage, a personal relationship between two individuals. Kelly-Gadol argues that as the feudal nobility consolidated its control over land, it undercut freely entered clientage in general and removed women from ownership relations, as well as from the political and personal prerogatives that had formerly been associated with vassalage. Men of the nobility, by contrast, became military and political arms, courtiers of a consolidated feudal ruling class in Renaissance and absolutist states. Women of this class became wives and ladies. As Kelly-Gadol shows, the courtly love of the Renaissance became asexual and spiritual as women were transformed from free vassal and unfree wife to unfree wife only.[3]

STRONG STATES AND RECREATED KIN CORPORATIONS

It is said that the rise of rural dispossessions and urban migrations begun by the early states of agrarian capitalism disrupted local and kinship networks and led to a weakening in family and kin groups. Unfortunately we know even less of early family among the European underclasses than we do of family among the nobility of feudal times. Yet it is a reasonable guess that some forms of corporate kinship prevailed among peasants and nobles in the rural villages of medieval and early capitalist Europe and that they persisted into modern times. As late as sixteenth-century England, and still later elsewhere in Europe, some (albeit unclear) corporate groups were responsible for pursuing (and being pursued in) blood vengeance (Stone 1975: 15). There is more information from a later period—early industrial capitalism—in

Europe and its later stages in both Euroamerica and the third world, which suggests that we would do better to ask how family and kinship changed rather than to assume that it disappeared. Sociologists and anthropologists have noted of proletarian families around the world that kinship networks exist and provide class-based lifelines and protective organizations (Caulfield 1974; Stack 1974; Young and Wilmott 1962; Joseph n.d.; Bott 1957). But the kinship networks of proletarians are clearly not the same as were the kin groups of precapitalist European underclasses.

To see proletarian kin networks as akin to the corporate groups discussed for African societies requires that proletarians have some kind of corporate estate. Yet a defining characteristic of proletarians is that they do not control productive means. Scott and Tilly (1975) speak of family wages among wage-earning classes of preindustrial Europe. They show that with industrialization, factory work by daughters was seen as a new variation on a traditional contribution to the family resources of the nonpropertied. Their point is echoed in recent studies of European immigrants to American factories (Lamphere 1978) and of twentieth-century women factory workers in Brazil (Safa 1978) and South Korea (Yoon 1976). It is implied as well in Stack's (1974) discussion of the claims on goods and services held by different members of kin networks among black Americans. In some ways the family wage Scott and Tilly describe can be seen as a corporate estate of proletarians, one to which all group members had some claim. But it is equally clear that it is in contradiction with the payment of individual wages. How proletarian families have worked with these contradictory demands needs research.

To pursue such an analysis of proletarian families as both protective and corporate groups requires pursuing also the changing relationship of proletarian families to means of production outside the sphere of capitalist production. It is quite clear that proletarianization and separation of families from their own productive means has been a long process, which is not complete even today. Braverman (1974) has shown how domestic production of use values persisted in premonopoly industrial capitalism and how its scope was drastically curtailed with the entry of monopolies into capitalist production of consumer goods. Yet the production of use values in the home persists in cooking, cleaning, shopping, and in all those activities necessary to transform wages into usable things. Those who regard the home as a nonproductive sphere and women's work in it as nonproductive today may live to mourn its passing once again as fast-food chains supersede home cooking and low wages force more mothers to join the rest of the proletarian family in the wage labor force.

To suggest the persistence—or continued re-creation—of corporate kinship groups among the underclasses is also to suggest the persistence, or continued re-creation of sisterly prerogatives. There are mentions of preindustrial women in riots, in marketing and selling roles, and as peasant spokespeople (Davis 1975: 146–48; Thompson 1971; Ehrenreich and English 1972), which evoke for me Igbo women's productive organization and sister relations and the sisterly prerogatives sustained by both. To pursue this line, to discover whether it is simply metaphor or something more, we need to learn about both work and kinship organization 'in preindustrial Europe. The bias toward upper-class women in the data may have led to undue explanatory weight on productive relations—control of productive means—at the expense of productive forces—or women's organizations as producers. To what extent did women of the producing classes in preindustrial as well as industrial times generate work-based collectives? What were the forces that gave rise to women's unions and union-like groups, to protective and mutual aid organizations in early industrial times? How did these relate to women's control over family estates?

Finally, this line of inquiry may locate the nineteenth-century women's movement in a larger perspective. I have suggested that from medieval times on, those prerogatives of autonomy, adulthood, and decision making that in African organizations stemmed from the sibling relationship stemmed in Europe from the wifely relationship and women's ownership of property. Capitalist transformation of productive estates, together with transformations of proletarian estates engendered by individual wages, establishment of extradomestic sites of production, and later by outlawing child labor, undercut wives' control over family estates. In this sense it is possible to see the women's rights movements of the nineteenth century as class-based attempts by women to recreate something of the sisterly prerogatives of preindustrial times by demanding control over such of the new productive means as were associated with their class—to control property and wages and to gain access to the new routes to security that developed in the nineteenth century: education and the licensed professions.

NOTES

1. Jack Goody (1969, 1976; Goody and Tambiah 1973) has written a great deal about these contrasts but has explained them by ahistorical reference to technological and ecological differences between Europe and Africa rather than by exploring historical processes of transition.

2. Clearly there is much to be asked about property inheritance beyond noting that European patterns provide for daughters' shares. To say that daughters were dowered is not to say that they always controlled their dowry. There are questions of historical changes and differences of class and geography. We need to know when daughters controlled their dowry and when husbands did so, when husband's and wife's properties were kept separate and when they formed a conjugal fund, when wives and widows were "couverte" and when they were "femmes soles," when wives inherited from husbands and when they did not. We also need to know the structure of property-owning groups in different times, places, and classes of Europe. Widespread patterns of partible inheritance would have dispersed family property. Yet Giesey (1977) has shown how such laws were widely circumvented among the wealthy in order to perpetuate family property in prerevolutionary France. Although most of the information comes from the nobility, Goody, Thirsk, and Thompson (1976) and Hilton (1975) have written on the peasantry in Europe during the later middle ages and in the transition to capitalism.

3. This applies to feudal nobility. It is not clear that peasants and other classes were affected in the same ways. Indeed Hilton suggests that English peasant women in the late middle ages sustained a certain amount of autonomy as part of, and perhaps as leaders in, the peasantry's success as a class in enforcing its claims against the English nobility (1975: 95–110).

BIBLIOGRAPHY

Aaby, Peter. 1977. "Engels and Women." *Critique of Anthropology* 3, 9 and 10: 25–53.

Adams, Robert M. 1966. *The Evolution of Urban Society*. Chicago: Aldine.

_____, and Hans J. Nissen. 1972. *The Uruk Countryside*. Chicago: University of Chicago Press.

Akinjogbin, I. A. 1967. *Dahomey and Its Neighbors, 1708–1818*. Cambridge: Cambridge University Press.

Alpers, E. A. 1968. "The Nineteenth Century: Prelude to Colonialism." In *Zamani: A Survey of East African History*, edited by B. A. Ogot and J. A. Kiernan, pp. 238–54. Nairobi: East African Publishing House.

_____, and Christopher Ehret. 1975. "Eastern Africa." In *The Cambridge History of Africa*, vol. 4, edited by R. Gray, pp. 469–536. Cambridge: Cambridge University Press.

Althusser, Louis, and Etienne Balibar. 1970. *Reading Capital*, translated by Ben Brewster. New York: Pantheon.

Anderson, Perry. 1974. *Lineages of the Absolutist State*. London: New Left Books.

Anene, Joseph C. 1966. *Southern Nigeria in Transition, 1885–1906*. Cambridge: Cambridge University Press.

Ardener, Shirley. 1973. "Sexual Insult and Female Militancy." *Man* 8: 422–40.

Ardrey, Robert. 1961. *African Genesis*. New York: Dell.

_____. 1966. *The Territorial Imperative*. New York: Atheneum.

Argyle, William J. 1966. *The Fon of Dahomey: A History and Ethnography of the Old Kingdom*. Oxford: Clarendon Press.

Asad, Telal, ed. 1972. *Anthropology and the Colonial Encounter*. Cambridge: Cambridge University Press.

Aswad, Barbara. 1967. "Key and Peripheral Roles of Noble Women in a Middle Eastern Plains Village." *Anthropological Quarterly* 40: 139–52.

Bachofen, J. J. 1861. *Das Mutterrecht*. Basel: Beno Schwabe.

_____. 1967. *Myth, Religion and Mother Right: Selected Writing of J. J. Bachofen*, translated by Ralph Manheim. Princeton: Princeton University Press.

Basden, George T. 1966. *Niger Ibos*. London: Frank Cass and Co.

Baxandall, Rosalyn; Linda Gordon; and Susan Reverby. 1976. *America's Working Women*. New York: Vintage.

Bennett, N. R. 1968. "The Arab Impact." In *Zamani*, edited by B. A. Ogot and J. A. Kiernan, pp. 216–37. Nairobi: East African Publishing House.

Bicchieri, M. G., ed. 1972. *Hunters and Gatherers Today*. New York: Holt, Rinehart and Winston.

Birdsell, Joseph. 1968. "Some Predictions for the Pleistocene Based on Equilibrium Systems among Recent Hunter-Gatherers." In *Man the Hunter*, edited by R. B. Lee and I. DeVore, pp. 229–40. Chicago: Aldine.

Birmingham, David. 1975. "Central Africa from Cameroun to the Zambezi." In *The Cambridge History of Africa*, vol. 4, edited by R. Gray, pp. 325–83. Cambridge: Cambridge University Press.

──────. 1976. "The Forest and the Savannah of Central Africa." In *The Cambridge History of Africa*, vol. 5, edited by John Flint, pp. 222–69. Cambridge: Cambridge University Press.

Boserup, Ester. 1965. *The Conditions of Agricultural Growth*. Chicago: Aldine.

──────. 1970. *Women's Role in Economic Development*. London: Allen and Unwin.

Bott, Elizabeth. 1957. *Family and Social Network*. London: Tavistock.

Bourne, H. R. Fox. 1903. *Civilisation in Congoland*. London: P. S. King and Son.

Braverman, Harry. 1974. *Labor and Monopoly Capital*. New York: Monthly Review Press.

Briggs, Jean. 1974. "Eskimo Women: Makers of Men." In *Many Sisters*, edited by C. Matthiasson, pp. 261–304. New York: The Free Press.

Brown, Judith K. 1970a. "A Note on the Division of Labor by Sex." *American Anthropoligist* 72: 1073–78.

──────. 1970b. "Economic Organization and the Position of Women Among the Iroquois." *Ethnohistory* 7: 151–67.

──────. Forthcoming. "Cross-Cultural Perspectives on the Female Life Cycle." In *Handbook of Cross Cultural Human Development*, edited by Robert Monroe, Ruth Monroe and Beatrice Whiting. New York: Garland.

Brown, Susan. 1975. "Love Unites Them and Hunger Separates Them: Poor Women in the Dominican Republic." In *Toward an Anthropology of Women*, edited by Rayna Reiter, pp. 322–32. New York: Monthly Review Press.

Burton, Sir Richard F. 1864. *A Mission to Gelele, King of Dahomey*. 2 vols. London: Tinsley Bros.

Campbell, Joseph. 1967. Introduction to *Myth, Religion and Mother Right: Selected Writings of J. J. Bachofen*. Princeton: Princeton University Press.

Carter, Gwendolen; Thomas Karis; and Newell M. Stultz. 1967. *South Africa's Transkei: The Politics of Domestic Colonialism*. Evanston: Northwestern University Press.

Caulfield, Mina Davis. 1974. "Imperialism, Family and Cultures of Resistance." *Socialist Revolution*, no. 20: 67–85.

Chagnon, Napoleon. 1968a. *Yanomamo: The Fierce People*. New York: Holt, Rinehart and Winston.

──────. 1968b. "Yanomamo Social Organization and Warfare." In *War: The Anthropology of Armed Conflict and Aggression*, edited by Morton H. Fried, Marvin Harris and Robert Murphy, pp. 109–59. Garden City: Natural History Press.

──────. 1976. "Yanomamo: The True People." *National Geographic* 150: 211–23.

Chase, Allan. 1977. *The Legacy of Malthus: The Social Costs of the New Scientific Racism*. New York: Knopf.

Chiñas, Beverly. 1973. *The Isthmus Zapotecs: Women's Roles in Cultural Context*. New York: Holt, Rinehart and Winston.

Clark, Alice. 1919. *The Working Life of Women in the Seventeenth Century*. London: George Routledge.

Cohen, Yehudi. 1974. "Culture as Adaptation." In *Man in Adaptation: The Cultural Present*, edited by Y. Cohen 2d ed., pp. 45–70. Chicago: Aldine.

Coquery-Vidrovitch, Cathrine. 1971. "De la traite des esclaves a l'exportation de l'huile de palme et des palmistres au dahomey: XIX$_e$ siècle." In *The Development of Indigenous Trade and Markets in West Africa*, edited by Claude Meillassoux, pp. 107–23. London: Oxford University Press.

Cox, A. H. 1950. "The Growth and Expansion of Buganda." *Uganda Journal* 14: 153–49.

Dalzel, Archibald. 1967. (Orig. 1793.) *The History of Dahomey*. London: Frank Cass.

Damas, David. 1968. "The Diversity of Eskimo Societies." In *Man the Hunter*, edited by R. B. Lee and I. DeVore, pp. 111–17. Chicago: Aldine.

Davidson, Basil. 1961. *Black Mother: The Years of the African Slave Trade*. Boston: Little Brown.

Davis, Elizabeth Gould. 1971. *The First Sex*. New York: G. P. Putnam's Sons.

Davis, Natalie Z. 1975. "Women on Top." In *Society and Culture in Early Modern France*, edited by N. Z. Davis, pp. 124–51. Stanford: Stanford University Press.

Davis, Paulina W. 1970. (Orig. 1871.) *A History of the National Women's Rights Movement*. New York: Source Books Press.

Davis, Shelton, and Robert Mathews. 1976. *The Geological Imperative*. Cambridge: Anthropology Resource Center.

Diner, Helen. 1965. *Mothers and Amazons: The First Feminine History of Culture*. New York: The Julian Press.

Divale, William, and Marvin Harris. 1976. "Population, Warfare, and the Male Supremacist Complex." *American Anthropologist* 78: 521–38.

_____, and Donald Williams. 1978. "On the Misuse of Statistics: A Reply to Hirschfeld et al." *American Anthropologist* 80: 379–86.

Draper, Patricia. 1975. "!Kung Women: Contrasts in Sexual Egalitarianism in the Foraging and Sedentary Contexts." In *Toward an Anthropology of Women*, edited by R. Reiter, pp. 77–109. New York: Monthly Review Press.

Durkheim, Emile. 1893. *The Division of Labor in Society*. New York: MacMillan.

Edgerton, Robert, and Francis Conant. 1964. "Kilipat: The 'Shaming Party' Among the Pokot of East Africa." *Southwestern Journal of Anthropology* 20: 404–19.

Edholm, Felicity; Olivia Harris; and Kate Young. 1977. "Conceptualising Women." *Critique of Anthropology* 3, 9 and 10: 101–30.

Ehrenreich, Barbara, and Dierdre English. 1972. *Witches, Midwives and Nurses*. Oyster Bay: Feminist Press.

_____. 1973. *Complaints and Disorders*. Old Westbury: Feminist Press.

Eisenstein, Zillah. 1977. "Constructing a Theory of Capitalist Patriarchy and Socialist Feminism." *Insurgent Sociologist* (Summer): 3–17.

Engels, Frederick. 1891. *The Origin of the Family, Private Property and the State.* Moscow: Foreign Languages Publishing House.

Evans-Pritchard, E. E. 1940. *The Nuer.* Oxford: Oxford University Press.

———. 1945. *Some Aspects of Marriage and the Family Among the Nuer.* Livingstone: Rhodes-Livingstone Institute.

———. 1965. "The Position of Women in Primitive Societies." In *The Position of Women in Primitive Societies and Other Essays,* edited by E. E. Evans-Pritchard, pp. 37–38. New York: The Free Press.

Fallers, Lloyd A., ed. 1964. *The King's Men: Leadership and Status in Buganda on the Eve of Independence.* New York: Oxford University Press.

Fallers, Margaret C. 1960. *The Eastern Lacustrine Bantu.* London: International African Institute.

Fee, Elizabeth. 1974. "The Sexual Politics of Victorian Social Anthropology." In *Clio's Consciousness Raised,* edited by M. Hartman and L. Banner, pp. 86–102. New York: Harper Torchbooks.

Fee, Terry. 1976. "Domestic Labor: An Analysis of Housework and Its Relation to the Production Process." *Review of Radical Political Economics* 8: 1–9.

Firestone, Shulamith. 1970. *The Dialectic of Sex.* New York: Bantam.

Fjellman, Stephen. 1977. "Hey, You Can't Do That: A Response to Divale and Harris' 'Population, Warfare and the Male Supremacist Complex.'" Paper delivered at the meetings of the Society for Cross-Cultural Research, East Lansing, Michigan.

Flexner, Eleanor. 1968. *Century of Struggle.* New York: Atheneum.

Forbes, Frederick E. 1966. (Orig. 1851.) *Dahomey and the Dahomans.* 2 vols. London: Frank Cass.

Forde, C. Daryll. 1963. *Habitat, Economy and Society.* New York: E. P. Dutton.

———, and G. I. Jones. 1950. *The Ibo and Ibibio-Speaking Peoples of Southern Nigeria.* London: International African Institute.

Fox, Robin. 1972. "Alliance and Constraint." In *Sexual Selection and the Descent of Man,* edited by B. G. Campbell, pp. 282–331. Chicago: Aldine.

Freuchen, Peter. 1961. *Book of the Eskimos.* Cleveland: World.

Fried, Morton. 1967. *The Evolution of Political Society.* New York: Random House.

———. 1975. *The Notion of Tribe.* Menlo Park: Cummings Publishing Co.

Friedl, Ernestine. 1967. "The Position of Women: Appearance and Reality." *Anthropological Quarterly* 40: 97–108.

Gailey, Harry. 1970. *The Road to Aba.* New York: New York University Press.

Gale, Faye, ed. 1970. *Woman's Role in Aboriginal Society.* Australian Aboriginal Studies 36. Canberra: Australian National Institute of Aboriginal Studies.

George, Margaret. 1973. "From 'Goodwife' to 'Mistress': The Transformation of the Female in Bourgeois Culture." *Science and Society* 37: 152–77.

Giesey, Ralph. 1977. "Rules of Inheritance and Strategies of Mobility in Prerevolutionary France." *American Historical Review* 82: 271–89.

Glassman, Carol. 1970. "Women and the Welfare System." In *Sisterhood Is Powerful,* edited by R. Morgan, pp. 102–14. New York: Vintage.

Goldman, Irving. 1970. *Ancient Polynesian Society.* Chicago: University of Chicago Press.

Goodale, Jane. 1971. *Tiwi Wives.* Seattle: University of Washington Press.

Goody, Jack. 1969. "Inheritance, Property and Marriage in Africa and Eurasia." *Sociology* 3: 55–76.

———. 1976. *Production and Reproduction: A Comparative Study of the Domestic Domain.* Cambridge: Cambridge University Press.

———, and S. J. Tambiah. 1973. *Bridewealth and Dowry.* Cambridge: Cambridge Univeristy Press.

Goody, Jack; Joan Thirsk; and E. P. Thompson, eds. 1976. *Family and Inheritance: Rural Society in Western Europe, 1200–1800.* Cambridge: Cambridge University Press.

Gordon, Linda. 1977. *Woman's Body, Woman's Right.* Baltimore: Penguin.

Gottschling, E. 1905. "The Bawenda: A Sketch of Their History and Customs." *Journal of the Anthropological Institute* 35: 365–86.

Gough, Kathleen. 1968. "New Proposals for Anthropologists." *Current Anthropology* 9: 403–36.

———. 1971. "Nuer Kinship: A Re-examination." In *The Translation of Culture,* edited by T. O. Beidelman, pp. 79–120. London: Tavistock.

———. 1975. "The Origin of the Family." In *Toward an Anthropology of Women,* edited by R. Reiter, pp. 51–77. New York: Monthly Review Press.

Green, Margaret M. 1964. *Ibo Village Affairs.* London: Frank Cass.

Haddon, Alfred C. 1910. *History of Anthropology.* New York: G. P. Putnam's Sons.

Hammond-Tooke, W. D. 1965. "Segmentation and Fission in Cape Nguni Political Units." *Africa* 35: 143–67.

Haraway, Donna. 1978. "Animal Sociology and a Natural Economy of the Body Politic." Parts 1 and 2. *Signs* 4: 21–60.

Harris, David R. 1972. "Swidden Systems and Settlement." In *Man, Settlement and Urbanism,* edited by P. J. Ucko, R. Tringham, and G. W. Dimbeby, pp. 1–18. Cambridge, Mass.: Schenkman.

Harris, J. S. 1940. "The Position of Women in a Nigerian Society." *Transactions of the New York Academy of Sciences* 2: 141–48.

Harris, Marvin. 1975. *Culture, People, Nature: An Introduction to General Anthropology.* 2d ed. New York: T. Y. Crowell.

Hart, C. W. M., and Arnold Pilling. 1960. *The Tiwi of North Australia.* New York: Holt, Rinehart and Winston.

Hartley, C. G. 1914. *The Position of Woman in Primitive Society: A Study of the Matriarchy.* London: E. Nash.

Henderson, Richard N. 1972. *The King in Every Man: Evolutionary Trends in Onitsha Ibo Society and Culture.* New Haven: Yale University Press.

Herlihy, David. 1976. "Land, Family, and Women in Continental Europe, 701–1200." In *Women in Medieval Society,* edited by Susan Mosher Stuart, pp. 13–46. University of Pennsylvania Press.

Herrnstein, Richard. 1971. "I.Q." *Atlantic Monthly* (September): 43–64.

Herskovits, Melville J. 1937. "A Note on 'Woman Marriage' in Dahomey." *Africa* 10: 335–41.

———. 1938. *Dahomey, An Ancient West African Kingdom.* 2 vols. New York: J. J. Augustin.

Higham, John. 1963. *Strangers in the Land.* New York: Atheneum.

Hilkey, Judy. 1975. "Masculinity and the Self-made Man in America, 1850–1900."
    Unpublished manuscript.

Hilton, Rodney H. 1975. *The English Peasantry in the Later Middle Ages*. Oxford:
    Clarendon Press.

Hindess, Barry, and Paul Hirst. 1975. *Pre-Capitalist Modes of Production*. London:
    Routledge and Kegan Paul.

———. 1977. "Mode of Production and Social Formation in Pre-Capitalist Modes of
    Production: A Reply to John Taylor." *Critique of Anthropology* 2: 49–58.

Hirschfeld, Lawrence; James Howe; and Bruce Levin. 1978. "Warfare, Infanticide,
    and Statistical Inference: A Comment on Divale and Harris." *American Anthro-
    pologist* 80: 110–115.

Hobsbawm, Eric. 1969. *Industry and Empire*. Baltimore: Penguin.

Hoebel, E. A. 1960. *The Cheyennes*. New York: Holt, Rinehart and Winston.

Hoffer, Carol. 1972. "Mende and Sherbro Women in High Office." *Canadian Jour-
    nal of African Studies* 1: 151–64.

Hunter, Monica. 1933. "The Effects of Contact with Europeans on the Status of
    Pondo Women." *Africa* 6: 259–76.

———. 1936. *Reaction to Conquest*. London: Oxford University Press.

Jacques, A. A. 1939. "Genealogy of Male and Female Chiefs of a Sotho Tribe." *Bantu
    Studies* 8: 377–82.

Jenness, Diamond. 1922. *The Copper Eskimo: Report of the Canadian Arctic Ex-
    pedition, 1913–18*. Ottawa: Acland.

Johnston, Harry. 1904. *The Uganda Protectorate*. 2 vols. London: Hutchinson.

Jones, Gwilyam I. 1963. *The Trading States of the Oil Rivers*. London: Oxford Uni-
    versity Press.

Joseph, Suad. n.d. "Does Poverty Have Public and Private Domains?" Unpublished
    paper.

Junod, H. A. 1920. "Some Features of the Religion of the BaVenda." *South African
    Journal of Science* 17: 207–20.

Kaberry, Phyllis. 1939. *Aboriginal Woman: Sacred and Profane*. London: G. Rout-
    ledge and Son.

Kagwa, Sir Apolo. 1934. *The Customs of the Baganda*. New York: Columbia Univer-
    sity Press.

Kay, Stephen. 1833. *Travels and Researches in Caffraria*. New York: Harper.

Kelly-Gadol, Joan. 1977. "Did Women Have a Renaissance?" In *Becoming Visible:
    Women in European History*, edited by R. Bridenthal and C. Koonz, pp. 137–64.
    Boston: Houghton Mifflin.

Kenyatta, Jomo. 1965. *Facing Mt. Kenya*. New York: Vintage.

Khaing, Mi Mi. 1963. "Burma: Balance and Harmony." In *Women in the New Asia*,
    edited by B. Ward, pp. 104–37. Amsterdam: UNESCO.

Kidd, Dudley. 1904. *The Essential Kaffir*. London: A. and C. Black.

Kirchhoff, Paul. 1959. "The Principles of Clanship in Human Society." In *Readings
    in Anthropology*, edited by Morton Fried, 2: 259–70. New York: T. Crowell.

Kiwanuka, M. S. M. Semakula. 1972. *A History of Buganda from the Foundation of
    the Kingdom to 1900*. New York: Africana Publishing Corp.

Knight, Chris. 1978. "The Origins of Woman: A Marxist-Structuralist View of the
    Genesis of Culture." *Critique of Anthropology* 3, 12: 59–87.

Kolata, Gina. 1974. "!Kung Hunter-Gatherers: Feminism, Diet, and Birth Control." *Science* 185: 932–34.

Kraditor, Aileen. 1971. *The Ideas of the Woman Suffrage Movement, 1890–1920.* Garden City: Anchor.

Krige, E. J. 1931. "Agricultural Ceremonies and Practices of the Balobedu." *Bantu Studies* 5: 207–41.

———. 1932. "The Social Significance of Beer Among the Balobedu." *Bantu Studies* 6: 343–57.

———. 1938. "The Place of the Northeastern Sotho in the Southern Bantu Complex." *Africa* 11: 265–93.

———. 1946. "Individual Development." In *The Bantu-Speaking Tribes of South Africa*, edited by I. Schapera, pp. 95–118. London: Geo. Routledge and Sons.

———. 1964. "Property, Cross-Cousin Marriage and the Family Cycle Among the Lovedu." In *The Family Estate in Africa*, edited by R. Gray and P. Gulliver, pp. 115–96. Boston: Boston University Press.

———. 1974. "Woman Marriage, with Special Reference to the Lovedu—Its Significance for the Definition of Marriage." *Africa* 44: 11–35.

———. 1975. "Asymmetrical Matrilateral Cross-Cousin Marriage—The Lovedu Case." *African Studies* 34: 231–57.

———, and J. D. Krige. 1943. *Realm of a Rain Queen.* London: Oxford University Press.

———. 1954. "The Lobedu of the Transvaal." In *African Worlds*, edited by C. D. Forde, pp. 55–82. London: Oxford University Press.

Krige, J. D. 1934. "Bridewealth in Balovedu Marriage Ceremonies." *Bantu Studies* 8: 135–51.

———. 1939a. "Some Aspects on Lovhedu Judicial Arrangements." *Bantu Studies* 13: 113–68.

———. 1939b. "The Significance of Cattle Exchanges in Lovedu Social Structure." *Africa* 12: 393–425.

Kruger, Ferdinand. 1936. "The Lovedu." *Bantu Studies* 10: 89–106.

Lamphere, Louise. 1974. "Strategies, Cooperation and Conflict Among Women in Domestic Groups." In *Woman, Culture and Society*, edited by M. Rosaldo and L. Lamphere, p. 97–113. Stanford: Stanford University Press.

———. 1978. "The Changing Role of Female Factory Workers: A Comparison Between Early and Recent French, Polish and Portuguese Immigrants." Paper prepared for National Institute of Education Research Conference on Educational and Occupational Needs of White Ethnic Women, Boston.

Lancaster, Chet, and Jane B. Lancaster. 1978. "On the Male Supremacist Complex: A Reply to Divale and Harris." *American Anthropologist* 80: 115–17.

Lancaster, Jane. 1975. *Primate Behavior and the Emergence of Human Culture.* New York: Holt, Rinehart and Winston.

Lane, Ann J. 1976. "Woman in Society: A Critique of Frederick Engels." In *Liberating Women's History*, edited by B. Carroll, pp. 4–25. Urbana: University of Illinois Press.

Law, Robin. 1978. "In Search of a Marxist Perspective on Pre-Colonial Tropical Africa." *Journal of African History* 9: 445–52.

Leach, Edmund. 1961. *Rethinking Anthropology.* London: Athlone Press.

Leacock, Eleanor. 1972. Introduction to F. Engels, *The Origin of the Family, Private Property and the State*, edited by E. B. Leacock, pp. 7–67. New York: International.

Lebeuf, Annie. 1971. "The Role of Women in the Political Organization of African Societies." In *Women of Tropical Africa*, edited by D. Paulme, pp. 93–120. Berkeley: University of California Press.

Lee, Richard. 1967. "Trance Cure of the !Kung Bushmen." *Natural History* (November): 30–37.

———. 1968. "What Hunters Do for a Living, or How to Make Out on Scarce Resources." In *Man the Hunter*, edited by R. B. Lee and I. DeVore, pp. 30–48. Chicago: Aldine.

———. 1969. "!Kung Bushman Subsistence: An Input-Output Analysis." In *Environment and Cultural Behavior*, edited by A. P. Vayda, pp. 47–79. New York: Natural History Press.

———. 1972a. "!Kung Spatial Organization: An Ecological and Historical Perspective." *Human Ecology* 1: 125–47.

———. 1972b. "Population Growth and the Beginnings of Sedentary Life Among the !Kung Bushmen." In *Population Growth: Anthropological Implications*, edited by B. Spooner, pp. 328–42. Cambridge: MIT Press.

———. 1972c. "Work Effort, Group Structure and Land Use in Contemporary Hunter-Gatherers." In *Man, Settlement and Urbanism*, edited by P. J. Ucko, R. Tringham, and G. W. Dimbleby, pp. 177–85. Cambridge, Mass.: Schenkman.

———. 1974. "Male and Female Residence Arrangements and Political Power in Human Hunter-Gatherers." *Archives of Sexual Behavior* 3: 167–73.

———. 1976. Introduction to *Kalahari Hunter-Gatherers*, edited by R. B. Lee and I. DeVore, pp. 3–26. Cambridge: Harvard University Press.

———, and Irven DeVore, eds. 1968. *Man the Hunter*. Chicago: Aldine.

———. 1976. *Kalahari Hunter-Gatherers*. Cambridge: Harvard University Press.

LeHerisse, A. 1911. *L'Ancien Royaume du Dahomey*. Paris: Emile Larose.

Leibowitz, Lila. 1975. "Perspectives on the Evolution of Sex Differences." In *Toward an Anthropology of Women*, edited by R. Reiter, pp. 20–35. New York: Monthly Review Press.

Leis, Nancy. 1974. "Women in Groups: Ijaw Women's Associations." In *Woman, Culture, and Society*, edited by M. Rosaldo and L. Lamphere, pp. 223–42. Stanford: Stanford University Press.

Leith-Ross, Sylvia. 1965. *African Women*. London: Routledge and Kegan Paul.

Lerner, Gerda. 1969. "The Lady and the Mill Girl: Changes in the Status of Women in the Age of Jackson." *American Studies* 10: 1–11.

———. 1971. *The Woman in American History*. Menlo Park, Calif.: Addison-Wesley.

Lestrade, G. P. 1930a. "Some Notes on the Political Organization of the Venda-Speaking Tribes." *Africa* 3: 306–22.

———. 1930b. "The Mala System of the Venda-Speaking Tribes." *Bantu Studies* 4: 193–204.

———. 1934. "Some Aspects of the Economic Life of the South African Bantu." *South African Journal of Economics* 2: 426–43.

Levi-Strauss, Claude. 1969. *The Elementary Structures of Kinship*. Boston: Beacon Press.

———. 1971. "The Family." In *Man, Culture and Society*, edited by H. Shapiro, pp. 261–85. New York: Oxford University Press.

Levine, David. 1977. *Family Formation in an Age of Nascent Capitalism*. New York: Academic Press.

Little, Kenneth. 1967. *The Mende of Sierra Leone*. London: Routledge and Kegan Paul.

Lorenz, Konrad. 1966. *On Aggression*, New York: Harcourt, Brace and World.

Low, Donald A. 1957. *Religion and Society in Buganda, 1875–1900*. East African Studies 8. Kampala: East African Institute for Social Research.

Lowie, Robert H. 1937. *The History of Ethnological Theory*. New York: Rinehart and Company.

———. 1961. *Primitive Society*. New York: Harper Torchbooks.

Lubart, Joseph. 1970. *Psychodynamic Problems of Adaptation—MacKenzie Delta Eskimos*. Ottawa: Department of Indian Affairs.

Lubbock, J. 1870. *The Origin of Civilization and the Primitive Condition of Man*. London: Longman's Green.

McCall, Daniel. 1961. "Trade and the Role of Wife in a Modern West African Town." In *Social Change in Modern Africa*, edited by A. Southall, p. 286–300. London: Oxford University Press.

McLennan, J. F. 1865. *Primitive Marriage*. Edinburgh: Adam and Chas. Black.

McNamara, JoAnn, and Suzanne Wemple. 1974. "The Power of Women Through the Family in Medieval Europe: 500–1100." In *Clio's Consciousness Raised*, edited by Mary Hartman and Lois Banner, pp. 103–18. New York: Harper and Row.

Maine, Sir Henry. 1861. *Ancient Law*. London: J. Murray.

Mair, Lucy. 1934. *An African People in the Twentieth Century*. London: Routledge and Kegan Paul.

Malinowski, Bronislaw. 1927. *Sex and Repression in Savage Society*. New York: Harcourt Brace.

———. 1929. *The Sexual Life of Savages in North-Western Melanesia*. New York: Harcourt, Brace and World.

Marie, Alain. 1976. "Rapports de parente et rapports de production dans les sociétés Lignageres." In *L'Anthropologie économique*, edited by F. Pouillon, pp. 86–116. Paris: Maspero.

Marks, Shula, and Richard Gray. 1975. "Southern Africa and Madagascar." In *Cambridge History of Africa*, vol. 4, edited by R. Gray, pp. 385–468. Cambridge: Cambridge University Press.

Marshall, Lorna. 1957. "The Kin Terminology System of the !Kung Bushmen." *Africa* 27: 1–24.

———. 1959. "Marriage Among !Kung Bushmen." *Africa* 29: 335–365.

———. 1960. "!Kung Bushman Bands." *Africa* 30: 325–55.

———. 1976. "Sharing, Talking and Giving." In *Kalahari Hunter-Gatherers*, edited by R. B. Lee and I. DeVore, pp. 349–71. Cambridge: Harvard University Press.

Martin, Marilyn K., and Barbara Voorhies. 1975. *Female of the Species*. New York:

Columbia University Press.

Marx Karl. 1964. *Pre-Capitalist Economic Formations*. New York: International.

Mason, Otis T. 1894. *Woman's Share in Primitive Culture*. New York: D. Appleton.

Maybury-Lewis, David. 1974. *Akwe-Shavante Society*. New York: Oxford University Press.

Mbeki, Govan. 1964. *South Africa: The Peasants Revolt*. Baltimore: Penguin.

Mead, Margaret. 1935. *Sex and Temperament*. New York: Wm. Morrow.

————. 1949. *Male and Female*. New York: Wm. Morrow.

Meek, C. K. 1937. *Law and Authority in a Nigerian Tribe*. London: Oxford University Press.

Meillassoux, Claude, ed. 1971. *The Development of Indigenous Trade and Markets in West Africa*. Oxford: Oxford University Press.

————. 1972. "From Reproduction to Production: A Marxist Approach to Economic Anthropology." *Economy and Society* 6: 93–104.

————. 1973. "On the Mode of Production of the Hunting Band." In *French Perspectives in African Studies*, edited by Pierre Alexandre, pp. 187–203. London: Oxford University Press.

————. 1975. *Femmes, greniers et capitaux*. Paris: Maspero.

Middleton, John, and G. Kershaw. 1965. *The Kikuyu and Kamba of Kenya*. London: International African Institute.

Miller, Jay. 1974. "The Delaware as Women: A Symbolic Solution." *American Ethnologist* 1: 507–14.

Millett, Kate. 1970. *Sexual Politics*. Garden City: Doubleday.

Mintz, Sidney. 1964. "The Employment of Capital by Market Women in Haiti." In *Capital, Saving and Credit in Peasant Societies*, edited by R. Firth and B. S. Yamey, pp. 256–86. Chicago: Aldine.

————. 1971. "Men, Women and Trade." *Comparative Studies in Society and History* 13: 247–69.

Mockler-Ferryman, Capt. A. F. 1892. *Up the Niger*. London: Geo. Philip and Co.

Molyneux, Maxine. 1977. "Andocentrism in Marxist Anthropology." *Critique of Anthropology* 3, 9 and 10: 55–82.

Montagu, Ashley. 1954. *The Natural Superiority of Women*. London: G. Allen and Unwin.

————, ed. 1956. *Marriage Past and Present: A Debate Between Robert Briffault and Bronislaw Malinowski*. Boston: Porter Sargent.

Morgan, Lewis H. 1877. *Ancient Society*. New York: World Publishing.

Morris, Desmond. 1967. *The Naked Ape*. New York: McGraw-Hill.

Mukasa, H. 1946. "The Role of the Kings of Buganda." *Uganda Journal* 10: 136–43.

Muller, Viana. 1977. "The Formation of the State and the Oppression of Women." *Review of Radical Political Economics* 9: 7–21.

Murdock, George P. 1937. "Comparative Data on the Division of Labor by Sex." *Social Forces* 15: 551–53.

————. 1949. *Africa: Its Peoples and Their Culture History*. New York: McGraw-Hill.

Murphy, Robert, and Julian Steward. 1956. "Tappers and Trappers: Parallel Process in Acculturation." *Economic Development and Cultural Change* 4: 335–53.

Murphy, Yolanda, and Robert Murphy. 1974. *Women of the Forest*. New York: Columbia University Press.

Nadel, S. F. 1942. *A Black Byzantium*. London: Oxford University Press.

_____. 1960. "Witchcraft in Four African Societies: An Essay in Comparison." In *Cultures and Societies of Africa*, edited by S. Ottenberg and P. Ottenberg, pp. 407–20. New York: Random House.

Newbury, Colin. 1961. *The Western Slave Coast and Its Rulers*. Oxford: Clarendon Press.

Nsimbi, M. B. 1956. "Village Life and Customs in Buganda." *Uganda Journal* 20: 27–36.

Nzimiro, Ikenna. 1972. *Studies in Ibo Political Systems: Chieftaincy and Politics in Four Niger States*. London: Frank Cass.

O'Brien, Denise. 1972. "Female Husbands in African Societies." Paper presented at the meeting of the American Anthropological Association, Toronto.

_____. 1977. "Female Husbands in Southern Bantu Societies." In *Sexual Stratification*, edited by Alice Schlegel, pp. 109–26. New York: Columbia University Press.

Okonjo, Kamene. 1976. "The Dual Sex Political System in Operation: Igbo Women and Community Politics in Midwestern Nigeria." In *Women in Africa*, edited by N. Hafkin and E. Bay, pp. 45–58. Stanford: Stanford University Press.

O'Laughlin, Bridget. 1974. "Mediation of Contradiction: Why Mbum Women Do Not Eat Chicken." In *Women, Culture and Society*, edited by M. Rosaldo and L. Lamphere, pp. 301–20. Stanford: Stanford University Press.

_____. 1977. "Production and Reproduction: Meillassoux's *Femmes, greniers et capitaux*." *Critique of Anthropology* 2: 3–32.

Omer-Cooper, J. D. 1969. *The Zulu Aftermath: A Nineteenth Century Revolution in Bantu Africa*. Evanston: Northwestern University Press.

Onwuteaka, V. C. 1965. "The Aba Riot of 1929 and Its Relation to the System of 'Indirect Rule.'" *Nigerian Journal of Economic and Social Studies* 7: 273–82.

Ortner, Sherry. 1974. "Is Female to Male as Nature Is to Culture?" In *Woman, Culture and Society*, edited by M. Rosaldo and L. Lamphere, pp. 67–88. Stanford: Stanford University Press.

Ottenberg, Phoebe. 1959. "The Changing Economic Position of Women Among the Afikpo Ibo." In *Continuity and Change in African Cultures*, edited by W. R. Bascom and M. J. Herskovits, pp. 205–23. Chicago: University of Chicago Press.

Perham, Margery. 1962. *Native Administration in Nigeria*. London: Oxford University Press.

Putnam, Anne. 1954. *Madami*. New York: Prentice-Hall.

Putnam, Patrick. 1948. "The Pygmies of the Ituri Forest." In *A Reader in General Anthropology*, edited by C. S. Coon, pp. 322–42. New York: H. Holt.

Raymond, Nathaniel, and Lila Leibowitz. 1974. "The Division of Labor and Authority in Collecting-Hunting Societies." Paper read at meetings of the Northeastern Anthropological Association, Worcester.

Reed, Evelyn. 1975. *Women's Evolution*. New York: Pathfinder.

Remy, Dorothy. 1975. "Underdevelopment and the Experience of Women: A Nigerian Case Study." In *Toward an Anthropology of Women*, edited by R. Reiter, pp. 358–72. New York: Monthly Review Press.

Rey, P. P. 1975. "The Lineage Mode of Production." *Critique of Anthropology* 3: 27–79.

Richards, Audrey I. 1966. *The Changing Structure of a Ganda Village*. Nairobi: East African Publishing House.

Riegelhaupt, Joyce. 1967. "Saloio Women: An Analysis of Informal and Formal Political and Economic Roles of Portuguese Peasant Women." *Anthropological Quarterly* 40: 109–26.

Ronhaar, J. H. 1931. *Women in Primitive Motherright Societies*. The Hague: Gröningen.

Rosaldo, Michelle. 1974. "Women, Culture and Society: A Theoretical Overview." In *Woman, Culture and Society*, edited by M. Rosaldo and L. Lamphere, pp. 17–42. Stanford: Stanford University Press.

_____, and Jane Collier. Forthcoming. "Politics and Gender in 'Simple' Societies." In *Sexual Meanings*, edited by S. Ortner and H. Whitehead.

Roscoe, John. 1966. *The Baganda*. New York: Barnes and Noble.

Ross, David A. 1965. "The Career of Domingo Martinez in the Bight of Benin, 1833–64." *Journal of African History* 6: 79–90.

Rowbotham, Sheila. 1972. *Women, Resistance and Revolution*. New York: Vintage.

_____. 1973. *Hidden from History*. London: Pluto Press.

Rubin, Gayle. 1975. "The Traffic in Women." In *Toward an Anthropology of Women*, edited by R. Reiter, pp. 157–210. New York: Monthly Review Press.

Sacks, Karen. 1974. "Engels Revisited: Women, the Organization of Production and Private Property." In *Woman, Culture and Society*, edited by M. Rosaldo and L. Lamphere, pp. 207–22. Stanford: Stanford University Press.

_____. 1976a. "State Bias and Women's Status." *American Anthropologist* 78: 565–69.

_____. 1976b. "Class Roots of Feminism." *Monthly Review* 27: 28–48.

_____. 1978. "Women and Class Struggle in Sembene's *God's Bits of Wood*." *Signs* 4: 363–70.

_____. 1979. "Causality and Chance on the Upper Nile." *American Ethnologist* 6: 437–448.

Safa, Helen. 1978. "Women, Production, Reproduction and Industrial Capitalism: A Comparison of Factory Workers in Brazil and the U.S." Paper prepared for the Conference on the Continuing Subordination of Women in the Development Process. Inst. of Development Studies. Sussex, Eng.

Sahlins, Marshall. 1968. *Tribesmen*. Englewood Cliffs, N.J.: Prentice-Hall.

_____. 1972. *Stone Age Economics*. Chicago: Aldine Atherton.

_____, and Elman Service. 1960. *Evolution and Culture*. Ann Arbor: University of Michigan Press.

Schapera, Isaac, ed. 1937. *The Bantu-Speaking Tribes of South Africa*. London: G. Routledge and Sons.

_____. 1956. *Government and Politics in Tribal Societies*. London: Watts.

Schlegel, Alice. 1972. *Male Dominance and Female Autonomy*. New Haven: HRAF Press.

_____, ed. 1977. *Sexual Stratification: A Cross Cultural View*. New York: Columbia University Press.

Schneider, David M., and Kathleen Gough, eds. 1961. *Matrilineal Kinship*. Berkeley: University of California Press.

Schweinfurth, Georg. 1873. *The Heart of Africa*. 2 vols. London: S. Low.

Scott, Joan, and Louise Tilly. 1975. "Women's Work and the Family in Nineteenth Century Europe." *Comparative Studies in Society and History* 17: 36–64.

Secoy, Frank. 1953. *Changing Military Patterns on the Great Plains*. Seattle: University of Washington Press.

Service, Elman. 1966. *The Hunters*. Englewood Cliffs: Prentice-Hall.

Shostack, Marjorie. 1976. "A !Kung Woman's Memories of Childhood." In *Kalahari Hunter-Gatherers*, edited by R. B. Lee and I. DeVore, pp. 246–77. Cambridge: Harvard University Press.

Silverman, Sydel. 1967. "The Life Crisis as a Clue to Social Functions." *Anthropological Quarterly* 40: 127–38.

Singer, Alice. 1973. "Marriage Payments and the Exchange of People." *Man* 8: 80–92.

Siskind, Janet. 1973. *To Hunt in the Morning*. New York: Oxford University Press.

———. 1978. "Kinship and Mode of Production." *American Anthropologist* 80: 860–72.

Skinner, A. 1916. *Political and Ceremonial Organization of the Plains Ojibway*. Anthropological Papers of the American Museum of Natural History 11: 475–512.

Slade, Ruth. 1962. *King Leopold's Congo*. London: Oxford University Press.

Slocum, Sally. 1975. "Woman the Gatherer: Male Bias in Anthropology." In *Toward an Anthropology of Women*, edited by R. Reiter, pp. 36–50. New York: Monthly Review Press.

Smith, Philip E. L. 1972. "Land Use, Settlement Patterns and Subsistence Agriculture: A Demographic Perspective." In *Man, Settlement and Urbanism*, edited by P. J. Ucko, R. Tringham, and G. W. Dimbleby, pp. 409–26. Cambridge, Mass.: Schenkman.

Smith-Rosenberg, Carroll. 1971. "Beauty, the Beast and the Militant Woman: A Case Study in Sex Roles and Social Stress in Jacksonian America." *American Quarterly* 22: 562–84.

———. 1974. "Puberty to Menopause: The Cycle of Femininity in Nineteenth Century America." In *Clio's Consciousness Raised*, edited by M. Hartmann and L. Banner, pp. 23–37. New York: Harper Torchbooks.

Soga, John H. 1930. *The South-Eastern Bantu*. Johannesburg: Witwatersrand University Press.

Solway, Jacqueline. 1976. "Social Organization of the !Kung Bushmen: A Re-Analysis." Unpublished paper.

Southwold, Martin. 1965. "The Ganda of Uganda." In *Peoples of Africa*, edited by J. L. Gibbs. New York: Holt, Rinehart and Winston.

———. 1968. "The History of a History: Royal Succession in Buganda." In *History and Social Anthropology*, edited by I. M. Lewis, pp. 127–52. London: Tavistock.

Speke, John H. 1937. *The Discovery of the Source of the Nile*. New York: Dutton.

Spencer, Herbert. 1884. *The Study of Sociology*. New York: D. Appleton and Co.

———. 1910. *The Principles of Sociology*. 3d ed. New York: D. Appleton and Co.

Stack, Carol. 1974. *All Our Kin*. New York: Harper Colophon.

Stanley, H. M. 1878. *Through the Dark Continent.* 2 vols. New York: Chas. Scribner's Sons.

Stayt, Hugh A. 1931. *The Bavenda.* London: International African Institute.

Steedman, Andrew. 1835. *Wanderings and Adventures in the Interior of Southern Africa.* 2 vols. London: Longman.

Steward, Julian. 1938. *Basin-Plateau Aboriginal Sociopolitical Groups.* Bulletin 120. Washington, D.C.: Bureau of American Ethnology.

Stone, Lawrence. 1975. "The Rise of the Nuclear Family in Early Modern England." In *The Family in History,* edited by Charles Rosenberg, pp. 13–58. Philadelphia: University of Pennsylvania Press.

Stuart, Susan Mosher. 1976. Introduction to *Women in Medieval Society,* edited by S. M. Stuart, pp. 1–12. Philadelphia: University of Pennsylvania Press.

Sumner, W. G., and A. G. Keller. 1932. *The Science of Society.* 4 vols. New Haven: Yale University Press.

Suttles, Wayne. 1960. "Affinal Ties, Subsistence and Prestige Among the Coast Salish." *American Anthropologist* 62: 296–330.

Tanner, Nancy. 1974. "Matrifocality in Indonesia and Africa and Among Black Americans." In *Woman, Culture and Society,* edited by M. Rosaldo and L. Lamphere, p. 129–56. Stanford: Stanford University Press.

Taylor, John. 1976. "Precapitalist Modes of Production (Part II)." *Critique of Anthropology* 2: 56–68.

Terray, Emmanuel. 1972. *Marxism and "Primitive" Societies.* New York: Monthly Review Press.

Theal, George M. 1915. *History of South Africa from 1795 to 1872.* London: G. Allen and Unwin.

Thomas, Elizabeth Marshall. 1959. *The Harmless People.* New York: Random House.

Thomas, William I. 1907. *Sex and Society.* Chicago: University of Chicago Press.

Thompson, E. P. 1971. "The Moral Economy of the English Crowd in the Eighteenth Century." *Past and Present* 50: 76–136.

————. 1976. "The Grid of Inheritance: A Comment." In *Family and Inheritance,* edited by Jack Goody, Joan Thirsk, and E. P. Thompson, pp. 328–60. Cambridge: Cambridge University Press.

Tiger, Lionel. 1969. *Men in Groups.* New York: Random House.

————, and Robin Fox. 1971. *The Imperial Animal.* New York: Holt, Rinehart and Winston.

Tillmon, Johnnie. 1976. "Welfare Is a Woman's Issue." In *America's Working Women,* edited by R. Baxandall, L. Gordon and S. Reverby, pp. 355–58. New York: Vintage.

Tilly, Louise; Joan Scott; and Miriam Cohen. 1976. "Women's Work and European Fertility Patterns." *Journal of Interdisciplinary History* 6: 447–76.

Tosh, John. 1970. "The Northern Interlacustrine Region." In *Pre-Colonial African Trade,* edited by R. Gray and D. Birmingham, pp. 103–18. London: Oxford University Press.

Turnbull, Colin. 1959. "*Legends of the BaMbuti.*" *Journal of the Royal Anthropological Institute* 89: 45–60.

_____. 1960. "The *Elima*: A Pre-Marital Festival Among the BaMbuti Pygmies." *Zaire* 14: 175–92.

_____. 1960a. "The *Molimo*: A Men's Religious Association Among the Ituri BaMbuti." *Zaire* 14: 307–40.

_____. 1962. *The Forest People*. New York: Natural History Library.

_____. 1965a. *Wayward Servants*. New York: Natural History Press.

_____. 1965b. *The Mbuti Pygmies: An Ethnographic Survey*. Anthropological Papers of the American Museum of Natural History 50: 145–282.

U.S. Department of Labor. 1974. *Women Workers Today*. Washington, D.C.: Women's Bureau.

Ukwu, U. I. 1969. "Markets in Iboland." In *Markets in West Africa*, edited by B. W. Hodder and U. I. Ukwu, pp. 113–250. Ibadan: Caxton Press.

Unomah, A. C., and J. B. Webster. 1976. "East Africa: The Expansion of Commerce." In *Cambridge History of Africa*, vol. 5, edited by John E. Flint, pp. 270–318. Cambridge: Cambridge University Press.

Van Allen, Judith. 1972. " 'Sitting on a Man': Colonialism and the Lost Political Institutions of Igbo Women." *Canadian Journal of African Studies* 6: 165–82.

_____. 1976. " 'Aba Riots' or Igbo 'Women's War'? Ideology, Stratification and the Invisibility of Women." In *Women in Africa*, edited by N. Hafkin and E. Bay, pp. 59–85. Stanford: Stanford University Press.

Walter, E. V. 1969. *Terror and Resistance*. New York: Oxford University Press.

Ward, Barbara, ed. 1963. *Women in the New Asia*. Amsterdam: UNESCO.

Washburn, Sherwood, and C. S. Lancaster. 1968. "The Evolution of Hunting." In *Man the Hunter*, edited by R. B. Lee and I. DeVore, pp. 293–303. Chicago: Aldine.

Watanabe, Hitoshi. 1968. "Subsistence and Ecology of Northern Food Gatherers with Special Reference to the Ainu." In *Man the Hunter*, edited by R. B. Lee and I. DeVore, pp. 69–77. Chicago: Aldine.

Webster, Paula. 1975. "Matriarchy: A Vision of Power." In *Toward an Anthropology of Women*, edited by R. Reiter, pp. 141–56. New York: Monthly Review Press.

Welter, Barbara. 1966. "The Cult of True Womanhood: 1820–1860." *American Quarterly* 18: 151–74.

White, Leslie. 1959. *The Evolution of Culture*. New York: McGraw-Hill.

Whyte, Martin K. 1978. *The Status of Women in Pre-Industrial Society*. Princeton: Princeton University Press.

Wilson, E. O. 1975. *Sociobiology: The New Synthesis*. Cambridge: Harvard University Press.

Wilson, Monica, and Leonard Thompson, eds. 1969. *The Oxford History of South Africa*, vol. 1: *South Africa to 1870*. New York: Oxford University Press.

Wolf, Eric. 1969. *Peasant Wars of the Twentieth Century*. New York: Harper and Row.

Wrigley, C. C. 1957. "Buganda: An Outline Economic History." *Economic History Review* 10: 69–80.

_____. 1964. "The Changing Economic Structure of Buganda." In *The King's Men*, edited by L. A. Fallers, pp. 16–63. New York: Oxford University Press.

Yoon, Soon Young. 1976. "You Can't Go Home Again: Migration of Korean Single, Young Female Workers." Paper presented at the meetings of the American Anthropological Association, Washington, D.C.

Young, Agatha. 1959. *Women and the Crisis*. New York: McDowell, Oblensky.

Young, Michael, and Peter Wilmott. 1962. *Family and Kinship in East London*. Baltimore: Penguin.

Zaretsky, Eli. 1976. *Capitalism, the Family and Personal Life*. New York: Harper-Colophon.

INDEX

About the Author

Karen Sacks, formerly Assistant Professor of Social Anthropology at Clark University, is with Drake University's Center for the Study of the Family and the State. Among her earlier publications are articles in such journals as *American Anthropologist* and *Monthly Review*.